A Field Guide for Genealogists

SECOND EDITION

D0872524

CLEARFIELD

First Edition, 2001

Second Edition printed for
Clearfield Company by
Genealogical Publishing Co.
Baltimore, Maryland
2003, 2004, 2007

ISBN-13: 978-0-8063-5219-0
ISBN-10: 0-8063-5219-1

Made in the United States of America

Table of Contents

vi

The following was taken from an internet family list site, author unknown, but it cried out to be included here. So to whoever composed this list, thank you for telling it like it is.

The Laws of Genealogy

The document containing evidence of the missing link in your research invariably will be lost due to fire, flood or war.

The keeper of the vital records you need will have just been insulted by another genealogist.

Your great-great grandfather's obituary states that he died, leaving no issue of record.

The town clerk you wrote to in desperation, and finally convinced to give you the information you need, can't write legibly, and doesn't have a copying machine.

The will you need is in the safe on board the "Titanic."

The spelling of your European ancestor's name bears no relationship to its current spelling or pronunciation.

That ancient photograph of four relatives, one of whom is your progenitor carries the names of the other three.

Copies of old newspapers have holes which occur only on last names.

No one in your family ever did anything noteworthy, always rented property, was never sued and was never named in wills.

You learned that Great Aunt Matilda's executor just sold her life's collection of family genealogical materials to a flea market dealer "somewhere in New York City."

Yours is the only last name not found among the 3 billion in the world famous Mormon Archives in Salt Lake City.

Ink fades and paper deteriorates at a rate inversely proportional to the value of the data recorded.

The 37 volume, sixteen thousand page history of your country of origin isn't indexed.

The critical link in your family tree is named "Smith."

Preface

You are sitting in a library and have just reached a dead end. Or maybe you have found a picture of some people that are purported to be ancestors of yours, but you just don't know who they are. Or you are doing research in a courthouse when you come upon a term in a will or a measurement in a land record that you don't understand. Maybe you find a newspaper from the dates and place where your ancestors lived, but you aren't sure what to look for in it.

In order to understand some of the things we run into as genealogists, it sometimes seems like we need to carry around a library with us. Of course, we just can't. Even if we could, some of us wouldn't know how to make the best use of it anyway.

Hopefully this little book will be a viable alternative--a useful tool which we can take with us in our purses or briefcases--that can help answer those little questions that come up.

Genealogy in General

Practical Uses of Genealogy

- Proving wills when the line of descent is needed
- Proving legitimacy
- Uncovering inherited diseases
- Understanding personalities, values and problem relationships within a family
- Tracing land ownership
- Passing the sense of place in history on to children
- Qualifying for descent or name based scholarships and grants
- Qualifying for historical societies based on descent
- Preparing oral and written histories for museums and libraries
- Tracing birth parents

What You Need to Know About an Ancestor

- Full name, including maiden
- Dates and places of birth, baptism, marriages, military service, death and burial
- Names of spouses, children, parents
- Family stories

What to Ask Relatives About Ancestors

While it may be easiest to get information from relatives by visiting them, sometimes inquiries have to be conducted by mail. If that is the case, always enclose a self-addressed stamped envelope. Likewise, if you are interviewing over the telephone, make sure you are the one paying for the call.

If you interview an elderly person, make sessions short. No one remembers well when tired, and an elderly person tires easily. But do not forget that a younger person might have the answers to your questions too.

Things you may want to ask about include

- names, places, and dates of birth, baptism, marriages, deaths, and burials of ancestors, parents and their siblings
- religion
- their occupations
- persons that others were named after
- any moves made while growing up
- the kind of houses lived in and the addresses
- nicknames

- old family records, letters, family Bibles, pictures or memorabilia that you can copy*
- descriptions of ancestors
- family scandals
- unique individual achievements
- names and addresses of other people, including relatives and old family friends, who might have information

*Photocopies are always preferable to hand copied versions. If someone is going to misinterpret the material, at least let it be you. You can always go back to the photocopy and see where you went wrong.

Phrase questions so that you get more than just a "yes" or "no" answer. For instance, ask the person you are interviewing to finish the following sentences.

When I was a child, the oldest person in my family was....
My parents would have been upset if they had known...
During the war, I...
The best time I had as a kid was when...
The family tradition that meant the most to me was...
Life was hard when...
We never talked much about...
One strange thing about my Grandparents was that...
In our family, education has always been...
Something I remember about my Great-grandparents is that...

Home Sweet Home

It is always easiest to begin with the current generation and work back one generation at a time. But remember, family lore, while interesting is not always gospel. Someone known as "Uncle Zeke" might be of no relation at all. Memories fade. Storytellers embellish. Families get confused. When there were three John Budds in a family, how can you be sure which one was the mariner?

The best clues for beginning a genealogical search are actual records right in your home or the homes of relatives. Often one person has become the unofficial family historian and/or pack rat. Ask that person to gather together anything which might help you. Some sources of genealogical information are listed below.

Account books / ledgers	Apprentice records
Address books	Auto licenses
Adoption papers	Autograph albums
Anniversary announcements	Awards
Appointment books	Baby books

Bank books
Bank statements
Baptismal certificates
Beneficiary records
Bills of sale
Bills
Birth announcements
Birth certificates
Birth notices
Bounty papers
Business licenses
Check stubs
Church bulletins
College degrees
College yearbooks
Communion records
Confirmation records
Contracts
Correspondence
Court actions
Deeds
Diaries / journals
Diplomas
Disability records
Discharge papers
Divorce papers
Driver's licences
Employment records
Engagement announcements
Engraved jewelry
Family albums
Family Bible
Family friends & neighbors
Family members
Family traditions
Financial records
Funeral memorial cards
Genealogies
Graduation announcements
Greeting cards
Guardian papers
Health records
Heirlooms
High school diplomas
High school yearbooks
Historical societies

Hometown newspapers
Hospital records
I.D. cards
Insurance policies
Internet
Interviews
Jewelry
Land grants
Leases
Letters
Local histories
Locket pictures
Marriage licenses
Medals
Membership records
Mementos
Military records
Military uniforms
Mortgages
Naturalization papers
New home announcements
Newspaper clippings
Notations in books
Obituaries
Old trunks
Oral histories
Ordination certificates
Passports
Photographs
Post cards
Postmarks
Prescription bottles
Professional licenses
Report cards
Resumes
Samplers
School yearbooks
School records
Scrapbooks
Social Security cards
Subpoenas
Summons
Sunday School records
Tax records
Traditions
Uniforms

Union papers
Vaccination records
Videos / home movies
Water rights

Wedding announcements
Wedding invitations
Wedding ring engravings
Wills

When You Think You Have Hit a Dead End...

Ask yourself -

Who were my ancestor's neighbors?	Land records, censuses
Who else was living with the family?	Censuses
What ship did he travel on and with who did he travel?	Ship records
Was he educated? If so, where?	Yearbooks, lists of students from the office of the superintendent of schools, censuses
Is there a family association?	Internet, *Everton's Genealogical Helper*

Where to Find the Information in Records

Most of the time, knowing where to find information is half the battle. Although all death certificates do not indicate religion, in some cases religion of the deceased can be determined by the listed place of interment. In the chart below,

B stands for Birth
M for Marriage
D for Death
I for Immigration Date

O for Occupation
F for Family Members
P for Physical Description
R for Religion

Source	Types of Records	B	M	D	I	O	F	P	R
Federal	Census	X	X		X	X	X		
	Selective and/or Military Service	X		X				X	
	Homestead Application	X							

4

Source	Types of Records	B	M	D	I	O	F	P	R
	Pension and/or Widow's Pension Application	X	X	X		X	X		
	Social Security Death Index	X		X					
	Naturalization and/or Citizenship	X			X			X	
	Emigration and/or Immigration				X	X	X	X	
State / Local Government	School Records	X					X		
	Driver's Licenses	X						X	
	Vital Statistics - Birth	X					X		
	Marriage		X				X		
	Death	X		X		X	X		X
	Business License / Apprenticeship						X		
	Probate Records			X		X	X		
	Land Records			X			X		
Personal	Family Bible	X		X	X	X	X		X
	Employment Records	X							
	Insurance Records	X	X			X			
Misc.	Hospital Records	X		X			X	X	X
	Physician's Records	X						X	
	Baptismal Certificate	X					X		X
	Newspaper Announcements	X	X	X			X		X
	Obituaries	X		X	X	X	X		X
	Cemetery and/or Tombstone Records	X		X			X		X

5

- Lay the proper groundwork. Don't skip generations.
- Don't keep your research in storage areas, such as basements and attics, prone to mold, fire and water damage.
- Don't store research on the floor. Pipes can burst, tubs overflow, and houses flood.
- When photocopying include the title page or the page with Library of Congress information for reference and later citation.
- Don't assume anything. Consider something as fact only when you have a primary source.
- Make sure your dates make sense. How old were the parents when they were married? Is there at least nine months between each child's birth, except in the case of twins?
- Seek original or unaltered reproductions of records and treat them carefully.
- Type or neatly write queries. Questions which cannot be read, cannot be answered.
- When sending a query, always include a self-addressed stamped envelope.
- Do not expect librarians, archivists, docents or curators to watch your children. And do not automatically expect your children to behave unattended in libraries, archives and museums.
- Copy everything remotely related to the surname. You never know when a connection can be made or when information can be traded.
- Cite your sources.
- Establish a filing system and stick with it.
- Double check all facts.
- Do your homework so you can understand the answers to the questions you ask.
- Remember, geographic names and boundaries change.
- Be creative with first name and surname spellings.
- Remember, everything in print is not fact.
- When dealing with conflicting information, do not assume the answer given the most frequently is the correct one.
- Don't believe everything your relatives tell you. Tales of royal descent are probably false.
- Store a second hard or disk copy of text and photographs off-site.
- Backup, backup, backup.

Genealogical Terms

Genealogy almost has a language of its own. When these terms are found in writings or records, they can be confusing to a newcomer to the field, especially since these words might have dissimilar meanings under common usage. For instance, an "orphan" in early records might have lost only one parent.

Some more frequently found terms are defined below.

ab nepos - a great-great-grandson

ab neptis - a great-great-granddaughter

accelerated - an index prepared by computer, such as a census index

aelaet - approximate age of (Latin)

agricultural schedule - a part of the 1850-1880 federal census which listed farmers and information concerning their farms

ahnenlist / ahnentafel - a charting system of ancestors, from the German "ahnen" (ancestor) and "tafel" (list). But is was first used in 1676 by Jerome de Sosa, a Spanish genealogist

ahnentafel numbers - numbering system used for identification on an ancestral chart

alias - the other name of a person who changed his/her name. The new name could be for a man who married into a distinguished family. The term was also used to signify illegitimacy in some parish records.

allied and associated families - families which intermarried, witnessed documents for each other, migrated together and lived near families being researched

ancestor - person from who one is descended

ancestor chart - chart showing a person and their ancestors

ancestral - relating to an ancestor

ancestral file - a database of names in genealogies on CD-ROM and the internet

Anglo-Saxon - also known as "Old English", referred to the language and time period between the invasion of the British Isles by Germanic tribes (c, 500 A.D.) and their defeat by William the Conqueror and the Normans (1066 A.D.)

archives - the storage place of older official records and historic documents. If capitalized, the word probably refers to the National Archives.

armiger - a person entitled to heraldic arms

armory - heraldry or a place where weapons are stored.

arms - parts: crest, wreath, mantle, helmet, shield, motto

ascendant - ancestor

ascendencia - ascendancy (Spanish)

bando - marriage banns (Spanish)

banns - public notice of a proposed marriage, usually but not always posted in the church

bautismo - baptism (Spanish)

Bible records - vital records, such as birth, death and marriage dates of family members, written on blank pages of the family Bible

birth certificate - documentation of birth

Bishops Transcript - one year's entries in a parish record which was sent to the Bishop

blazon - the verbal description of the family coat of arms

boda - wedding (Spanish)

broadsides - large papers printed to usually be used for advertising, similar to posters and hand bills of today. They frequently contained information of genealogical importance.

casamiento - marriage (Spanish)

cascading pedigree chart - series of charts that cover multiple generations for an individual. The last person of each chart becomes the first person on another chart.

catastro - census (Spanish)

census - periodic tally of the population

census enumerator - person who counts or lists inhabitants of a region

census index - alphabetical listing of names enumerated in a census

Certified American Lineage Specialist - a person holding a certification of skill in genealogy

Chino - term used periodically to describe the offspring of a Black and Native American, or the offspring of a Mulatto and Chinese

Christian name - first name given at birth

chronology - grouping of events in order of occurrence

Church of Jesus Christ of Latter-day Saints (LDS) - the Mormon Church

circa - approximate date

citation - page or section reference, support or proof

clan - a social unit consisting of several families claiming descent from a common progenitor and following the same hereditary leader in the Scottish Highlands

closed-end question - questions which can be answered with a short statement of fact

coat of arms - shield with distinct symbols or emblems painted in defined colors identifying one person and his descendants. Originally it was a garment embroidered with these heraldic devices.

collateral relatives - persons who share an ancestor but do not descend from one another. For example, descendants of Benjamin Franklin's sister are collateral relatives of Benjamin Franklin.

compiled record - information gathered together from oral history, original records or other compiled records

connubial - pertaining to marriage

consanguinity - related by blood

county formation date - date the county was created from previously existing counties or Indian lands crest - figure attached to the top of the helmet. The symbol was usually taken from the shield.

death notice - brief mention of death, briefer than an obituary

decedent - a deceased individual

decem - ten

demography - the study of attributes of various human populations, their vital and social statistics

descendant - immediate and/or direct progeny

descendant chart - chart showing a person and all their descendants

direct heir - someone in an individual's direct line of descent or ascent

dit - also known as; alias (French)

domestic - someone who does housework, but not always as a servant

Doomsday Book - register of English land ordered by William the Conqueror and continued until 1783

double dating - recording a date using both the Julian and Gregorian calendar years, such as 5 February 1720/21

dowry - the money, goods and property a bride brings to the marriage

Duitsh man - refugee from the Low Countries who settled in Colchester, England and set up a church in the 1500's

dyet - diet, food

edad - age (Spanish)

emigrant - person who leaves one country to reside in another

emigration - the withdrawal or migration of persons from their country of residence to another

endogamy - the practice of marriage within a small group, such as a caste, family, or village; inbreeding

enterré - buried (French)

enumerate - to count

enumeration order - house to house sequence of census entries

ephemera - papers not intended for posterity that have survived and are used for historical purposes

epoch - event of distinction usually defining the beginning and/or end of a "period"

era - an indefinite period of time characterized to notable historical events

escutcheon - the shield on which is indicated rank of the bearer of the arms. It has two parts.
1. Field - the surface or background
2. Charges - patterns and/or symbols

esquire - originally fourteen year and older gentleman ranking just below a knight from chivalric times. Later an esquire was one who held office under the crown. More recently, it has become a term for a gentleman in business and an unofficial title of respect.

esse - is

evidence - proof

exogamy - the practice of marrying an individual from out of a person's own social or family group

falleció - deed (Spanish)

family group sheet - page recording members of a family unit

Family History Centers - smaller branches of the Family History Library

Family History Library - genealogical library in Salt Lake City operated by The Church of Jesus Christ of Latter-day Saints (LDS or Mormon) Church

Family Tree Maker - a commercial genealogy program

footnote - additional information to material appearing on a page. It is usually found at the bottom of the page or, sometimes, at the end of the chapter or book as "endnotes."

fiveteen - fifteen

forebear - forefather, ancestor

fortnight - 14 days

fraternal order - organization of people with similar beliefs or club membership

freeborn - born to a free person.

freeman - a man who is freed from bondage or slavery; or who was an elected citizen of a town given the right to vote and conduct business

Friends - members of The Society of Friends, a.k.a. "Quakers"

fuget hora - the hour is fleeting

funeral gifts - gifts given to those invited to attend a funeral

funeral rings - rings worn in the 1600's and 1700's in memory of a dead friend

gazetteer - a geographical dictionary

genannt - also known as; alias (German)

Genealogical Data Communication - the format created by the LDS Church which allows transfer of genealogical data via software

Genealogical Society of Utah - an division of the Family History Department of the LDS Church

genealogy - study of ancestors and family history. It comes from the Greek "genea" meaning "race" or "family."

generation - a group of people born within a usual time span between the birth of a father and his first child, making the interval of uncertain length. There may be three or four generations in a one hundred year time period.

gentle birth - a person born into a family of high standing, but not of nobility

gentleman - a respectful term to denote someone not of noble birth, but having the right to a coat of arms

given name - person's first name

godparent - man or woman who sponsors a child at baptism

griff - term used primarily in Louisiana to denote a person of Black and Mulatto or Native American and Mulatto ancestry

heirloom - item of special value handed down through generations of a family

heraldry - the designing and granting of a coat of arms

heritage - something that is passed on or belongs to a person by reason of birth

historical and genealogical societies - groups of people brought to together because of a common interest in a family name, locality or ethnic group, who work to preserve and make available records of historic value

hoja de servicio - record of government service (Spanish)

home guard - men in a region organized to defend an area in an emergency

Homestead Act of 1862 - federal law defining generous terms for people to acquire and settle land

housekeeper - in early times, a male or female property owner

Huguenot - French Protestant

ibid. - found in the same place (as in book, chapter and page) as the last reference

iglesia - church (Spanish)

immigración - immigration (Spanish)

immigrant - person arriving in a country with the intentions of settling there

immigration - the movement to one country from another

indentured servant - someone who voluntarily or involuntarily was obligated to work for another person for a specific time period in exchange for passage to America or for money. An indentured servant had no rights until the sum owed had been paid.

inhumacion - burial (Spanish)

inmate - a man living in a home of another, but not necessarily an institution

issue - offspring

instant - "this month", as in "your letter the 15th inst."

interlibrary loan - process of one library borrowing books from another library for patron's use

International Genealogical Index - database of names with information from private records and primary sources

irregular unit - informal group of armed men organized for an expressed purpose

Josephite - follower of the Reorganized Church of Jesus Christ of Latter Day Saints

junior - the younger of two person having the same name, living in the same community

jurisdiction - having authority to carry out specific duties

kith and kin - friends, neighbors and family

late - deceased

Law of Pews - determination by the state as to whether church pews were considered personal estate or real estate

legacy - a gift of property or money received through a will

Library of Congress - depository of information created for the US Congress. It is open to the public

lineal descendant - in direct line of descent, such as grandfather, father, son

loose papers - legal documents relating to one subject gathered into packets and filed at the courthouse. For example, all claims, inventory and other records pertaining to the probate of a will are gathered together in a packet.

Loyalist - a person who continued their loyalty to England during the American Revolution, a Tory

macadam - popular type of road in the 1800's. The road had a convex base of packed earth overlaid by two 4-inch layers of graded stones. Finely ground pebbles covered the stones. Tar was added as a top layer, creating tarmac.

maiden name - a female's family name/surname at birth

manuscript collection - assorted unpublished papers held by an archives or library

maternal line - descent on the mother's side

matrilineal - descent runs through the female line

Mestizo - a term often used for the offspring of a Caucasian and a Native American

Metis - any person of mixed Native American and Caucasian descent

migrant - a person who changes residence

Military Death Index - database of men and women who died in the Korean and Vietnam Wars

microfiche - photographic cards of reduced pages of printed material. A special machine is needed to read them.

migrate - to move

microfilm - photographic rolls of reduced pages of printed material. They need a special reader.

militia - local armed forces organized for emergencies

modified register - book of one's descendants

moiety - a half portion

mortality schedule - enumeration of deaths from the twelve months preceding the censuses, generally from 1850-1880. It lists name, county, age and cause of death for each person.

morte - dead (French)

mort né - stillborn (French)

motto - a saying or war cry shown on a ribbon below the shield, except in Scotland where the motto appears above the shield

mourir - to die (French)

muerte - death (Spanish)

mug book - slang for a county or commemorative history with biographies containing portraits

Mulatto - a term used for the offspring of Caucasian and Negroid parents

muster rolls - lists of all able-bodied men, usually between the ages of 16 and 60, eligible for militia duty and owned their own weapons

nacido muerto - stillborn (Spanish)

nació - birth (Spanish)

naissance - birth (French)

National Archives - US repository of documents

National Highway - a road built in the early 1800's which ran from Baltimore, through Pennsylvania, West Virginia, Ohio, Indiana and into Illinois

naturalization - the procedures to become a citizen

near friend - blood relative who is also a close friend

necrology - register book of deaths

necrosis - decay of bones or tissue

ne - original or birth name of a man

nee - maiden name

New England - the six most northeastern states

New Style - refers to dates after the change from the Julian to the Georgian Calendars

next of kin - closest blood relative

nickname - informal name, usually a version based on the given name, surname, place or physical feature. It can be a familiar form of a name or a source of ridicule.

noces - wedding (French)

obituary - a published announcement of a person's death

Old Dominion - Virginia

Old Style - refers to dates prior to the change from the Julian to the Gregorian Calendars. The new year began in March prior to then.

open-ended questions - questions which can be answered in essay form

oral history - verbal account of events

original record - information recorded by an eyewitness at or close to the time of the event

orphan - a child who has lost at least one parent

padre no conocidos - parents unknown (Spanish)

page - the 7-14 year old son of a gentlemen. The boy was raised in the home of a person of superior title and acted as a servant

paleography - study of ancient forms of writing

Palatinate - area in Germany west of the Rhine River

panteón - cemetery (Spanish)

parent county - county from which another county was formed

parentesco - relationship)Spanish)

parto - birth (Spanish)

passenger list - usually a list of names of ship passengers

paternal line - descent on the father's side

patronymic - name derived from paternal ancestor (Jacobson, the son of Jacob)

patroons - wealthy Dutch farmers who had been granted land in New York and New Jersey by the Dutch government

pedigree - chart indicating lineage or ancestral line

pedigree chart - genealogical form for recording lineage

peerage - British nobility included in books containing peers' rank, genealogy, history and titles

pension - a stipend provided to military veterans or the elderly

per annum - Latin for "per year"

per diem - Latin for "per day"

period - time between two dates

periodical - publication released at recurrent intervals

Personal Ancestral file - popular genealogical computer program

personal property - moveable property, not attached to the land

pioneer - early settler in an area

plantation account - records pertaining to the business of a plantation

population schedule - completed census questionnaire

Prerogative Court of Canterbury - English court which settles estates of people owning land in England, but reside elsewhere

primary sources - information recorded by someone directly involved at the time of the event. On a death certificate, the name, date of death, cause of death, place of death are primary pieces of information. The names of the deceased person's parents are not. Courtroom testimony is a primary source.

primogenitor - earliest known ancestor, originator of a line of descent

primogeniture - right of the eldest child to inherit

progenitor - direct descent from an ancestor

proof - documents used as evidence

Prussian - resident of the Kingdom of Prussia, a northern European county which contained much of present-day Germany and existed between 1701-1871

public house - a tavern

purpure - purple

query - a question requesting exchange of information

record - an account of an important event

redemptioner - colonial emigrant who agreed to serve as a bonded servant to pay for his voyage

regestros paroquiales - church records (Spanish)

register - a recorded listing of names and/or dates

regular soldier - a military man serving duty in the "standing army"

removed - moved

repository - receptacle or place where something is stored

Revolutionary War - American War of Independence fought 1776-1783

secondary record - created from other sources

secondary source - information recorded after an event or by someone not directly involved in the event. Family genealogies are secondary. On a death certificate, names of parents of an elderly deceased person are secondary information.

senior - the elder of two persons with the same name living in the same community

sepulchered - buried in a rock or stone vault

shoppes - any building were goods are produced

sic - Latin for "thus" or "as written"

slave - a person who is owned by and considered property of another

slave schedule - portion of the 1850 and 1860 federal census listing slave owners with number, sex and age of slaves owned

Social Security Death Index - index of Social Security Death Benefits paid

sollars - attic/upper room in a house

Soundex - system of name code of one letter and three numbers used to keep the same and similar names together

source - origin of information, the record or person furnishing data

source citation - note indicating origin of information

spinster - a never married, single lady or a person who spins thread

sterk /stirk/ styrke - between one and two years old

surname - family or last name

tax record - list of area taxpayers

te - the

tithable - income subject to tax or for support of a church

Tory - a person who continued their loyalty to England during the American Revolution (a Loyalist) or a member of the British Tory political party

ultimo - last, as in "your letter of 15th ult." (Latin)

United Empire Loyalist - Americans who remained loyal to the King of England

vecino - head of household (Spanish)

verbatim - word for word

visitation - stay for official inspection

vital records - public records of birth, marriage, death

viz - from "videlicet" meaning "namely" (Latin)

Whig - early American political party which supported the American Revolution

widow's pension - stipend received by a woman because of her deceased husband's military service or employment

Works Progress Administration / Works Project Administration - governmental program begun during the Great Depression of the 1930's. Many WPA workers compiled guides to vital records and interviewed early settlers about their lives.

Familial Terms

Family relationships could become quite complicated in small communities. One convoluted family lineage belong to Thomas Jefferson. His daughters Martha and Maria married their cousins. Martha's first husband was her second stepmother's first husband's younger brother. And that was Jefferson's legitimate family. His probable seven children by his slave Sally Hemings just complicated relationships even more.

Added to that, terms used today did not always have the same meaning. And words used in colonial documents were not always taken from common usage.

ab napos - great-great grandson

ab neptis - great-great granddaughter

abueia - grandmother (Spanish)

abuelo - grandfather (Spanish)

ancestor - a person from whom one is descended

aunt - formerly used in front of a given name to show respect to an older, close family friend - not necessarily a relative

base born - illegitimate

base son - son born to an unmarried woman

bastard - illegitimate

bisabuelo - great grandfather (Spanish)

brother / sister - a sibling. But the terms can also denote an in-law or step sibling be used to show close friendship, or indicate a fellow church member. They can indicate a member of a religious order or merely a member of the same community.

collateral ancestor - direct ancestor's extended family, such as aunts, uncles, brothers, sisters and cousins of the ancestor

conjugi - spouse

consanguinity - descended from a common ancestor; shared blood

consort - spouse

cónyuge - spouse (Spanish)

cousin - in colonial times, a nephew or niece, or sometimes any familial relationship, blood or otherwise, except for mother, father, brother or sister. It did not necessarily mean a common grandparent. Although, now
- First cousins share two grandparents
- Second cousins share two great grandparents
- Third cousins share two great-great grandparents
- Half-cousins are the children of half-siblings (children who share only one parent).
- Double cousins are the children of two sets of siblings who have married. They share two complete sets of grandparents.
- A first cousin once removed is one generation from being first cousins, i.e. a cousin's child

cousin German - a child of an aunt or uncle (first cousin)

cuate - twins (Spanish)

dowager - a widow who inherited property from her dead husband

descendants - progeny of a particular ancestor

father / mother - a parent. But father or mother can also indicate an in-law.

forebearer - an ancestor

hermana - sister (Spanish)

hermano - brother (Spanish)

hermano politico - brother-in-law (Spanish)

hija - daughter (Spanish)

hijo - son (Spanish)

hijo adoptivo - adopted child (Spanish)

illegitimate - conceived out of wedlock

illegetimus - illegitimate (Spanish)

in-law - any familial relationship resulting from marriage in colonial times

issue - children

junior / senior - used to differentiate between two people with the same name, whether or not there was a familial relationship. The term could also be used with women's names.

kindred - blood-related persons

legitimate - issue of valid marriage

lineal - of direct descent

madrestra - stepmother (Spanish)

madre - mother (Spanish)

madre politica - mother-in-law (Spanish)

marido - husband (Spanish)

maternal - pertaining to mother

medio hermano - half-brother (Spanish)

mother-in-law - a person's stepmother or spouse's mother

natural - usually refers to an illegitimate child.

nephew / niece - from Latin *nepot / nepos* meaning "grandson" and "granddaughter". In colonial times the terms were frequently used for those relationships.

now wife - refers to the current wife, whether or not the husband had been previously married

nuera - daughter-in-law (Spanish)

padre - father (Spanish)

padrinos - godparent (Spanish)

padro politico - father-in-law (Spanish)

padrastro - stepfather (Spanish)

paternal - belonging to the father

patritius - paternal

primo - cousin (Spanish)

primo carnal - first cousin (Spanish)

progenitor - originator of a line of descent

progeny - children

relict - widow or widower

sibling - brother or sister

spouse - husband or wife; joined in legal matrimony

sobreno - nephew (Spanish)

still born - dead at birth

tio - uncle (Spanish)

uxor - wife

vidua - widow

widow / widower - woman / man whose spouse had died and who remained unmarried

yerno - son-in-law (Spanish)

𝒽𝓸𝓊𝓈𝑒𝒽𝑜𝓁𝒹 𝒢𝑜𝑜𝒹𝓈

Did you ever wonder what those things mentioned in an estate inventory were? Or perhaps you have found a letter and can understand only half of it, even though the letter was written in English.

adz - extremely sharp hoe-shaped ax

ambry - large cupboard

andiron - pair of metal log supports used in hearths

appurtenances - rights attached to owning land, such as having grazing rights

ardent spirits - alcoholic beverages

armoire - large, two-door cabinet used as a cupboard

arrow back chair - primitive plank-bottomed chair with arrow shaped spindles

backsyde - outbuildings

bays & says - type of wool cloth

beaker - glass or cup

becker - wooden serving dish

bed warmer - long handled metal pan with lid which holds coals and is placed under bed covers to warm them

bedstead and cord - bed frame and rope-strung instead of slat support

beehive clock - small 19th century shelf clock resembling a beehive

bell seat - early 18th century chair with a bell-shaped or rounded seat

blunderbuss - a short gun with a large bore and a flaring nozzle which fired several small metal balls at a time

boluter - sieve

bovenlyf - corset (Dutch)

brandlet - trivet

brasier - metal pan

breakfront - wooden cabinet

Brown Bess - smooth bore flintlock musket.

bucket bench - cupboard with doors below and rimmed shelf and work surface above

broiler - long handled scissor-like

kitchen utensil

calamus - reed used as a writing pen

carbine - a gun more powerful than a usual pistol. The name came for the interior diameter of the pistol. Later carbines were short rifles used by the calvary.

carbiole - an early, stuffed arm chair

cartonnier - an open sided, small cupboard with compartments which sat on writing tables. It was used for storing papers.

caudle cup - two handed, silver cup

chaffer - chaffing dish, a metal dish with candle or hot coals underneath or around it to keep food warm

chattels - personal property

chifforobe - a double door bedroom chest with drawers on one side and space to hang clothes on the other

chiffonier - tall narrow chest of drawers, sometimes with an attached mirror

clarence - closed carriage with four inside seats and an outside driver's seat

closed cupboard - cupboard with doors

closestool - stool holding a

chamber pot

coal oil - kerosene

combaes - blanket (Dutch)

commode - decorated chest of drawers

cony - rabbit

counterpane - bedcover woven in squares

dornix - heavy damask

dresser - originally a table or board used for preparing food

8d nales - eight penny nails

fauteuil - a chair with arms

fender - iron plate used to keep coals from falling on the floor

fixt - fixed

flatiron clock - a small 19th century shelf clock resembling a flatiron

flatware - table ware with no cutting edge, i.e. spoons and forks

fleakes - fence-making hurdles

flintlock - gun fired with a vice which holds a piece of flint. When it struck against the hammer or steel, it produces a spark, which ignites the charge and fires the gun.

flock - wool used to stuff pillows and mattresses

four poster - a bed with four corner posts sometimes used to support a canopy

form watch - an oddly shaped watch

fowler - sporting, rifle-like firearm

freedom box - hinged box containing papers giving freedom to a person in the 17th and 18th centuries

garnish - set of dishes, usually made of pewter

gearing - harness for horses

gilt - gold plated

grease lamp - an easily carried lamp in which animal fat and a twisted rag wick were used

gredyron - gridiron, for tools for cooking over a fire

girandole - branched candlestick

handirons - andirons

harpsichord - a keyboard, but string plucked instrument similar to the piano

highboy - tall chest

hogshead - large vessel

hoodbox - instrument, hautbois / oboe

hovel - open shed or outhouse

husslements / husty / hushelles /

husoulment - minor household goods

hutch - a ventilated chest or bin used to store food

joyned - stool

keeler - broad wooden vessel in which milk or cream were set to cool

kettle - an open cooking pot

koe - cow (Dutch)

kombaars - rug (Dutch)

lanthorne - lantern

looking glass - mirror

low boy - dressing table

messuage - dwelling with surrounding land and out buildings

musket - smooth bored, long arm, large caliber gun

open betty - see "grease lamp"

opstal - small structure on a piece of land; outbuildings (Dutch)

pale - fence stake

peel - long handled shovel used to put bread in the oven

pepper box - early pistol

pillow beers / drawers - pillow cases

ploegh - plow (Dutch)

porringer - bowl

press - enclosed cupboard

pricket - candlestick holder with a spike to hold the candle

quearne - hand mill for grinding grain

quicksett - hedge

quissions - cushions

sheers - plow shares

shoppes - house or building where merchandise is produced

sideboard - dining room furniture holding items for food service

skomar - skimmer for removing ashes from hearth

slot / slut - see "grease lamp"""

sollars - attic

spytt - spit for roasting meat

standard - a chest or the support for a lamp or candlestick

stupuet - pan or skillet

tarletan - thin muslin

trade tokens - brass or copper tokens issued by tradesmen used like coupons

treen ware - wooden ware

trevytt - trivet

truckle bed - trundle bed

trug - basket with a fixed handle

tunnel - funnel

turnout - carriage with horses and equipment

valons - valence

virginalls - rectangular harpsichord; a keyed musical instrument similar to a legless spinet piano, popular in the 16th and 17th centuries

voider / voyder - a large dish

wainscoting / waynscotte - wood paneling

Abbreviations

E.E. Thoyts called it "courthand" because so many abbreviations appeared in old deeds and other court records. Frequently census takers used abbreviations when the place of birth, relationship to head of the house or occupation was to be recorded. Others appeared on tombstones. The reason for these abbreviations was simply to save time and space. They varied in punctuation and capitalization.

As with spellings, abbreviations could take on quite a creative flair. In some cases, the letter or letters at the end of an abbreviated word were raised high¹.

The easiest abbreviations and contractions had straight or curved lines over the word to indicate a portion of the word had been omitted. Where a letter was duplicated, as the "m" in "hammer," the second "m" might have been dropped and a short horizontal line would have been placed over the first "m." Eventually, the straight line stood for an omitted "m" or "n."

Although contractions of two words were other forms of abbreviating, they were not the ones recognized today "T'err" was a contraction to "to err." "The other" might have become "T'other."

Modern day genealogists have also come up with their own form of "courthand." These abbreviations might also be misunderstood by the novice.

The abbreviations listed below were only the most common old and new forms used. That is not to say that what is shown in capital letters here might not be found in lowercase elsewhere.

& - and (derived from "et")

&c - and so forth

&caske - with cask

*/x - born

o-o common-law marriage

-30- the end

= married

$ - Spanish or US dollar

@/a) - at, as in "sold @ $1.00 per pound"

a. - about, age, acre

AAGHS - Afro-American Genealo-gical and Historical Society

a.a.s. - died in the year of his/her age

AASP - American Antiquarian Society Proceedings

ab. - about, abbey

abbr. - abbreviation

abd. - abdicated

Abp. - Archbishop

abr. - abridged

abs. / abstr. - abstract

abt. - about

acad. - academy

acc - accusative

accot/acct - account

ackd. - acknowledged

actg. - acting

AD - *Anno Domin*

Ad - adopted

AdCl - adopted child

AdD - adopted daughter

ADC - Aide-de-Camp

adj. - adjoining, adjutant, adjourned

adm / admin/ admr.- administration, administrator

29

Admon - letter of
administration

admx - female
administrator

adv - adverse
(against)

ae - age

AF & AM - Ancient
Free and Accepted
Masons

aff. / afft. - affidavit

aforsd - aforesaid

afs. - aforesaid

aft. - after

AG - Accredited
Genealogist

ag. lab - agricultural
laborer

AGLL - American
Genealogical Lend-
ing Library

AGRA - Association
of Genealogists and
Record Agents

agt - agent, against

AJGS - Association
of Jewish Genealo-
gical Societies

a.k.a. - also known
as

AKIA - A Klansman
I am

AL - American
Legion

al - aunt-in-law

ald. - alderman

alleg. - allegiance

a.l.s. - autographed
letter signed

als - alias, also

an/ano, - year, as in
"Ano 1582"

anc. - ancestor,
ancient

annot. - annotated

ano. - another

anon. - anonymous

ant / antiq -
antiquities

AOP - American
Order of Pioneers

APG - Association
of Professional
Genealogists

APJI - Association
for Protection of
Jewish Immigrants

app. - apprentice,
approximately,
appendix, appointed

appl. - appealed,
applied

appr. - appraise-
ment, appraiser

approx-
approximately

apptd. - appointed

appx. - appendix

A R - Anno Regni
(year of reign)

ar. co. - artillery
company

arr. - arrived

ASCII - American
Standard Code for
Information
Interchange

ASG - American
Society of
Genealogists

asgd. - assigned

ASGR - Association
of Germans from
Russia

asr. - assessor

assn. / assoc. -
association

Asst - assistant

at - attendant

atba - able to bear

30

arms

attchn - attachment

atts. - attorneys

atty. - attorney

a.w.c. - letter of administration with will and codicil attached

AWOL - absent without leave

b. - born, brother, bondsman, banns book,

ba. - bachelor, baptized

bal./ ball. - balance

bap. / bapt. - baptized

bbl - barrel

Bboy - bound boy

B.C. - before Christ

bcer - birth certificate

BCG - Board of Certified Genealogists

b.d. / bdt. - birth date

bd. - bound, buried

bec. - became, because

bef. - before

beq. - bequeathed

bet. / betw. - between

Bgirl - bound girl

BIA - Bureau of Indian Affairs

BIGHR - British Institute of Genealogy and Historical Research

b.i.l. / BI - brother-in-law

biog. - biography

bks - barracks, books

BLM - Bureau of Land Management

BLW - Bounty Land Warrant

B.M. - Bench Mark

bndsmn - bonds-man

bo - boarder

b/o - brother of

bp. - birthplace, baptized

bpl. - birthplace

BPOE - Benevolent & Protective Order of Elks

bpt. - baptized

Br. - British

br. / bro. - brother

B.S. - bill of sale

bu. / bur. - buried

c. - cousin, circa (approximately)

ca. - circa

CAILS - Certified American Indian Lineage Specialist

cal - calendar

CALS - Certified American Lineage Specialist

Cap - captain

CAR - Children of the American Revolution

CC - company commander, county clerk

CCP - Court of Common Pleas

cd - continued

CDA - Colonial Dames of America

CDIB - Certified Degree of Indian Blood

CDXVII - Colonial Dames of the 17th Century

cem. - cemetery

cen. / cens. - census

cent. - century

cert. - certificate

c.f. - compare

CG - Certified Genealogist

CGI - Certified Genealogical Instructor

CGL - Certified Genealogical Lecturer

CGRS - Certified Genealogical Record Specialist

CH - courthouse

ch. - children, chief, church, chaplain

Cha - chamber maid

chh. - church

chan. - chancery

chl/chldn - children

ch/o - child of

chr. / chris. - christened

cie - compagnie (company)

cir. - circa

cit. - citation, citizen

civ. - civil

CJ - county judge

clk./clke - clerk

CO - commanding officer, Colonial Office

co. - company, county

cod. - codicil

CofA - Coat of Arms

col. - colonel, "colored" (early term for person of African heritage)

comm. - commissioners

comp. - company

complt - complaint

cont. - continued

contr. - contract

corp - corporal

cort/crte - court

Couns - counsellor

cous. / csn. - cousin

coven. - covenant

CRA - Church Records Archives

crspd. - correspondence

c.s. - copy signed

CSA - Confederate States of America

C.T.A. - Cum testamento annexo/ "with will attached"

cwt - hundred weight (equal to one hundred twelve pounds)

d. - daughter, died, days,

da. - daughter, days

DAB - Dictionary of American Biography

DAC - Daughters of the American Colonies

DAR - Daughters of

the American
Revolution

dau. - daughter

DB - Doomsday
Book

DC - Deputy Clerk

DCG -
Descendants of
Colonial Governors

DCW - Daughters
of Colonial Wars

Dea / deac. -
deacon

dec. / dec'd / d'd -
deceased

defdt - defendant

dep.- deputy,
deposed, depot

desc. - descendant

DFPA - Daughters
of Founders and
Patriots of America

d. & h. - daughter
and heir

di. - diocese

dil. - daughter-in-
law

d-i-l - daughter-in-
law

dis ./ dischd. -

discharged

discip. - discipline

dist. - district

div. - divorced,
divided

DNB - Dictionary of
National Biography

d/o - daughter of

do. / dto. - ditto

doc. / docum. -
document

dom. - domestic

DOW. - died of
wounds

dpl - place of death

DR - Daughters of
the Revolution,
death record

dr. - dram, doctor,
debtor

drest - dressed, as
in meat

d.s. - died single,
document signed

ds. - daughters

dsct - descendant

d.s.p. - *descessit
sine parole* (died
without issue)

d.s.p.l. - died
without legitimate
issue

d.s.p.m. - died
without male issue

d.s.p.s. died without
surviving issue

dt. - date

dtr. - daughter

d. unm. - died
unmarried

dvm - *decessit vita
matris* (died in the
lifetime of his
mother)

dvp - decessit vita
patris (died in the
lifetime of his
father)

DVR - Society of
the Descendants of
Washington's Army
at Valley Forge

d.y. - died young

dyet - food

e. - east

ecux. - executrix
(female executor)

E.D. - for census
Enumeration
District

ed. - editor

e.g. - *exemplie gratia* (for example)

Emp. - employee

en - engineer

Eng./Engl. - England, English

enl. - enlisted

Ens. - ensign

ensu. - ensuing

equiv - equivalent

esp - especially

Esq. - Esquire

est. - established, estimate, estate

establ. - established

estd - estimated

et al. - *et alia* (and others)

etc. - *et cetera* (and so forth)

et ux/uxor - and wife

et. vir. - and husband

exc. - exchange, except

exec. / exor./ exr. - executor

excelly - Excellency

exit. atta, - signed attached

exox. / exx. - executrix

exs. - executors

f. / fa. - father

F&AM - Free & Accepted Masons

F.A. - Field Artillery

FaH - farm hand

FaL - farm laborer

fam. - family

FARC - Federal Archives and Records Centers

FASG - Fellow of the American Society of Genealogists

FaW - farm worker

FB - foster brother

F.B. - Family Bible

FBI - full blooded Indian

f.e. - for example

fem - female

FF - foster father

ff. - following pages

FF'S - First Families

FFV - First Families of Virginia

FGRA - Family Group Record Archives

FGS - Federation of Genealogical Societies

fgs - family group sheet

FHC - Family History Center

FHL - Family History Law

FIGRS - Fellow of the Irish Genealogical Research Society

f-i-l / fil. / fl - father-in-law

fl - flourished, flows

f.m. - free mulatto

fm - Foster Mother

f.n. - free Negro

FNGS - Fellow of the National Genealogical Society

34

f/o - father of

fo. - folio

FoB - foster brother

FOP - Fraternal Order of Police

FoS - foster sister

FPC - Free Persons of Color

foll. - following

FR - Family Registry

Fr - French

freem. - freeman

g. - grand, great

ga - great aunt or grand aunt

GAR - Grand Army of the Republic; Union Army veterans

G.B. - Great Britain

gch. / gcl. - grand-child

gd - granddaughter

gdn. - guardian

GEDCOM - Genealo-gical Data Communication

Gen/Genll - General

gen. - generation, genealogy

Gent. / Gentln-Gentleman

Germ. - German

gf - grandfather

ggf - great grand-father

ggm - great grand-mother

GGSA - German Genealogical Society of America

GH - Genealogical Helper Magazine

GIM - Genealogical Institute of Mid-America

GLC- Genealogical Library Catalog

GLO - General Land Office

gm. - grandmother

gml - grandmother-in-law

gn - grand or great nephew or niece

Go - governess

Gov/Govr- governor

gp. - grandparent

GPAI - Genealogical Periodical Annual Index

GPC - Genealogical Publishing Company

gr. - great, grand, graduate, grant

g.r. - grave record

grf. - grandfather

Grk - Greek

grnd jur - grand jury

grs. / gs - grandson

g.s. - grave stone

GSG - Genealogical Speakers Guild

GSU - Genealogical Society of Utah

GSW 1812 - General Society of the War of 1812

Gt. Br. - Great Britain

gt. gr. - great grand

GTT - Gone To Texas

gu - great uncle

gua - guardian

gvn. - given

gz. - gazetteer

h. - husband, heir

hb - half-brother

hdgrs.- head-
quarters

He. - herder

HEIC - Honorable
East India Company

her. - heraldry

hers. - herself

Hg - hired girl

Hh - hired hand

Hk - Housekeeper

hlg - hireling

HM - His / Her
Majesty

HMS - His / Her
Majesty's Service or
Ship

hims. - himself

hist. - historian,
history

h/o - husband of

hon./honora./
honble. - honorable

hon. dis. -honorably
discharged

HSA - Huguenot
Society of America

hund - hundred

hus. - husband

I - inmate

i. - issue

IA - modern
abbreviation for
Iowa

Ia. - old abbreviation
for Iowa

ibid. - *ibidem* (the
same reference)

i.e. - *id est* (that is)

IGI - International
Genealogical Index

illus. - illustrated

inc. - incorporated,
incomplete

incl. - included

Ind. - Indians

IND.S.C - Indian
Survivors'
Certificates

Ind. T. / Ind. Ter. -
Indian Territory

Ind. W.C. - Indian

Widows' Certificate

inf. - infant, infantry,
information

inh. - inherited

inhab. - inhabitant

inq. - inquiry

inqst - inquest

inst. - institute,
instant, *instans*
(present, as in "this
month" or last, as in
"last Monday")

int. - intentions,
interred, interest

inv./invt. - inventory

IOF - Independent
Order of Foresters

IOOF - Independent
Order of Odd
Fellows

JA - Judge
Advocate

JNH - Journal of
Negro History

JP - Justice of the
Peace

Jr. / junr. - junior

ju. - *jure uxoris*
(right of wife)

jud. / judic. - judicial

jur. - *jurat* (voucher signifying a record was drafted by the person who signed it)

k. - killed, king

KIA - killed in action

kn. - known

knt. / kt. - knight

K. of C. - Knights of Columbus

l. - lodger, license, left descendants, law

la. / labr. - laborer

Lat. - Latin

Lau - launderer

lb. - pound

LBC - Letter Book Copy

LC - Library of Congress

ld. - land

ldr. - leader

LDS - Church of Jesus Christ of Latter-day Saints

L.I. - Long Island

lib. - library

lic. - license

Lieut. - lieutenant

li. / liv. - lived

lit. - literally

lnd. - land

loc. cit. - *loco citato* (in the place cited)

LOM - Loyal Order of Moose

l.p. - local preacher

LPC - Likely to become public charge

L.S. - *Locua sigilli*: place for a seal

ltd. - limited

m. - month, mother, married, meter, male, thousand

m/1 m1 - married first

mag. - magistrate

Maj. - major

Man. - manager

masc. - masculine

mat. - maternal

matys./majt. - majesty's

m.bn. - marriage banns

MCA - Microfilm Corporation of America

MCC - Microfilm Card Catalog

MCD - Municipal Civil District

md. - married

mdm - madam

mem. - member, memorials

ment. - mentioned

messrs. - plural of mister (Mr.); messieurs,

Mex.S.C. - Mexican Survivors'Certificate

Mex.S.O. - Mexican Survivors' Originals

Mex.W.C. - Mexican Widows' Certificate

MG - Minister of the Gospel

m.h. - meeting house

MGH - Middle High

German

m.i. - monument inscription

mi. - miles

MIA - Missing in Action

mil. / milit. - military

min. - minister

m-in-l / ml - mother-in-law

MLG - Middle Low German

MLW - Military Land Warrant

mng - meaning

m.o. - mustered out

mo. - mother, month

MOPH - Military Order of the Purple Heart

mors. - death

mov. /mvd. - moved

MQ - *Mayflower Quarterly*

MR - marriage record

mrkd - marked,

branded

ms./mss. - manuscript

mtg. - mortgage, meeting

M.W.A. - Modern Woodmen of America

my/d. - my daughter

N. - Negro, North

n. - name, nephew, north

NA - not available, National Archives, Native American, North America, non allocatur (not allowed)

na. - naturalized

NARA - National Archives & Records Administration

n.d. - no date

N.E. - New England, Northeast

NEH - National Endowment for the Humanities

NEHGR - New England Historic Genealogical Register

NEHGS - New England Historic Genealogical Society

neph. - nephew

nfi - no further information

nfk - nothing further known

NGS - National Genealogical Society

NHPRC - National Historical Publications and Records Commission

ni - niece

NIGR - National Institute of Genealogical Research

n.k. - not known

nm. - name

nmed - named

NN - not named

not. - noted

not md - not married

no. vo. - *nolens volens*, with or without consent

NP - Notary Public

n.p. - no place

nr. - not recorded, near

NS - New Style Calendar (Gregorian), Nova Scotia

NSCDA - National Society of the Colonial Dames of America

NSDAR - National Society, Daughters of the American Revolution

NUCMC - National Union Catalog of Manuscript Collections

nunc - nuncapative will (oral will, written by witness)

nupr-a-ae - bride or wife

N.W. - Northwest

NW. Terr. - Northwest Territory

n.x.n. - no Christian name

o. - oath, officer

O.B. - Order Book

ob. / obit. - obituary

O.C. - Orphans Court

o.c. - only child

occ. - occupation

O.E. - Old English

off. / offic. - official

OM - Organized Militia

o.p. - out-of-print

op. cit. - *opere citato* (work cited above)

ord. - ordained, ordinance

orig. - original, origin

OS - Old Style Calendar (Julian)

o.s.p. - died without issue

o.t.p. - of this print

p. - post (after), page, per, parent, pence, patient

p:poll - per person

Pa - partner

p.a. - power of attorney

par. - parish, parent

pat. - patent, paternal

pc - pedigree chart

PCC - Prerogative Court of Canterbury

pchd. - purchased

PE - presiding elder

perh. - perhaps

petitn. - petition

petr - petitioner

pg. - page

ph. - parish, physician

PI - Preliminary Inventories

pish - parish

PJP - Probate Judge of the Peace

pl - plural

PLB - Poor Law Board

plt. - plaintiff

P.M. - afternoon, Post Mortem (after death)

P.O. - Post Office

POA - Power of

Attorney

POE - Port of Entry

Por - porter

poss. - possibly

POW - prisoner of
war

p.p. - *propria
persona* (person
who represents
himself)

pp. - pages

pr. - per, proved
(will), prisoner,
principal, probated

p.r. - parish record

PRO - Public
Record Office

pro. - probate,
proved (will)

prob. - probable

prop. - property

propr. - proprietor

P.S. - Patriotic
Service

psentmt -
presentment made
to a grand jury

p'sonl - personal

pt. - point, petition,

pint

pte.- part

ptf. - plaintiff

pu - pupil

pub./publ. - public,
published/er

pvt. - private

pymt. - payment

q. - *Quarto*
(oversized book)

Q.V. - quod vide
(which see)

q.y. - query

r. - rector, roomer,
river, road, resided,
removed

R. - Range, Rabbi,
King or Queen
(Roi), Rector

R.C. - Roman
Catholic

rcdr. - recorder

rcpt. - receipt

RD - release of
dower rights

rec. - record

rect - receipt

ref. - reference,

referred

Reg Gen - Registrar
General

rel. - relative

reld. - relieved

relict - *relicta /
relictus* (widow /
widower)

rel-i-l - relative in
law

rem. - removed,
moved

ren. - renunciation

rep. - reprinted,
representative

repud. - repudiated

reqt. - request

res. - residence,
research

ret. - retired

Rev. - Reverend,
Revolutionary War

RG - Registered
Genealogist

rgstr. - registrar

RIP - Rest in Peace

rinq. - relinquished

RR - railroad

Rt.Honab - Right Honorable

rt. - dower right

s. - son, survivor, shilling, south

s.a.- *sine anno* (without a year)

s. and h. - son and heir

SAR - Sons of the American Revolution

SASE - self-addressed stamped envelope

sb - stepbrother

scl - Step child

SCV - Sons of Confederate Veterans

sd. / s'd - said

SDA - Seventh Day Adventist

sec. - secretary, second, security, section

Senr. / Sen. / Sr. - senior

serg./sgt - sergeant

Serv./servt. - servant

sett. - settlers

sev. - several

sf - stepfather

sh. - shortly, ship, share

si - sister

sib. - sibling

sic - exactly as written

sil./sl - son-in-law

sin. - *sine* (without)

sis. - sister

sm. - stepmother

sm. - small

sn. - *sine* (without)

s/o - son of/sister of

SO - Survivors' Originals

soc. - society

s.p. - *sine prole* (without offspring)

s.p.l. - *sine prole legitima* (without legitimate offspring)

s.p.m. - *sine prole mascula* (without male offspring)

spr. - sponsor

srnms - surnames

SS - *Supra Scriptum* (as written above)

ss - stepson

st. - saint, street

ster / sterl - sterling

Su - superintendent

suc - succeeded (followed)

suff - suffix

suite - lawsuit

Surg. - surgeon

surnm - surname

surv. - survived

SUV - Sons of Union Veterans

sw. - swear

T./Tp./Twp. - Township

Ten. - tenant

terr. - territory

test / testa / testes - testament witness)

thot. - thought

TIB - Temple (Records) Index Bureau

tn. - town, township

tobo - tobacco

top. - topographical

to-w - to wit

t.p. - title page

tr. - translation, troop

transcr.-transcribed

treas. - treasurer

TRIB - Temple Records Index Bureau

twp - township

ty. - territory

u / unc. - uncle

UDC - United Daughters of the Confederacy

ult. - *ultimo* (last month)

unasgd. - unassigned

unit. - united

unk. - unknown

unm. - unmarried

unorg. - unorganized

USCG - United States Coast Guard

USCT - United States Colored Troops

USMC - United States Marine Corps

USN - United States Navy

USWPA - United States Public Works Administration

utl - *ultimo* (late)

ux - uxor (wife)

v./vs. - versus

v.a. - *vixit annos* (lived stated number of years)

var. - variation

VFW - Veterans of Foreign Wars

Vi - visitor

VIP - Very Important Person

virdt / verd - verdict

Virga - Virginia

Vis./Visc.- Viscount, Viscountess

vit. - vital

viz. - *videlicet* (namely)

vol. - volunteer, volume

v.r. - vital records

vs. - versus

v.s. - vital statistics

w. - wife, will, west, widow

W.B. - Will Book

wch - which

W.D. - War Department

w.d. - will dated

wd - widow, ward

wf/o - wife of

wh. - which, who

WIA - Wounded in Action

wid. - widow

wit. - witness

wk(s) - weeks

Wkm - workman

W.O. - Widow's Originals

w/o - wife of

W.O. - Warrant Officer

WOW - Woodmen of the World

w.p. - will probated

WPA - Works Progress (Projects) Administration

WRHS - Western Reserve Historical Society

W.S. - Writer to the Signet

wt / wth - with

wtn. - witness

ww. - widow

ww/o - widow of

wwr. - widower

X - Christians, Christ, used in lieu of a signature

x ch - exchange

Xn. / Xtian - Christian

Xped. / Xr. Christened

Xt. - Christ

xt. - next

xt.crt. - next term of court

Xty. - Christianity

y. - year

yd. - graveyard

ye - the

yen - then

yr. - younger, year, your

yt. - that

Organizations Which Might Have Genealogical Information

Frequently societies and organizations keep genealogical-type information about members. A few possible sources would be organizations involved with

Brotherhoods	Charities	Reform groups
Fraternities	Service groups	Occupations
Ethnic groups	Military units	Hobbies
Religions	Family Names	Professional
Insurance	Patriotic groups	societies

Acceptable Proofs of Relationship

The best records were created during a person's lifetime. Those can include

- Birth records listing parents, unless there was a probable reason for the informant to misrepresent the facts
- Church records of christenings, marriages and burials
- Death certificates filled out by spouses or parents

- Marriage records listing parents of the couple
- Land records which include "To my son/daughter" or "children of the deceased
- Military pension records in which the veteran has listed his wife and children
- Tombstones which include relationships, but only if the stones were produced immediately after the deaths
- Court records, such as orphans and divorce court records, which state relationships
- Documents, such as a family Bible, which lists names, dates and relationships, but only if the information was documented directly following the event.

Unacceptable Proofs of Relationship

- Family history or tradition*
- The mother was younger than twelve or older than fifty
- Census records which did not record relationship to head of household (and even then the information might be incorrect)
- Obituaries listing children, siblings and spouse
- County histories*
- Men named "junior" or "senior." Those titles merely indicated an older and a younger man with the same name living in the same town
- Children born less than nine months apart, except for twins
- Printed genealogies, such as those in Compendium of American Genealogy and DAR Lineage Books which have not been verified
- Family group sheets compiled by individuals

*Family and area histories are dependent upon the validity of the information collected and how much the researcher allowed his own opinions and bias to enter the work. In addition, adopted and step children were frequently listed as natural children.

Topic Sources and Additional Reading

Allen, Desmond Walls and Carolyn Earle Billingsley. *Beginner's Guide to Family History Research.* Bountiful, Utah: American Genealogical Lending Library, 1991.

Archives and Manuscript Repositories in the District of Columbia. <www.loc.gov/coll/nucmc/dcsites.html>. Library of Congress <lcweb@ loc. gov> Updated August 12, 1998.

Baxter, Angus. *In Search of Your British and Irish Roots.* New York: William Morrow and Company, 1982.

Carter, Michael, ed. *The Encyclopedia of Popular Antiques.* London: Octopus Books, 1980.

CyberTree Genealogy Database Home Page <home.sprynet.com/sprynet/ lgk71>. Printout dated 14 January 2000.

DeJong, Eric. Country Things. New York: Weathervane Books, n.d.

Drake, Paul. *What Did They Mean By That?: A Dictionary of Historical Terms for Genealogists.* Bowie, Maryland: Heritage Books, 1994.

Family TreeMaker. Online Genealogy How-To "Word Meanings". Broderbund Software, <www.familytreemaker.com> Copyrighted 1996-1998.

Fitzhugh, Terrich V.H. *The Dictionary of Genealogy.* London: A&C Black, 1994.

GENUKI: UK & Ireland Genealogical Information Service. <www.genuki. org> Revised 11 June 2000.

Gormley, Myra Vanderpool. "Shaking Your Family Tree: Examining Evidence to Prove a Pedigree" <ancestry.com> Online. Link exchange. Reprint of 7 August 1997. Los Angeles: Los Angeles Times Syndicate. Printout dated 26 July 2000.

Greenwood, Val D. *Researcher's Guide to American Genealogy.* Baltimore: Genealogical Publishing Company, 1990.

Harland, Derek. *Genealogical Research Standards: Basic Course in Genealogy* Vol II. The Genealogical Society. Salt Lake City: The Church of Jesus Christ of Latter-Day Saints, 1963.

Hey, David, ed. *The Oxford Companion to Local and Family History.* New York: Oxford University Press, 1996.

Hinkley, Kathleen W. "Alphabet Soup: Understanding the Genealogical Community". Learn About Genealogy. Genealogy.com. <www.genealogy. com/33_Kathy.html>. Copyrighted 1998.

Howells, Cyndi. Cyndi's List of Genealogy Sites on the Internet <www.cyndislist.com> Hosted by RootsWeb. Cyndi Howells, Webmaster <cyndihow@oz.net> Revised 24 July 2000.

Jacobson, Judy. *Genealogist's Refresher Course*, 2nd ed. Baltimore: Clearfield Company, 1996.

Larson, Frances. *The Genealogist's Dictionary*. N.p. 1986.

Linkopedia. Genealogy Tools <www.linkopedia.com/genealogy_tools.html> Copyrighted 2000.

Mills, Elizabeth Shown. Evidence, Citation and analysis for the Family Historian/ Baltimore: Genealogical Publishing Company, 1997.

NGS Online Course. <www.ngsgenealogy.org> National Genealogical society. 4527 17th Street North; Arlington, Virginia 22207. Copyrighted 2000.

Phillips, Phoebe, ed. *The Collectors Encyclopedia of Antiques*. New York: Crown Publishers, 1977.

Powers, Juanetta. What Do Those Initials Mean? In LANDON-D Digest Vol. 00. #40. Listserve message from <mollie@gtec.com> to LANDON-D Digest. <LANDON-L@rootsweb.com> 08 June 2000

Richley, Pat Isaacs. "Lesson 21 Interviewing Relatives". Dear MYRTLE'S Genealogy for Beginners. MyFamily.com. <www.ancestry.compuserve.com/lessons/beginners/beginners. Copyright dated 1998-2000.

Schulze, Lorine McGinnis. Organizing Genealogical Materials. <www.rootweb. com/~ote/organize.htm> The Olive Tree Genealogy. Revised 3 January 1998. Copyrighted 1996-2000.

Smith, Kenneth L. Estate Inventories: How to Use Them. N.p., 1984.

Tylcoat, Dave and Sue Tylcoat. Glossary <ourworld.compuserve.com/homepages/dave-tylcoat>. Printout dated 13 September 1999.

Wadsak, Horst A. *Unexplained Encounters in Genealogical Research*. N.p. 1981.

Webster's Ninth New Collegiate Dictionary. Springfield, Massachusetts: Merriam-Webster Publisher, 1983.

Wells, David A. *John Timb's Things Not Generally Known: A Popular Handbook of Facts Not Readily Accessible in Literature, History and Science*. New York: D. Appleton and Company, 1857. Reprint. Gale Research Company, 1968.

West, Edmund. *Our Ancestors Nicknames*. Lineages, 1996.

Names

Given Names

Six Most Common Male Given Names
Boston 1630-1634

John	Richard	Edward
William	Thomas	Robert

Three Most Common Female Given Names
Massachusetts Bay Colony 1630-1670

Mary	Elizabeth	Sarah

Translated Male Given Names

A number of immigrants Anglicized their names when they arrived in America. So when an ancestor was born in a foreign country their name and/or their children's names could appear in the translated or the original forms. Uncle Ludvig became Uncle Louie and, for some unknown reason, Uncle Svertrup became Uncle Earl. Alberto might have become Albert. Do you know who Jose Quenedi Chico would have become if his name were translated? Joseph Kennedy, Jr. Translations for some of the names given to men are below.

English	French	German	Spanish	Hungarian	Polish
Andrew	Andre	Andreas	Andres	Andi	Andrezej
Anthony	Antoine	Anton	Antonio	Antal	Antek
Charles	Carles	Karal	Carlos	Kalman	Karol
Christopher	Christophe	Christoph	Christobal	Kriska	Krysig
Daniel	Daniel	Daniel		Dani	Danek
David	David	Tab/David	David	David	Dawid
Edmund	Edmond	Edmund	Edmondo	Odi	Edmund
Francis	Francois	Fraenzel	Chico	Ferenc	Franciszek
Frederick	Frederic	Friedrich/ Fritz	Federico	Frici/ Frigyes	Fredek

English	French	German	Spanish	Hungarian	Polish
George	Georges	Jeurgen/ Jeorge	Jorge	Genovaya	Jerzy
Gregory	Gregoire	Gregor	Gregorio	Gergely	Grezgorz
Henry	Henri	Heiner	Enrico	Henrik	Henriek
Lawrence	Laurant/ Eustache	Lorenez	Lorenzo	Lenci/ Lorant	Inek
Lewis	Louis	Ludwick/ Ludwig	Luis	Lajcs/Laji	Ludwiczek/ Lutek
Jacob	Jacobus Jacques	Jakob/ Jackel	Diego	Jakab	Jakwoek
James	Jacques	Jacob	Jaime	Imre	Dymitry
John	Jean	Johann/ Hans/Haen	Juan	Jancsi	Jan
Joseph	Josephus	Beppi/ Josef	Jose	Joska	Josef/Jozef
Mark	Marc	Markus	Marco	Marci	Mareczek/ Marek
Matthew	Mathieu	Matthias/ Mathe	Mateo	Mate	Maciei/ Mates
Michael	Mickael	Michel	Miguel	Mihal	Machas/ Michal
Paul	Paul	Paul	Pablo	Pal	Inek
Peter	Pierre	Peter/ Paraskivas	Pedro	Peter	Pitrus
Phillip	Philippe	Philipp	Felipe	Fulop	Fil
Raymond	Raymond	Raimund	Raymundo		Mundek
Richard	Richard	Richard	Ricardo	Riczi	Rye
Robert	Robert	Robert	Roberto	Robert	Robert
Stephen	Etienne	Stefan/ Steffel	Estave	Isti	Stefan
Thomas	Thomas	Thomas	Tomas	Tamas	Slaweek
Victor	Victor	Viktor/ Victoir	Victorio	Geiza	Woltpr

English	French	German	Spanish	Hungarian	Polish
Vincent	Vincent	Vinzenz	Vincente	Vincze	Vincenty
William	Guillaume	Wilhelm	Guillemo	Vili	Bole

Abbreviations for Male Given Names

Besides common abbreviations, a straight line running horizontally through the tall letters of a word, or a colon placed at the end usually indicated the name had been abbreviated. Other times a small last letter above the line denoted an abbreviation.

Aarn	Aaron	Jno	Jonathan
Ab/Abra	Abraham	Jos	Joseph
Alexr	Alexander	Leond	Leonard
Andw	Andrew	Matthw	Matthew
Benj/Benja	Benjamin	Nich	Nicholas
Cha/Chas	Charles	Nicols	Nicholas
Christr	Christopher	Patrk	Patrick
Ebenr	Ebenezer	Rich	Richard
Ed	Edmund	Robt	Robert
Edw	Edward	Saml	Samuel
Fra/Fran	Francis	Tho/Thos	Thomas
Geo/Go	George	Tim	Timothy
Gilrt	Gilbert	Wilfd	Wilford
Hen	Henry	Xian	Christian
Ja/Jas	James	Xpher/Xr	Christopher
Jer/Jere	Jeremiah	Zacha	Zachariah

Unusual Nicknames

The word "nickname" derived from "eke" (alternative) name. Although given names and nicknames can be interchangeable in documents, it seems almost impossible to ascertain the root of some of those names. Although most people think "Nan" is a nickname for "Nancy," but it doesn't have to be. It could also stand for "Hannah" or "Ann".

Eugene Fields wrote a poem that corroborates the problem simply.

> Father calls me William,
> Sister Calls me Will,
> Mother calls me Willie,
> But the fellers call me Bill.

Female Nicknames

Abbie	Abigail / Tabitha	Addie	Adelaide

Allie	Alice	Fally	Eliphal
Babby	Barbara	Fan(ny)	Frances
Babs	Barbara	Florrie	Florence
Barba	Barbara	Floss(ie)	Florence
Becca	Rebecca	Frankie	Frances
Bee	Beatrice	Fronie	Saphronia
Bella	Arabelle/Isabella/	Fytie	Sophia
	Rosabel	Gail	Abigail
Bertie	Bertha	Gatty	Gertrude
Bessie	Elizabeth	Genie	Eugenia
Beth	Elizabeth	Ginger	Virginia
Betsy	Elizabeth	Ginnie	Virginia
Betty	Elizabeth	Greta	Margaret/Margaretta
Biah	Abiah	Gussie	Augusta
Biddy	Bridget/Obedience	Hanna	Anne/Anna
Bitsy	Elizabeth	Hat(tie)	Harriet
Briney	Sybrina	Hepsy	Hepsibah
Caddie	Caroline	Hermie	Hermione
Callie	Caroline	Hettie	Ester/Henrietta/
Charlie	Charlotte		Hester/Mehitabel
Cindy	Cynthia/Lucinda	Ib	Isabella
Cleda	Cleophas	Jenny	Jane/Janet/Jeanette/
Crece(y)	Lucretia		Jennet/Genevieve/
Daisy	Margaret		Virginia
Delia	Adelia/Adele/Bedlia/	Jill	Julia
	Cordelia/Fidelia/	Kate	Catherine
	Phidelia	Kay	Catherine
Dimmis	Damaris	Kersty	Christina
Dody	Dorothy	Kit	Catherine
Dolly	Dorothy	Kizzie	Kesiah
Donia	Fredonia	Lena	Angelina/Caroline/
Dora	Eudora/Theodora/		Madeleine/Helena/
	Dorothy		Magdalena/Paulina/
Dosia	Theodosia		Selina
Dot(ty)	Dorothy	Letty	Letitia
Edie	Edith/Edwina	Libby	Elizabeth
Edith	Adeline	Linda	Melinda
Effie	Euphemia	Lindy	Melinda
Eliza	Elizabeth	Lisa	Elizabeth/Lise
Ella	Eleanor/Elenora	Livy	Olive/Olivia
Ellie	Eleanor	Liza	Adeliza/Elizabeth
Elsie	Alice/Elizabeth/	Lizzie	Elizabeth
	Ellen/Helen	Lolly	Charlotte
Em(my)	Emeline/Emily/	Lotty	Charlotte
	Hester	Lou	Louetta/Louisa/
Etta	Henrietta/Marietta		Lucinda

51

Lucy	Lucinda/Lucretia/		Honora/Honoria
	Lucia/Lucelle	Ollie	Olive/Olivia
Lynn(e)	Belinda/Melinda	Patsy	Martha/Patience
Madge	Margaret	Patty	Martha/Patricia
Mae	Mary	Peg(gie)	Margaret
Maggie	Margaret	Penny	Penelope
Maisie	Mary/Margaret	Polly	Mary
Mamie	Mary	Reba	Rebecca
Manda	Amanda	Rita	Margaret
Mandy	Amanda	Sadie	Sarah
Marty	Martha	Sal(ly)	Sarah
Mat(tie)	Martha	Sammy	Samantha
May	Mary	Suchy	Susan/Susanna/
Meg/	Margaret		Susannah
Megan		Sukey	Susan
Mellie	Amelia/Melanie/	Susanna	Susan
	Permelia	Tempy	Temperance
Meta	Margaret	Tess(ie)	Teresa
Midge	Margaret	Tibbie	Isabella
Milly	Amelia/Millicent	Tillie	Matilda/Mathilda/
	Mildred		Temperance
Mina	Wilhelmina	Tina	Christina
Minnie	Wilhelmina	Tishie	Letitia
Moll(y)	Mary	Titia	Letitia
Nabby	Abigail	Trina	Catherine
Nan(ny)	Ann/Hannah/Nancy	Trissie	Beatrice
Nana	Ann	Trixie	Beatrice
Nellie	Eleanor/Eleanora/	Trudy	Gertrude
	Ellen/Helen	Vicy	Lewvisa
Nettie	Henrietta	Virgie	Virginia
Nina	Ann	Willie	Wilhelmina
Nib	Isabella	Winnie	Winifred
Nora	Eleanor/Eleanora/		

Male Nicknames

Ab	Abijah/Abner	Bob	Robert
Abe	Abraham	Cager	Micajah
Abram	Abraham	Chan	Chauncey
Algy	Algernon	Chas	Charles
Augie	August	Chuck	Charles
Barney	Barnabas	Claas	Nicholas
Bat	Bartholomew	Cuddy	Cuthbert
Bert	Albert/Cuthbert/	Cy	Cyrus
	Herbert	Dick	Richard
Bige	Abijah	Dirch	Cerrick

Dirck	Theodoric	Lem	Lemuel
Dob(bin)	Robert	Les	Leslie/Lester
Dode/Dody	Theodore/Theodorick	Lig(e)	Elijah
Dolph	Randolph/Rudolph	Lije	Elijah
Dyer	Obediah	Lish	Elisha
Eben	Ebenezer	Lorry	Lawrence
Ed	Edgar/Edmund/	Mal	Malachi/Malcom
	Edward/Edwin	Monty	Montague
Eli	Elias/Elijah/	Mose	Moses
	Elisha	Nab	Abel
Eph	Ephraim	Nat(ty)	Nathan/Nathaniel
Eppa	Epaphroditus	Ned	Edward
Ez	Ezra	Newt	Newton
Fanny	Nathaniel	Obed	Obediah
Fate	Lafayette	Obi	Obediah
Fayette	Lafayette	Ollie	Oliver
Ferdie	Ferdinand	Paddy	Patrick
Finnie	Phineas	Pleas	Pleasant
Frankie	Francis/Franklin	Quill	Aquila
Fred	Alfred/Frederick/	Reg(gie)	Reginald
	Winifred	Riah	Zachariah
Gene	Eugene	Rias	Zachariah
Gil(lie)	Gilbert	Rich	Richard
Gus	Augustus	Robbin	Robert
Hal	Harold/Henry	Rod	Roderick/Rodney/
Ham	Hamilton		Rodriguez
Hank	Henry	Rodge	Roger
Hans	Johan	Ron	Aaron/Ronald
Harry	Henry	Rye	Zachariah
Hi	Hiram	Sam	Samson/Samuel
Hiley	Hiram	Sandy	Alexander
Hy	Hiram	Si	Josiah/Silas/
Ike	Isaac		Silvester
Irv	Irvin/Irving	Sy	Silas
Izzy	Isidore	Tad	Thaddeus/Theodore/
Jack	Jackson/John		Theodorick
Jamie	James/Jameson	Ted	Edward/Theodore/
Jed	Jedediah/Jeduthan		Theodorick
Jerry	Gerald	Theo	Theophilus
Jock	John	Tiah	Azariah
Jude	Judah	Tony	Anthony/Antoine/
Judy	Judah		Antonio
Kiah	Hezekiah	Tys	Matthias
Kit	Christopher	Vet	Silvester
Ky	Hezekiah	Winnie	Winifred
Lazar	Eleazer		

| Zach(y) | Zachariah | | Zeke | Ezekiel |
| Zander | Alexander | | | |

Two Kids - One Name

Many times two children within the same family were given the same first names. Likely explanations include -

1. The first born child with the name had died ; i.e. Edwin Smith (b. 1822 d. 1831) was the brother of Edwin Smith (b. 1832).
2. The two children had different mothers.
3. The first name was the same, but the middle name was different (i.e. Mary Francis Knight was the sister of Mary Anne Knight.
4. Because of finances or death, relatives had taken in a child with the same name as one of their own children, i.e. John Budd raised his son Christopher and his nephew Christopher Budd, Jr.
5. And occasionally, particularly in German and Dutch families, children of the same parents, living within the same families at the same time were indeed given the exact same names.

Sources for Early American Given Names

Early American names were truly descriptive of the times. The thirteenth and last child in one family was named "Finis." The child of an unwed mother was named Asad Experience Wilson. And yet another family named their children alphabetically, from Alan through Kathryn. Whether the name ended up to be Ernest Thanksgiving Johnson, Fly Debate Roberts, Sea Delivered Sylvester or George Washington Reddick, thought was put into the naming of these children.

Abstract Messages	Pardon	Wait	Guile	Reason
	Submit	Takeheed	Fight-the-good fight	
Ancestry	Cherokee Kelly			
Animal Qualities	Bernard (bear courage) Leonard (lion courage)			
Biblical	Solomon	Esther	Rachel	Abraham
	Jesus	Moses	Bathsheba	Zebulun
Characteristics	Wealthy	Worthy	Manly	Artful
Classics	Cicero	Ptolomy	Mozart	Aschylus
Emotions	Happy	Resolved	Friendly	Relief
	Freelove	Faintnot	Reconcile	Love
Family Surnames	Cayce McCracken Valentine Budd Cole Porter			

Feelings	Mourning	Comfort	Endure	Hate
Feminine version of Father's Name	Paulina	Josephine	Jessie	Georgianna
Food	Preserved Fish	Jam Pye		Tuna White
Gender specific by spelling only	Marian/Marion Gail/Gale	Carol/Carroll Frances/Francis	Jean/Gene Carrie/Cary	
Heroes	Napoleon	Lafayette	Jefferson	Lincoln
Literature	Dryden	Gulliver	Juliet	Othello
Non-gender specific	Meredith	Robin	Whitney	Pat
Occupation / Rank	Major	Miner	Doctor	Taylor
Places (Typonymic)	America Arizona	Bahama Property	Indiana Israel	Ceylon Tennessee
Religious Fervor God	Thanklord Christian	Hosanna Thankful	Epiphany Hallelujah	Grateful-to- Evil
Unusual	Fountain Orange Increase	Trial How Long Not	Cinderella Eleven Wait a while	Avoid Illness Bright
Virtues	Thankful Preserved	Silence Sobriety	Prudence Discretion	Charity Obedience

And just when you think you have it all figured out, you will find

Thomas Marietta Abernathy, daughter of James Polk
and Lula Jones Abernathy
and
Thomas Hazel Stewart, son of Aaron and Sarah Brock
Stewart

Surnames

The word "surname" stemmed from "sire name" (father's name) and didn't really come into use until after the Norman Conquest in 1066. Fixed surnames began at the top of society and worked slowly down the rungs of the social ladder. Finally, circa 1485, England instituted a law requiring everyone to adopt a surname. Many were chosen based on town, color, arts, science or office.

By the time surnames really became popular and spellings of them were standardized, it was long overdue for future genealogists. Think how taxing it would have been to untangle the following will without surnames.

> Joseph Brown of Mansfield, N.J. bequeathed
> $20 each to names sakes Joseph Brown
> Woolman, Joseph Brown Conrow, and Joseph
> Brown Hunt.

But even with surnames, it could be troublesome finding an ancestor. Governments provided for legal changes of names. But circumstances and jurisdictions varied from country to country and state to state.

Persons having the same name often caused confusion. For example, four men named Christopher Youngs were all living in the small town of Southold, Long Island at the same time.

Conversely, difficulties also occurred when families adopted different surnames. Upon arriving in the United States, members of the Dutch Lambert Huybertse family from Dolderbrink, took the various surnames of Lambetse, Lambertsen, Lambertzen, Huybertse, Brink and, for some reason, Terpenning. Other families in the Old World ended up with a variety of surnames when individuals used different means to settle which was to be their name.

Father's Given Name	His Child's Given Name	Surname Taken	Source of Surname
David Daniel		LeClerke	a scholar
	William	DeMalpas	name of his father's estate
	Phillip	Gogh	"red" for his hair color
	David	Golborne	name of his estate
	John	Goodman	name given by others due to excellence of his character
Richard		DeCotgrave	name of his estate
	William	Little	of diminutive stature
	Richard	Kenclarke	"knowing scholar"
	John	Richardson	son of Richard

Sources of Surnames

When adopting a surname for themselves, people had different ideas about how to go about it. So surnames today have a wide range of origins.

Animals	Fuchs (Fox)	Lion	Wolf
	Dove	Pigeon	Birdseye
Biblical	Adams	Christianson	Danielczyk
	Estevez	Shimkus	Himmel
			(Heavenly)
Colors	Dunne (Grey)	Russell (Russet)	Green
	Wynne (White)	Brown	Black
Directions	Southcott	Easton	Westlake
	Norman	Escott	Norbert
Father's Given	Jacobson	ap David	Olsen
	O'Brien	Fitzhugh	Kristiansdottir
Geographic	Wood	Lane	Field
	Ford	Beach	Ridge

Home settings "Castle" may have been the name taken by someone who lived in or near a castle.
"Field" may have come from an open, treeless piece of land.
"Moore" probably originated with the wastelands , "Moors", of Northern England or Scotland

Hometowns Jean Morin de Loudon (John Morin of the city of Loudon, France) became Jean de Loudon and, finally Jean Loudon
David Deal may have come from the Deal Valley in Kent County, England

Nature	Hazlewood	Turnipseed	Snow
	Mayberry	Rain	Kmayk (Pebble)
Occupations	Schmidt (Smith)	Shepherd	Baurer (Farmer)
	Koch (Cook)	Parson	Mueller (Miller)
Titles	Knight	Pope	Schultz (Mayor)
	Richter (Judge)	Koenig (King)	Marshall

Physical Characteristics	Rufus Whiteman	Schwarz (Black) Lange (Long)	Gross (Large) Klein (Small)
Personal Characteristics	Friend Pilgrim	Goodfellow Keen	Rascal Hardy

But sometimes it is not that easy to uncover the origin of a name. For instance, the Scottish name Mathieson may have come from the pet name "Mathie" for "Matthew". Or it may have come from the Scottish "MacMhathian", the English "Maddison" or "Mathewson", the Dutch "Matthysen" or the Irish "MacMathan". "Mathan" meant "bear" and Scottish clan names such as "M'Mathan" (son of the bear) were introduced between 1300 and 1450. But before that, there was the old Gaelic name of "Mathghamhuin". "Mathison" was also found in Norway. So how did the name "Mathieson" evolve?

Surname Prefixes, Suffixes and Conjunctions

Because of America's "melting pot" nature, our surnames represent a broader spectrum of languages and ethnicities than anywhere else on earth. Many times that variety is demonstrated by the prefixes and suffixes on American surnames.

Prefix or Suffix	Meaning	Language	Example
a	daughter of	Polish / Czech	Barta
accio	bad	Italian	Boccaccio
aitis	son of	Lithuanian	Adomaitis
ak	son of	Slovak	Kopchak
anok	son of	Brelorussian	Marcishanok
ap	son of	Welsh	ap David / Pritchard (from "ap Richard")
at / att / atte	of	Saxon / English	Attwood
az	son of	Portuguese	Juaraz
bach / baugh on	brook	German	Wittelsbach
bauer	builder / farmer	German	Bauer Verlag
beau	fair	French	Beauchamps

Prefix or Suffix	Meaning	Language	Example
ben	son of	Hebrew	Ben David
berger	person living on a hill or mountain	German	Berger
bin	son of	Arabic	Bin Ladin
binte	daughter of	Arabic	Binte Syed Hassan
brad	broad	English	Bradley
by	location	English	Bywater
cki	son of	Polish	Czaplicki / Drzewucki
cock	pet form	English	Hitchcock
de /de la / del	of	French & Spanish	Jean Morin de Loudon
de / di / d'	son of	Italian	di Luca
degli	of the	Italian	Degli Angeli
dochter	daughter of	Dutch	Jansdochter
dottir / datter	daughter of	Scandinavian	Kristiansdottir
ek	son of	Slovak	Simek
enke	son of	Ukrainian	Kovalenke
er	location	English	Downer
es	son of	Portuguese / Spanish	Garces
escu	son of	Romanian	Petrescu
evich	son of	Slavic	Sergevich
ez	son of	Spanish / Basque	Hernandez
Fils / Files	son of	French	Filson
Fitz	son of	Irish	Fitzgerald
hol / holt	wood	English	Holcombe
ian	from	Armenian	Hagopian

Prefix or Suffix	Meaning	Language	Example
ic	son of	Slovak	Simovic
ides	son of	Greek	Christides
ies	son of	English	Davies
ing / ins	son of	English	Robbins
kins	son of	English	Perkins
la / le	the	French	La Sarge
Mac / Mc / M'	son of	Irish / Scottish	MacDonald
maier / mair / mayer / mayr / meier / meir/ meyer	farm manager	German	Meyers
man / mann	servant of	German	Hermann
na	son of	Russian	Ivanovna
nen	son of	Finnish	Mattinen
O'	grandson of	Irish	O'Brien
off	from	Bulgarian	Petroff
oglu	son of	Turkish	Misiroglu
one	large	Italian	Capone
ov	son of	Russian / Czech	Romanov
ovich	son of	Russian / Yugoslavian	Mikhailovich
ovna / ova	daughter of	Russian	Petrova
polites	son of	Greek	Polites
putra	son of	Hindustani	Himalaya Putra
ram	raven	German	Bertram
rich	mighty	German	Friedrich
s	son of	English / Welsh	Davis
se	son of	Dutch	Oelofse / Pieterse

Prefix or Suffix	Meaning	Language	Example
sen / son	son of	Scandinavian	Jakobsen
ski / sky	son of	Polish / Russian / Czech	Kaminski
sohn	son of	German	Jakobsohn
stein	stone	German	Frankenstein
szen	son of	Dutch	Claaszen
under	location	English	Underhill
Van	of / from	Dutch	Van Dyke
verch	daughter of	Welsh	verch Gruffydd
wicz	son of	Polish	Abrahamowicz
wiec	one who	Polish	Mysliwiec
win	friend	English	Goodwin
witt	white	German	Witt
y	and	Spanish	Wamba y Garces
z	son of	Dutch	Borgertz
zen	son of	Dutch	Lambertzen

Reasons Surnames Have Changed

When searching for names in indexes or lists, variations in spellings must be considered. A name may be found spelled several spellings within the same document. But which is correct? Reasons surnames have changed through the years are given below.

1. Sometimes names were changed by necessity - real or perceived. For instance,

* Names were originally written in a different type of script, such as Arabic (ﻧﺎﻳﺮﺑ), Cyrillic (ВаЙёШ), or Greek (ΎύŸϋΏώ).
* Criminals chose aliases
* Children were adopted
* Persons, such as those of German ancestry during World War I, feared mistreatment.

61

- Illegitimate children could, at various times, carry the surname of the biological father, the mother, or the mother's husband (in the case of adultery or later marriage).

2. Historically, most, but not all, women changed their names upon marriage.

3. The custom of children taking their father's given name as their surname is still prevalent in some parts of the world. In Norway, Jakob Pedersen had Albert Jakobsen who emigrated in 1915. Instead of continuing to give his children his first or given name as their surname, all of Albert's children took the Jacobson name in the United States.

4. Names were translated when families immigrated.
- A German named Pfarrar became a Parsons.
- A Spaniard named Zorra became a Fox.
- A Pole named Mularz became a Mason.

5. While many ancestors changed their surnames themselves, frequently, customs and immigration officials had a lot to do with which surname we use today. They were the ones who recorded the name of each immigrant and wrote down what they thought they were told. Some names were simplified or Americanized.
- Mathieson became Matheson
- Wodospad became Wood
- Krolowa became Kroll

6. Foreign accents have played a major component as to how names were recorded in the United States. Records not only reflected the accent of the speaker, but also the hearing capabilities of the listener.
- Yonson became Johnson
- Smythe became Smith

7. An ancestor who could not read or write, could not be expected to correct misspellings of his name by an immigration officer, census taker or county clerk. Names were
Misspelled
• Landon	Lanckton	Langton
• Metcalf	Metcalfe	Midkiff

Written phonetically
• Robbinson	Robbenson	Robinson
• Allen	Allyn	Alan

Had interchanged vowels
• Landon	Landin	Landen

And had interchanged consonants
- Gerald became Jerald

- Carson became Karson
- Shoemacher became Shoemaker

8. And, unfortunately, sometimes names were mistakenly recorded because of
Carelessness
- Smith became Smit
- Schoenbeck became Shonbeck
Illegible handwriting
- Davis vs. Dawes
- Conner vs. Commer
Typographic errors (letters dropped, doubled or transposed)
- Judge became Jugde
- Harpole became Harpol or Harpool

Where to Find a Maiden Name

Cemetery plot
Children's death certificates
Children's names
Children's marriage licenses
Church records
Citizenship application
County history / biography

Divorce papers
Family Bible records
Marriage license
Obituary
Widow's pension
Wills and probate records
Woman's death certificate

Census records since 1850 have shown relationships of everyone in the home to the head of the household, including in-laws. But probably the most overlooked of the suggestions listed above are the given and middle names of a woman's children and grandchildren. One example is George Walker Bush who was given his grandmother's maiden name for his middle name. Another is Kate Cole, the mother of Cole Porter.

Titles

Caballero   a Spanish nobleman or gentleman

Deacon   title ranking above "Goodman" and "Mister"

Don   the Spanish term for "Mister"

Dona   the Spanish term for "Mrs."

Esquire   originally an "esquire" was a knight's attendant. Later, it was used by lawyers to signify their level of education.

Freeman one who had received full rights of citizenship. Citizenship was usually conferred upon adult males who had the consent of fellow town dwellers, or had inherited or married into some land. A freeman had to have an adequate income and be able to pay all town taxes.

Gentleman a descendant of an aristocratic family who were entitled to bear a coat of arms, owned land and did not perform manual labor. The term could also refer to a retired man.

Gentlewoman
wife of a gentleman

Goodman a solid member of the community who ranked above freeman, but below a gentleman was known as a "Goodman". His wife was known as "Goodwife". In documents either could have been referred to "Goody" as in "Goody Vail."

Graf the Germanic equivalent of "count" was "Graf". In fact, the surname "DeGraf" means "the Count."

Hacendado
Spanish term for the owner of a large private estate

Heer Dutch title of respect, such as "lord" or "mister"

Herr leader, master or ruler in early Germanic times

Hidalgo a Spanish nobleman

Husbandman
a small landholder or a tenant, who may also have had to work for others, just below a yeoman

Juffrou Dutch title of respect equivalent to "Madame" or "Lady"

M. the French term for "Mister"

Madame the French term for "Mrs."

Mademoiselle
the French term for "Miss"

Mister a title used by sea captains, members of the military, government officials, school masters, distinguished merchants, physicians, magistrates, the clergy, and any freeman with two college degrees in New England

Mistress (Mrs.)
    any married or unmarried female in the family of a male entitled to the title "Mister"

Mll   the French abbreviation for "Miss"

Seigneur   the French version of "Squire", or the "lord of the manor"

Sieur   a French landowner of lesser rank then a Seigneur. The word "Sieur" eventually became "monsieur."

Spinister   term usually used for an unmarried woman beyond customary marrying age, but also used for a married woman or widow transacting business on her own behalf

Squire   originally a title awarded to a member of the British gentry of lower ranking then a knight, but above a gentleman. In America, "Squire" was a term applied to the principal landowner in the area

Yeoman   farmer who worked his own land but had more land then a husbandman

Place Names

Originally, place names in the North American Colonies were named for British peers (Georgia, Williamsburg, Jamestown) or places (Plymouth, New Hampshire, New York), with a smattering of Indian names (Delaware, Narragansett, Ticondaroga) thrown into the mix. Then, after the Revolution, towns were named after an early settler, hometowns of first settlers, Revolutionary War heroes or even the postmaster's wife or daughter.

As time passes, finding some places becomes more difficult. In many instances, names have been changed and boundaries have moved. Possumtown in Monroe County, Mississippi, ended up as Columbus in Lowndes County. In World War I, the citizens of Brandenburg, Texas, decided to exhibit their patriotism by changing the town's name to "Old Glory."

Pieces of counties have broken off, sometimes joining pieces of other counties; or becoming counties themselves. Sumter County, Mississippi, was organized out of land from three other counties. Later, Sumter citizens changed their county's name to Webster.

Difficult place names can be easily misspelled in records. Did Great-grandpa mean Nacogdoches, Texas, or Natchitoches, Louisiana, when he listed "Nachidoches" as a birth place in the Family Bible? And who would have thought that a place pronounced "Chew′ la" would be spelt "Tallulah"?

Place Name Prefixes and Suffixes
(European Origins)

Sometimes some hints about an area can be learned from the prefixes and suffixes of a place's name.

aber	mouth of river
ach	flowing water
acker	farm or acre
acre	yard or small enclosure or field
agua / acgua	water
alt	old
angra	bay
art	high
arroyo	stream or creek
at	at
au / aue	meadow or low place
bach	brook or creek
bad	spa, resort or place with a springs
baer / boer / by / bry / bua	to dwell in or near
bahn	road
bally	town or village
bas / bassel / basso	low
baum	tree
beck / bek	brook or creek
bel	beautiful
ben / beorg / berg / berge / bergen	mountain or hill
bi / by	beside
blad / blatt	leaf
bo	farm
boca	mouth or estuary
bode	abode
bois	wood
borg / borough / burg / bury	fortified town or castle or fortress
born	stream or spring
borstel / bostel	living place
botle / bottle	abode or house
brink	grassy place
bronn / brunn	spring
bruch	swamp or moor
bruck / brueck / brucken / brugg	bridge

by	farm or village
campo	plain
cap / capo	cape
carrick / craig / crick / crau	rock or ridge
caster / cester / chester	site of Roman occupation
cerro / champ	hill
cima / cime	peak
cite / citta / ciudad	town or village
combe / cum	depression in a hillside
corne / corno	peak
costa / cote	coast
cumb	valley
dal / dale / dahl / dell	valley
deich	dike
den / dene / denu	woodland pasture for animal
dic / ditch / dyke	ditch
don / dun	place of height, like a hill, fort, or earthwork
dorf / dorp	hamlet or village
eau	water
eck	corner of a mountain or bend in a river
eglwys / eglos / eaglais	church
eich / euche	oak
est / este	east or eastern
et	at
feld / felde / field	house by field
fells	cliff
fiore	flower
ford / fjord / fuhrt / furt / furth	crossing, ford or arm of the sea
frieden	peace
fuente	spring or well
gale / gill	ravine or narrow lane
gard	farm
garth	yard or small enclosure or field
gasse	alley or narrow street
glyn	valley
golf / golfe / gulfo	gulf
grad	town or city
grand / grande / gross	big
grave	grove
gren	branch
hafen	port or harbor
hagen / hain	grove

hall / healh	stone house or steep hill
ham / heim / hen	home of
hard / hardt / hart	hard or firm
haus / heim / holm	house
haut / hoch	high or upper
haven	port or harbor
heilig	holy
hoeck	corner
hof / hofe / hoff	farm or manor or courtyard
hoh	ridge
hop	small bay or pool of water
ile / ilha / insel / isla/ isle / isola	river island
ing	belonging to... or place of...
kappel / keeill / kil / kirchen / kirk	church or chapel
lac / lago	lake
lagoal / laguna	lagoon
lan / llan	cemetery
land	land or farm
lea / lee / leigh / ley / loo / ly	untilled land, valley or meadow
lof / love	leaf
lo / loh	thicket
loma	hill
lund	grove
maes / mag / magh / mat	house by field
mar / meer / mer / more	sea
moel / mont / monte	mountain
moos / mos	marsh
muehl / muhl / muhle	mill
nant	stream or narrow valley
ness	cape or headland
neu / neuf / neuve / nieuw / nouveau / novy / ny	new
nord / norte	north
ofer	ridge
oog	island
or	river or seashore
oost / ost	east
pach	brook or creek
paso / pass / passo	pass
pen	hilltop
pointe / ponta / punta	point
porto	port
reich	realm or empire
reka / rio / rivier / riviere	river
reuth / ried	cleared area

ridge / rigge / rigge / rudge	ridge
rop / rup	farm
san / sankt / santa / santo / sao	saint
sculf / shel / skel / skel	shelf or lodge
stad / stadt / statt	city or town
tal / thal	valley
terra / terre / tierra	land
thorpe	farm
thwaite	cleared area
ton / tun	homestead, settlement or town
tre / treb / tref / trev / troff	hamlet or village
val / valle / vlai	valley
vall / ville /	field
wahl	field
wald / walde	forest or woods
wall / weald	home by the wall
way	path or roadway
weiler	village
werk	factory or works
wich / wick	dwelling place
winkler	corner
worth	homestead
wyl	village
zell	monastery or monk's cell

Sources for Place Names

Most North American place names can be traced to Colonial European (Spanish, Dutch, English, French) or Native American origin. But they all do seem to fall into certain categories.

Descriptive	Detroit (straits)	Three Rivers	Mt. Pleasant
	Dismal Swamp	Baton Rouge	Oktibbeha ("stinking water")

Named for Other Places	London, Ontario	Birmingham, Alabama
	Paris, Texas	New Hampshire

Directions	Sudbury	North Dakota
	West Palm Beach	Easthampton

People	Koscuisko	San Antonio	Austin
	Lake Champlain	Hagerstown	Pontiac

Events	Gun Barrel City	Broken Arrow	Cannon Ball
	Council Bluffs	Fishkill	Cripple Creek

Native American	Tombigbee Cherokee	Ontario Monongahula	Miami Souix City
Humorous / Strange	Bad Axe French Lick Truth or Consequences	Santa Claus Sleepy Eye	Soddy-Daisy Kill Devil Hill
Inspirational	Palestine St. Augustine	Purgatory Solomon	Bethlehem Faith
Ancient History	Memphis Cincinnati	Carthage Ypsilanti	Cicero Hannibal
Locations Combined	Texarkana (on Texas / Arkansas border) Michiana (Michigan / Indiana) West Memphis, Arkansas		
Mythological	Troy Neptune City	Olympus El Dorado	Phoenix Delphos

Topic Sources and Additional Reading

Carlberg, Nancy Ellen. *Overcoming Dead Ends*. Anaheim: Carlberg Press, 1991.

Connecticut State Library. "A Listing of Some 18th and 19th Century American Nicknames" History and Genealogy Unit. <www.cslnet. ctstateu.edu/nickname.htm>. Revised March 24, 1999.

Costello, Margaret F. "A Child by Any Other Name" *NEHGR Nexus* .New England Historic Genealogical Society. Boston Massachusetts. Vol. CXLVII No. 585. (January 1993).

Fitzhugh, Terrich V.H. *The Dictionary of Genealogy*. London: A&C Black, 1994.

Flores, Norma P. and Patsy Ludwig. *A Beginner's Guide to Hispanic Genealogy*. San Mateo, California: Western Book / Journal Press, 1993.

Handybook for Genealogist's. Logan, Utah: Everton Publishers. 1999.

Hanks, Patrick and Flavia Hodges. A Dictionary of First Names. Oxford: Oxford University Press. 1988.

Hill, Barbara. "Fifteen Ways to Find a Maiden Name" (Reprint from *The Diggers Digest*, Vol 11 No.4). *South Dakota Genealogical Society Quarterly* Vol 4 No. 1. (July, 1885).

Hook, J.N. *All Those Wonderful Names: A Potpourri of People, Places, and Things*. New York: John Wiley & Sons, 1991.

Hook, J.N. *Family Names: How Our Surnames Came to America*. New York: MacMillan, 1982.

Global Gazetteer. <www.knowledge.co.uk/geodata> Designed by Knowledge computing. ALLM Systems Marketing. Revised 25 June 1999.

Jacobson, Judy. *Genealogist's Refresher Course*. 2nd ed. Baltimore: Clearfield Company, 1996.

Larson, Frances. *The Genealogist's Dictionary*. N.p. 1986.

National Atlas of Canada. <atlas.gc.ca> Online. National Resources Canada GeoAccess division. Copyrighted 2000.

National Geographic Map Machine. <www.nationalgeographic.com/resources/ngo/maps> National Geographic Society. Copyrighted 2000.

Robb,Amanda H. and Adam Chester. Encyclopedia of American Family Names. New York: Harper Collins, 1995

Room, Adrian. *Placenames of the World: Origins and Meaning of the Names for Over 5000 Natural Features, Countries, Capitals, Territories, Cities and Historic Sites*. Jefferson, North Carolina: McFarland & Company, 1997.

Rose, Christine. "Nicknames" *Everton's Genealogical Helper*. Utah: Everton Publishing, Mar-Apr 1987 p.11-15.

Surnames, What's in a Name? <clanhuston.com/name/name.htm> Broken Arrow Publishing. Copyrighted 1996-1998

Swift, Esther Munroe. *Vermont Place-Names: Footprints of History*. Brattleboro, Vermont: The Greene Press, 1977.

Thode, Ernest. *German-English Genealogical Dictionary*. Baltimore: Genealogical Publishing Company, 1992.

Libraries

Cataloging Systems

Most libraries in America use the Library of Congress or the Dewey Decimal Classification systems which arrange collections by subjects dictated by call numbers. Under the Library of Congress System, some sections that would interest genealogists would be -

C	Aux. Sciences of History	E	American History
CR	Heraldry	F	State & Local History
CS	Genealogy	H	Social Sciences
CT	Biography		

Under the Dewey Decimal System, sections of interest to genealogists include -

300	Social Sciences	920	Biography & Genealogy
900	Geography & History	970	North America

Types of Libraries

Public Libraries

Local

The genealogy and local history collections of most local public libraries are proportionate to the size of the town. No matter how small, they still should have city directories, cemetery records and local history books. Occasionally, local citizens will have donated their own family group sheets.

State

The State Library or Commission collects statistical, historical and genealogical information relating to the state. Collections could include material about immigrants, religious and minority groups; vital records; and collections of state, regional and even federal publications and documents. Normally there is a cooperative set-up between local libraries and state library commissions allowing local libraries to borrow books from the state.

National

Although the Library of Congress is a public library, more information about its importance to genealogical work is listed under Genealogy Libraries below. Many books published in the United States can be located in the three buildings of the Library of Congress. The library's catalog is easily accessed via the internet and there are a variety of guides to LOC holdings, such as

-The Black Press Held by the Library of Congress
-Stars and Stripes, Library of Congress Holdings
-Handbook for Foreign Genealogical Research: a Guide to Published Sources in English
-Surnames: A Selected List of References about Personal Names in the Library of Congress
-Telephone and Research Guides in the Library of Congress: a Finding Guide
-17th & 18th Century Foreign Newspapers: Holdings of the Library of Congress
Reading rooms which could have genealogically relevant material include
    Local History and Genealogy Reading Room
    Microform Reading Room
        American periodicals from 1741-1900
        City directories
        Census indexes
    Geography and Map Reading Room
        Historic and modern US and foreign maps
        Land ownership maps
        US and foreign gazetteers
    Prints and Photographs Reading Room
    European Reading Room

Genealogical Libraries

State Historical and Genealogical Societies
- Illinois State Genealogical Society
- Massachusetts Historical Society
- State Historical Society of North Dakota
- Virginia Genealogical Society

Regional History Libraries, such as
- New England Historic Genealogical Society
  In Boston, their library has histories and genealogies concentrating on New England and Massachusetts.
- Long Island Historical Society
  In Brooklyn Heights, New York, this society library concentrates on the settlement of Long Island, New York.
- Phillips Library, Peabody Essex Museum
  In Salem, Massachusetts, the old Essex Institute was consolidated with the Peabody Museum making a large collection of antiquities, historic objects and books. The Phillips Library has become the home of original documents photographs, graphic material, historical manuscripts such as diaries and logbooks. The library also owns state, county

and town histories of New England States and 400,000 rare books.

National Genealogical Libraries
- The Family History Library of the Church of Jesus Christ of Latter-day Saints
  The Family History Library in Salt Lake City is the largest genealogical library in the world. LDS library contains
  - -270,000 family histories
  - -2,000,000 rolls of microfilm
  - -300,000 books
  - -400,000 microfiche

  The library and its 1800 smaller Family History Centers have microfilm and microfiche readers; copiers; computers and printers. There are sections on
  - -Family genealogies, histories & biographies,
  - -Scottish Church Records,
  - -Military Index from the Korean and Vietnam Wars
  - -Social Security Death Index
  - -Family Registry listing organizations and individuals interested in sharing information
  - -Original records from all over the world
  - -Thousands of county, state and regional records

- Daughters of the American Revolution Library
  Their holdings include over 100,000 books and thousands of files, including personal letters, and unpublished genealogies pertaining to genealogical and historical research. Instead of the Dewey Decimal or Library of Congress Classification Systems, the Daughters of the American Revolution use "call words." Under their cataloging system, one catalog card and corresponding book spine might read

Call Words	Meanings
MS	State
Counties	Subject
Oktibbeha	County Name
Car	Author - first three letters of surname

Or in the case of a genealogy, the card and book spine might read

Call Words	Meanings
Families	Category
Cox	Subject Family
Jac	Author - first three letters of surname

In addition to books, the DAR Library also has Ancestor Cards and Patriotic Index entries giving information concerning Revolutionary War Veterans. Much of the DAR's information covers those who served during Revolutionary War. Types of service recognized by the DAR includes

-Federal, state or county military or militia,

-Patriotic Service (PS) demonstrated by signing the oath of allegiance and donating supplies to the war effort,

-Civil Service (CS) shown by serving as a town or county official or on a jury during the conflict.

The Ancestor Card might look something like this

```
LAST NAME, FIRST NAME        Rank, Commanding Officer
    birth date; place        Pensioner
    death date; place
    residence during Rev. War
    names of spouses
```

A Patriotic Index Entry would include the name, birth year and place, death year and place, marriages, state of service and if the patriot received a pension.

- National Genealogical Society
  The NGS library in Arlington, Virginia has a collection of genealogies, local histories, Bible records, census indexes and periodicals on genealogy-related topics. Its circulating library is housed in the Special Collections Department at the St. Louis County Library Headquarters in Missouri.

- The Library of Congress
  It collects and publishes work, but original records are at the National Archives. As the national library, LC has an extensive collection of
  -Loyalist claims on microfilm
  -Family genealogies on microfilm and in book form
  -Guides for particular ethnic and foreign groups
  -Local histories

-Genealogical and historical periodicals
-Military Index from the Korean and Vietnam Wars
-Indexes to genealogical periodicals
-Social Security Death Index
-US city directories
-Published censuses and census indexes

The Library of Congress in Washington, D.C. encompasses three buildings - the Jefferson, Madison and Adams Buildings - connected by underground tunnels and walkways. The collection includes more than 17 million books and almost 95 million special collection items such as manuscripts, maps, photographs, recordings and film. So getting around can be confusing. For genealogists, there are a few things to remember.

1   Most genealogical and local history books are in the Jefferson Building. Many books and periodicals needed for research are on the open shelves of that reading room. Other books are delivered to researchers by "runners".

2   If possible, before ever going to the library, go to the Library of Congress internet web page and do title, author or subject searches for needed material. Write down the following information for each book you want to see and put them in order of importance in a notebook.

LOC number
Author
Title
Volume

This will save a great deal of time once you get to the Library.

3   Upon entering, get a Reader Registration Card. Every researcher has to have one. It will save time and money to get a copy card at the same time.

4   Books that are not on the open shelves get to patrons faster if the patron is in the building and reading room where the materials are kept. In this case, the Local History and Genealogy Reading Room is in the Jefferson Building.

5   In the reading room, find a labeled desk site. Each study space is labeled to help librarians get books to the correct patron. There are computer and hard copy catalogs in each reading room. There should also be supplies of call slips (brown colored for the local history room).

- Fill out the call slips with the book information required, your reader registration card number and your desk number.
- Give the request slips to the "runner" for the room. There is a limit in number of requests accepted per hour. Many times it takes the full hour to retrieve the books, so begin requesting books as soon as you arrive.
- While waiting for your books to be delivered, begin browsing the open shelves. They are primarily divided by geographic subject - and the CD's available in the reading room.

University Libraries

Main Library

While they can be public, these libraries can also be connected to private universities. In general, the university library will have the holdings expected to be needed for advanced education, including large history and biography sections and newspaper files. Large universities might have more than one library.

Special Collections

A university could have a library whose collection is particularly dedicated to the medical school, law school or some other professional school. But some have other specialized collections like the Quaker Collection at Whittier College or the Bentley Historical Library at the University of Michigan. At least one section of any university library system should be set aside for the study of local history, where might be found Federal censuses, tax lists, Union or Confederate records and histories of counties and people in the region.

Archives

The University Archives is the place, usually in the library, where papers of early settlers, dignitaries and less notable persons, and university officials are kept. It should also be the storage area for pictures which have been donated to the university and historical documents; including newspapers, yearbooks and letters of recommendation; concerning the university itself.

Speciality Libraries

Speciality libraries are ones concerned with groups of people, such as those brought together by place of birth, religion or fraternal organization. They often have materials not found anywhere else. Examples include

Stanford University's Chicano Reference Library
The Mennonite Historical Library

Types of Genealogy Books

How to and Where to:
- *Bibliography of American County Histories*
- *China Connection: Finding Ancestral Roots for Chinese in American* by Low
- *Directory of Historical Organizations in the united States and Canada*
- *Genealogical and Historical Guide to Latin American* by DePlatt
- *Genealogical and Local History Books in Print*
- *How to Work with a Professional Genealogist*
- *Genealogical Libraries Within 300 Miles of Starkville* by the Oktibbeha County Historical and Genealogical Society
- *Genealogies in the Library of Congress*
- *Genealogist's Refresher Course* by Jacobson
- *How to Find Your Family Roots* by Bear and Demong
- *Special Collection in Libraries in the Southeast* edited by Howell
- *The Source: A Guidebook of American Genealogy* by Szuchs et. al.

Censuses
- *Michigan Censuses 1710-1830: Under the French, British, and Americans* ed. by Russell
- *Census of India 1931*
- *Index of 1840 Federal Population Census of Indiana*
- *Census of Pensioners for Revolutionary or Military Services*

Local Histories
- *Austin Colony Pioneers* by Ray
- *Historical Sketches of Oktibbeha County, Mississippi* by Carroll
- *Massachusetts Bay Connections: Historical and Biographical Sketches of the Towns and Communities of the Massachusetts Bay Colony* by Jacobson
- *Historical Sketch of Southold Town* by Case

Genealogies
- *Compendium of American Genealogy: the Standard Genealogical Encyclopedia of The First Families of America* edited by Virkus
- *The Hotchkiss Family* by Cowdell
- *Landon Genealogy: The French and English Home and Ancestry* by Landon
- *Long Island Genealogies* by Bunker
- *Encyclopedia of Jewish Genealogy*

Cemetery Records
- *Cemetery Locations in Wisconsin*
- *Historical Cemetery Records of Bradley County, Tennessee*
- *The Jay Cemetery, Rye, New York*

Governmental Records
- *Genealogical Records in Texas* by Kennedy and Kennedy
- *List of Freemen of Massachusetts 1630-1691* by Paige
- *Probate Records of Norway* by the Genealogical Society of the Church of Jesus Christ of Latter-Day Saints, Inc.

Lineage Books
- *The Lineage of Litchfield*
- *Index of the Rolls of Honor in the Lineage Books of the NSDAR*
- *National Society Sons and Daughters of the Pilgrims Lineage Books*

Ship Records
- *American Passenger Arrival Records* by Tepper
- *Passenger List - R.M.S. "Maitai"*

Periodicals
- *Everton's Genealogical Helper*
- *Mississippi Genealogical Exchange*
- *The New England Historical and Genealogical Register*

Vital Records
- *Alabama County Divorce Reports 1908-1937*
- *Arkansas Marriage Record Index: Early to 1850*
- *Chicago and Cook County Vital Records - Birth Index 1871-1916*

Places Other Than Usual Genealogy Books to Find Information in University or Public Libraries

Although the genealogy/local history section is an obvious stop for most genealogists visiting the public library, hidden treasures can be found in almost all the sections. Particular attention should be paid to the sociology, history, geography, biography and reference sections.

A discussion of what might be found in each of the following can be found below the list.

Newspapers	Cemetery records
Published histories	Church histories
Unpublished family histories	Indexes
Obituary collection	Biographies/Diaries

Vertical (V) files	Directories
City and county directories	Governmental records
Local county censuses	Encyclopedias/Dictionaries
Mortality schedules	Maps
Country histories	Non-paper sources

Newspapers

Newspapers can be a rich source of genealogical information, especially when official records have been destroyed. They are particularly helpful in tracing the female line, which is generally more difficult to trace.

Places in the Library Having Genealogical Information Taken from Newspapers

On the whole, they are more legible and easier to read then handwritten records. However, most are not indexed and those newspapers not yet microfilmed can be yellowed and brittle to use.

* Collections of obituaries.
* Vertical Files (files of news articles kept by subject).
* Books of news articles from a specific era or a specific newspaper, such as *Genealogical Data from Colonial New Haven Newspapers* compiled by Scott and Conway
* Loose and/or microfilm pages of newspapers catering to ancestors as specific readers. They may be based on
  Community   Ethnic Origin
  Nationality   Religion

Genealogical Information Found in the Newspaper

You never know where an ancestor might pop up in a newspaper. On December 11, 1925, the Starkville News published letters to Santa that had been sent in that small town and two neighboring communities. Second grader Harold Heflin of nearby Longview didn't ask for anything for himself. He wanted Santa to bring oranges to his "Grannie" and a rattle for Martha Lou Scottie who was "just three months old and hasn't any mamma. She lives with her grandma, Mrs. White."

Type of Article	Example of Type of Information Found
Clubs & Organizations	• Attendees • Memberships Example - "Officers installed in Romeo Lodge, I.O.G.T. No. 150 are Eliza Phelps, R. Selfridge..."

Type of Article	Example of Type of Information Found
Visitations to and from Family Members	• Names of relatives and relationships • Residences • Hints at ages Example - "Mrs. J.R. Storment visited her daughter, Mrs. French in Eustace, Texas..."
Announcement of Birth	• Name and sex of child • Place and date of birth • Parents • Religious affiliation • Godparents • Other relatives Example - "Mary Walpole of Southold gave birth to 1 male and 2 female babies; the 2 females have survived and will constitute a 2nd set of twins, making a total of 10 living children to a woman only 28 years of age, herself a twin."
Parties	• Dates of special occasions • Names of friends and relatives • Residence Example - "Mrs. J.P. Castles celebrated her birthday Friday by having a few of her lady friends and her sister Mrs. M.A. McKnight.."
Announcement of Marriage	• Names and ages of couple • Parents names • Location of wedding • Religious affiliation • Witnesses and attendants • Out of town relatives • Life history Example - "Jane Spence and Kevin Lane... married October 2 at St. Luke's Catholic Church in Athens, Georgia. Parents are Mr. and Mrs. Guy Spence of Athens and Mr. and Mrs. M.H. Lane of Irving, Texas. Attendants were the bride's sister Brenda Noebel..."

Type of Article	Example of Type of Information Found
Announcements of Death (Obituary)	• Name of deceased and nickname • Age at death • Dates of birth and death • Place and cause of death • Military and life history • Names of deceased and surviving relatives • Religious affiliation • Times, date and places of funeral and burial Example - "Asia Tucker born Nov. 2, 1870 in Chumby, Texas passed away May 30. She worked for Well Made Novelty Co. for 35 years... was proceeded in death by her husband of 42 years Madison Tucker, survived by son George Tucker, daughter Ruby Bailey both of Arlington."
Illnesses	• Residence • Possible causes of death and/or unemployment Example - "Mr. John H. Smith was continued to his room this week with fever."
Newcomers	• Previous residences • Family members • Occupation Example - "Stephen H. Davis formerly of Brooklyn, has moved... just east of the village..."
Reunions	• Family reunions -names and residences • Military reunions-names and units • School reunions-names and date of graduation Example - "Seven of the nine children of James Cunningham of Romeo met in his home to celebrate a visit by son Robert Cunningham. The son is on... furlough from the United States warship Brooklyn..."

Type of Article	Example of Type of Information Found
Estate Sales	• Name of deceased • Approximate date of death • Executor • Residence Example - "Col. Graham, trustee, sold the real estate of the late Elisha Holloway. The 107 acre tract was sold to Geo. Ward."
Anniversaries & Birthdays	• Names of celebrants • Date of birth or marriage • Place of residence • Names of relatives Example - "Mrs. J.P. Johnson celebrated her birthday Thursday..."
Business Notices	• Advertisements • New business openings • Business dissolution • Slave sales • Land speculator's announcements • Apprentice Examples - "Carpenter's Grocery's Going-Out-Of-Business Sale"
School News	• Staff names • Graduation participants • Casts in school plays • Achievements • Grades and approximate ages of students Example - "The anniversary of Henry W. Longfellow will be celebrated by the 11th grade at the school building... Recitations will be delivered by Jennie Reid, Mark Starkweather..."
Arrest & Court Reports	• Change of Names • Adoptions • Land Sales • Divorces • Probate • Arrests • Criminal and civil cases Example - John McMann was "brought up for whipping Juda McMann, his darling wife..."

Type of Article	Example of Type of Information Found
Public Notices	• Names of government officials • Tax rolls • Bankruptcy • Notice of debtors • Legal advertisements for runaway slaves • Military deserters • Undelivered mail Examples - 1, "Joshua Borlock of Norfolk; his creditors are ordered to appear before Elijah Hall Esqur." 2. Six Cents Reward... Runaway from subscriber in August last, Isaac Purnall, an indented apprentice to the carpenter business... seventeen years of age.
News Articles	• Names • Ages • Residence • Physical description • Achievements Examples -1. Marston Cabot died when "splitting posts, accidentally cut off one of his legs and died a few hours later" 2."Captain Larew was kill'd and 20 of his men kill'd and wounded."3."Charles F. Beebe won the purse amounting to $9 that was shot for at the shooting match..."

Periodicals

Genealogical periodicals can range from newsletters to full publications. The subject can be as small as a single community to as wide as all surnames someone might study.

The *Genealogical Periodical Annual Index* (GPAI) is key to genealogical literature. It is a comprehensive English language catalog of surname, locality, topical and book review articles. The 1995 edition included nearly 350 publications and 13,000 citation.

As with other genealogical sources, names may appear under a variety of spellings. A sample listing from 1995 was

LARICK, Henry b 1844, w Sarah Elizabeth Humiston,

OH, IA, hist sketch NFB 27: 2:21

Referring to the front, it is explained that NFB stands for "Newsletter, Fellowship of Brethren Genealogists" and an address is given for the newsletter.

Periodicals catalogued in GPAI can be found in large genealogical libraries or smaller libraries in the area of interest. They may also be borrowed Inter-library Loan or back issues may be purchased directly from the publisher

Published and Unpublished Histories

Whether a general history giving group histories and migration patterns, or a history of a specific place, a surprising amount of information can be found in them.

* *Highland Clans and Tartans* by Munro
* *Historical Development of Land Use in Starkville, Mississippi, a Small University City* by Mitlin
* *History of the Romeo Community School District 1824-1976* by Buzzeli
* *Michigan Voyageurs* by Russell
* *The Puritans in America* edited by Heimert and Delbanco
* *Valley of the Lower Thames 1640 to 1850* by Hamil

Obituary Collection and Cemetery Records

Frequently compiled by local genealogical societies, these records contain an abundance of vital information.

* *Civil War Soldiers Buried in Arkansas' National Cemeteries* by Knight
* *Linn County Iowa Cemeteries: College Township*

Church Histories

In addition to giving a mini history of the community, church histories almost always contain membership rolls and occasionally they will even list baptism, marriage and burial records.

* *Historical Resources: Diocese of Connecticut*
* *History of the Baptist in Arkansas 1818-1978*
* *Hopewell Baptist Church, Yalobusha Association*
* *The Jesuit Relations and Allied Documents: Mission of the Hurons of Detroit, 1733-56*

Indexes

The information you need might be readily available if you just know where to go to find it.

* Federal Census Indexes arranged by state and year. But, be careful, the number following the name might be the either original page number or a new page number.
* Union and Confederate Veterans

Biographies / Diaries

Biographies and diaries contain names of friends, family members and neighbors. They also include details of their subject's life.
- *Sadye H. Wier: Her Life and Work* by Wier and Lewis
- *John Askin Papers* edited by Quaife
- *Journal Comprising an Account of the Loss of the Brig Commerce of Hartford (Con.) James Riley, Master Upon the Western Coast of Africa August 28th, 1815...* by Robbin
- *Who's Who*
- *Winthrop's Journal "History of New England" 1630-1649* ed. By Hosmer

Vertical (V) Files

Vertical Files may include newspaper clippings, charts, pamphlets, loose papers and unbound manuscripts relating to a topic. Vertical Files are arranged alphabetically by topic.

City and County Directories

Although there are any number of directories that have been drawn up by clubs, churches, companies and schools, some are a little more unique then usual, such as

Servicemen's Album: Oktibbeha County Mississippi: World War II

Libraries attempt to maintain old and current official city and county directories, which fall into one of two classes -

1. Reverse / criss-cross directories with three separate listings - by name, by address and by telephone number. From a series of criss-cross directories, a genealogist might learn an ancestor's

    Changes of address and approximate dates
    Neighbors
    Place of employment
    Approximate date of death
    Length of residence in community
    Middle names or initials
    Spouse's name

    A genealogist could also determine the number of people living in the residence and if the ancestor is a renter or owner of the home.

2. Telephone books with names of people, businesses, and governmental agencies with telephone numbers and modified addresses. Although not as much, some of the same information could be derived from a series of telephone books as from a criss-cross directory.

Local County Censuses

Frequently some enterprising genealogist has decided to copy census type information into book form, making the information more accessible. Examples include -
* *1850 US Census: Oktibbeha County Mississippi* ed. by Schunk

Mortality Schedules

Mortality Schedules were rolls enumerating all deaths from the twelve months preceding a census, generally from 1850-1880. The schedule included each deceased person's name, county, age and cause of death.

Directories

Directories, such as those below, list persons, places and groups, giving the genealogist addresses to contact for more information.
* *American Blue Book of Funeral Directors*
* *Baird's Manual of American College Fraternities*
* *Catalog of City, County, and State Directories Published in North America*
* *Directories in Print*
* *Directory of Archives and Manuscript Repositories in the United States*
* *Directory of Churches and Religious Organizations in* (Name of State)
* *Encyclopedic Directory of Ethnic Organizations in the United States*
* *Guide to Records of Immigrant Society Agencies in the United States*
* High School and College Yearbooks
* *National Directory of Address and Telephone Numbers*
* *National Trade and Professional Association of the United States* - an annual list of professional, labor, trade, scientific and technical unions and societies.

Governmental Records

Any number of governmental records have been copied into book form. Some examples include -
* Abstracts of Choctaw County, Mississippi Records compiled by Wiltshire
* *Announcement of the Romeo Public School, 1903-1904, With annual Report of the Board of Trustees for the Year 1903,*

Containing Statistical History of Fractional District No. 1, Of Washington and Bruce From 1827 to 1903
- *Historical Data Relating to Counties, Cities and Towns in Massachusetts* prepared by Cook
- *Muddy River and Brookline Records 1634-1838 By the Inhabitant of Brookline, in Town Meeting*
- *Territorial Papers of the United States* by the US Government Printing Office. Multi-volume, multi-territory, multi-year

Encyclopedias / Dictionaries

Understanding the history of a group, makes understanding an individual ancestor so much easier.
- Dictionaries of name meanings, such as *The Origin and Signification of Scottish Surnames* by Sims
- *Encyclopedia of Associations*
- *Encyclopedia of Jewish Genealogy*
- *Greenwood Encyclopedia of American Institutions*
- *Harvard Encyclopedia of American Ethnic Groups*
- *International Encyclopedia of Secret Societies and Fraternal Orders*

Maps and Gazetteers

Because communities can be small and they can change their names or even fade away, gazetteers, in particular, are necessary tools for the genealogist.
- *North Carolina Gazetteer* by Powell
- *Atlas of Winnebago County, Iowa* by Stark

Non-Paper Sources

Microform refers to any film bearing micro-photographic reproduced printed material. It is used to preserve and store cumbersome volumes in minimum space, such as census records, newspapers and special collections.
- Microfiche are miniaturized photographs of documents or book pages on four by six inch sheets containing as many as thirty pages of text. Microfiche machines make the sheets readable.
- Microfilm are miniaturized photographs of documents, book pages or other graphic material printed on reels which can be read on microfilm machines.

A computer is an electronic machine capable of receiving and processing data.

- CD-Roms are small record-like disks which can be "read" by the computer. Genealogical books, marriage records, social security indexes, ship records and other information have been put on CD-Roms and can be purchased for use at home. Many libraries also keep genealogical CD's for patron's use.
- Search engines on the internet find online sites relating to any topic. Many libraries, including the Library of Congress, have put their catalogs online.

Getting a Book Your Library Does Not Own

Libraries can borrow books and other materials from each other. This is called "interlibrary loan." Each library system should have an interlibrary loan librarian. While many public libraries will not lend genealogical books because they can be rare, fragile or out-of-print, State Library Commissions are more likely to lend them.

After an interlibrary loan librarian has obtained a listing of what libraries own a particular book and has found that none will lend it, there are still two steps that can be taken.

1. If a library nearby has the book, a quick trip there can be made.
2. Also, most libraries are willing to photocopy pages of books for even non-patrons as long as the copying falls within the copyright law guidelines and the patron pays for the cost of copying and postage.

Topic Sources and Additional Reading

American Library Directory 1997-1998. 50th edition. New Providence, New Jersey: R.R. Bowker, 1998.

British Library. <www,bl.uk/index.html> The British Library Board. The British Library's Online Information Server. Copyrighted 1999.

Carlberg, Nancy Ellen. Overcoming Dead Ends. Anaheim: Carlberg Press, 1991.

Fielding, Anna Lisa, comp. and ed. and Leslie K. Towle, ed. Genealogical Periodical Annual Index. Vol. 34. Bowie, Maryland: Heritage Books, 1995.

Genealogical Research at the Library of Congress. Washington, D.C: US Government Printing Office, 1993.

Hey, David, ed. *The Oxford Companion to Local and Family History.* New York: Oxford University Press, 1996.

Hoffman, Mariam. Genealogical and Local History Books in Print. 4 Vol. Baltimore: Genealogical Publishing Company, 1995-1997.

Jacobson, Judy. *Genealogist's Refresher Course.* 2nd ed. Baltimore: Clearfield Company, 1996.

Library of Congress Home Page. <lcweb.loc.gov> Library of Congress. Printout dated 20 July 2000

Scott, Kenneth and Roseanne Conway, comp. *Genealogical Data from New Haven Newspapers.* Baltimore: Genealogical Publishing Company, 1979.

Scott, Peter. Hytelnet on the World Wide Web <www.lights. com/hytelnet> Northern Lightsd Internet solutions <pscott@library. berkley.edu> Printout dated 26 July 2000.

Shadrick, I. *Libraries for Genealogists.* Banning, California: I. Shadrick, 1987.

"The Value of Newspapers". *The Genealogical Helper.* Utah: Everton Publishing, January-February 1978 p. 15.

Photographs

Identifying People in Photographs

A picture can indeed be worth a thousand words. A picture, be it photograph or portrait; of a man, a woman and seven children of varying ages; has no names on it. If it looks like a family unit, it probably is one. The man and woman are probably married and the children can be roughly aged.

While identification is possible, that data does not guaranty identification. Nevertheless, the photograph can furnish additional clues. For example, the date the photograph was taken can be determined by the

- Type and size of photograph
- Type of photograph case, if there is one
- Comparison to other photographs of ancestors
- Photographer information on the photograph, including name, address and other markings
- Tax stamps appearing on photographs taken in the North between August 1864 and August 1865 (The money was used to help support the Civil War. Dealers were obliged to affix the stamps to all photographs except for those smaller than the stamp.)
- Notations made by owners on the back of the picture
- Hair styles
- Approximate ages of subjects
- Fashion*
- Other items in the picture, such as telephone, furniture, light fixtures, mode of transportation (Obviously a telephone could not have appeared in a picture prior to its invention).

*Remember, the less financial security a family has, the more likely the styles worn in pictures are behind the times. For instance, a dress may have been made to last longer or handed down to a younger child.

The Basics of Dating a Picture by the Photographic Process

The earliest principles of photography originate with Aristotle and the *camera obscura*, when Aristotle noticed the crescent shape of an eclipsing sun in the gaps between the leaves of a tree. But true attempts at photography with a camera were not begun until the 1800's in England and France.

1790 - 1850	silhouette
1839 - late 1860's	daguerreotype
1844 - 1930's	tintypes / ferrotype

1845 - c.1855	calotype
1849 - 1925	stereograph
1850 - 1860 & 1880's	salt prints
1850 - 1870	hyalotype
1851 - 1870	ambrotype
1853 - 1902	wet-paint print
1854 - 1885	carte de visite
1855 - 1865	melainotype
1865 - 1890's	woodburytypes
1866 - 1920	cabinet card
1870 +	postcard
1885 - 1910	cyanotype
1889 +	nitrate-based plastic roll film
1898 +	Kodak family camera
1900's	albumen print
1939 +	non-flammable plastic film

Types of Photographs

albumen prints - glossy paper photographs

ambrotype - produced as a glass image with a black background. In fact, many found today can be identified by the flaking away of parts of that background. The thin negative against the black background appears as a positive. By 1860, this offspring of wet plate photography was the most extensively used method of photography. Like daguerreotypes, ambrotypes had a protective case and gilt borders. However, ambrotypes were much more fragile then daguerreotypes. The glass was fragile, making the them difficult to carry safely. Exposures took up to 20 seconds, compared to the daguerreotypes which took 2 seconds. Often color was added to the lips, cheeks or jewelry.

cabinet cards - photographs on large (6 1/2" by 4 1/2") card stock. Because of the size, blemishes were more visible, so retouching was first used on cabinet cards. There are a number of ways to date cabinet cards. Note that there are time overlaps with the various styles.
Card Colors

•	White (yellowed with age) card stock	1858-1869 & 1871-1874
•	Gray or tan	1861-1866
•	Gray	1872-1880
•	Yellow	1869-1874
•	Pastels	1873-1910
•	Colors on faces and back of mounts	1880-1890

•	Glossy, creamy colored back and buff colored faces	1882-1888

Card Borders

•	Red or gold rules, single and double lines	1866-1880
•	Wide gold borders	1884-1885
•	Gold beveled edges	1885-1892
•	Metallic green or gold border	1890-1892
•	Colorless impressed outer border	1896

Card Edges

•	Beveled	1875-1900
•	Notched	1894-1900

Card Corners

•	Square	1866-1880 & 1902-1910
•	Square with scalloped sides	1880-1890
•	Rounded corners, single line	1889-1896

Card Size

•	Regular	1869-1920
•	Larger	1880-1906

Card Backgrounds and Props

•	Furniture	1860-1866
•	Background drape	1860-1868
•	Columns	1860-1870
•	Books, vases, urns	1860-1870
•	Steps	1870-1880
•	More elaborate sets	1870-1890
•	Tropical props	1890-1900
•	Bicycles	1890-1900
•	Automobiles	1900's

Other

•	Small simple type imprints on back	1860-1867
•	Painted	1861-1900
•	Advertisement on the back	1869-1879
•	Intricate fonts with curlicue lines	1870-1900
•	Rustic	1875-1885
•	Elaborate ads or flowers on the back	1890-1900
•	Pebbled or rough stock	1900-1920

calotype - the first paper photograph, there were approximately a dozen users in the early and mid 1840's. Using a two-step process, a negative image was made on light-sensitive paper then printed on sensitive paper to make a positive. Invented by Englishman William H. F. Talbot, the problem with the process was that residual chemicals remained and fixing was deficient. So most of those that have survived today have very faded, discolored images.

carte de visite - paper photograph produced on 4 1/4" by 2 1/2" card stock

cyanotype - blue tinted

daguerreotype - named for Frenchman Louis J. M. Daguerre, the daguerreotype was the first major, yet practicable, photographic process. More expensive to produce then the ambrotype, this was an early photograph with a mirror-like quality which was produced on silver or silver-covered, highly polished copper plate. First, it was held to a sheet of glass by a foil looking decorative frame. It was then fit into a case which was like a small double frame, padded with silk or velvet. The cases could be used to date daguerreotypes. Cases which were
- Preserved and ornate around the picture   1850's
- Made of bark-like wood   1849-1854
- Plastic with clear designs on the front   after 1854
- Highly decorated   1861-1865.

The silver finish frequently tarnished like silverware. Magnets would stick to daguerreotype.

hyalotype - glass plate positive known in the 1870's as "magic lantern slides" because they were able to be projected on a wall.

postcards - photographs of people or places which were made into postcards and mailed to friends and family. Obviously, if a postcard has been post marked, copyrighted or hand-dated, dating is easy. However, if none of those appear on the card, the following might help
Types of cards -
- Pioneer - dated from before officially   1899
  prior to sanctioned cards
- Lithographs - matte surface, some made   1900 +
  glossy with albumen coating.
- Real photographs - printed on photographic   1900 +
  paper with place for message and address
  and the word "Postcard" on the back
Characteristics of cards -
- Undivided backs - sometimes with "Address   1901-1907
  Only On This Side" on back, message space
  on the front
- Early divided - line in middle of back or 1/3   1907-1915
  from left edge. Usually contained instructions
  of where to put the address and message and
  a "Post Card" label at the top, center back
- White bordered, divided back - had "Post   1915-1955
  Card" on right of the back, a white edge 1/8 -
  1/4 inch wide and a stamp box

- Marble textured   1920-1940
- Linen surface - textured card, smooth or rough 1930-1955
to touch. Most have white, yellow or beige
borders

Stamp box -
- "Place Stamp here, One Cent Domestic,   pre-1930
Two Cents Foreign"
- "Place One Cent Stamp Here"   1930-1952
- "Place Stamp Here"   1952 +

salt prints - unshiny, sepia brown and purple photographs on regular paper using silver nitrate

silhouettes (a.k.a. "portraits in profile" and "profiles a la Pompadour) - Less costly than portraits (2 for 25 cents in 1805), silhouettes were easy to do quickly. An estimated 250,000 were made, primarily in New England. There were three types.
- hollow cut - traced and cut out of ivory colored paper and backed with black paper or silk. This was most common in New England.
- cut and paste - full length silhouettes cut freehand from black paper with scissors and mounted on ivory colored paper. They were sometimes dressed up with a sepia wash.
- painted - hair and clothing details of silhouettes frequently painted with bronze paint

stereograph card - 3 ½" by 7 ½" card stock showing identical side by side images that were viewed through a binocular-like device which fused the images. These sold for only a few cents.

tintype / ferrotype - a positive photograph made by thinly distributing nitrate over a narrow black iron plate, making it magnetic. Since they were cheaper to manufacture, tintypes were sold for between a penny and a quarter each. Tints were added to cheeks and jewelry. There were a number of types.
- Melainotypes - the earliest tintype produced.   1855-1860
They were manufactured on heavy metal and
stamped "Neff's Melainotype Pat 19 Feb 56"
along the edge.
- Civil War Period - Between 1/6 and 1/4 inch   1861-1865
plate, they frequently can be dated by the
Potter's Patent paper holders or the uncancelled
tax stamps on the back. The War Retail Tax
Stamps date them to between August 1, 1864
and August 1, 1865.

- Brown Period - chocolate-tinted surfaces.   1870 - 1885
  These pictures also began to include rustic
  backdrops and rural props.
- Gem Period - small portraits (postage stamp   1863 - 1890
  size) flourished. These tintypes were made
  popular by Gem Galleries and could be stored
  in albums, lockets or other jewelry.
- Carnival Period - tintypes photographed at   1875 - 1930
  public gatherings. Usually there were painted
  backdrops and novelty props.
- Postmortems - deathbed portrait of loved one   1800's

wet-paint print - a large contact print identifiable by uneven flow of
chemicals to edges of the glass. They were expensive and large
(between 11" by 14" and 20" by 24"). These cameras were taken out of
the studio and photographed large expanses.

woodburytypes - red tint to entire photograph. The picture is very sharp
when the color is filtered out.

Hair Styles

Differentiating Between Boys and Girls

Before 1900, small children of both genders were put in skirts and
girls oftentimes wore their hair cropped until puberty. So it can be difficult
to determine the sex of small children in early pictures. Then, to add to
the difficulty, at the turn of the century, Little Lord Fauntleroy sausage
curls became popular on boys.

But there is one way to differentiate between boys and girls. Most
of the time, girls parted their hair in the middle, while boys did not part
their hair in the middle until the 1900's.

Older children wore wigs very early on and then hairstyles similar
to their parents. After 1900, boys mainly wore their hair short while girls
wore their hair bobbed, braided or pulled into a ponytail.

Hair Styles Among the Poor

In the 1700's, less affluent men generally wore smaller wigs then
wealthier men. The wigs of the poor also were normally made of
horsehair with natural hair interweaved. Poorer women pulled their hair
back in a high or a low bun under a cap with some curls showing.

Men's Hair Styles

Men were clean shaven throughout the 18th century. During the 1700's, men wore wigs over a shaved head or very short hair. Until 1795, wigs were powdered for formal and ceremonious occasions. Before powdering, the wigs were heavily greased. But after a "wax tax" was levied, powdering declined.

1700-10   "Pigeon Wings" (loose curls were worn over the ears).

1710-20   The "Tie Wig" (the curl of the wig was held back with a black ribbon, either with a large black bow or a single braid with a smaller ribbon) became popular.

1720-30   Men wore full bottomed wigs (the front hair in two very exaggerated raised peaks with a center part).

1730-40   Toupee/ toupet / foretop became popular.

1750-70   "Buckles" (wigs with rolls of horizontal curls which covered the ears and the rest of the wig was pulled back) were lightly powered.

1770-80   Natural hair was worn with one roll above each ear and tied in the back with a ribbon.

1780-90   "Hedgehog" style wigs (sides and top were brushed out in spikes) became popular with both men and women. Natural hair was worn with one roll over each ear and tied back.

1780-1810 A single, broad curl, often dressed ear to ear around the head.

1790-1800 Styles ranged from short cropped to side rolls to shaggy, falling to shoulders.

In the 1800's, wigs were gone except for among the elderly. Generally, men's hair was shorter, but full and high in front. Between 1830 and 1870, center parts began at the nape of the neck for some styles.

1800-10   Short hair was brushed toward the face. Longer hair was worn in the wilderness. Men continued to be generally clean shaven.

1810-20	A little longer and tidier hair with more curls or waves became popular. Sideburns or side whiskers on the cheeks were stylish.
1820-40	Men wore closely curled hair with loose waves on the forehead and short back hair. Some hair was parted and puffed on top. Some men wore small moustaches, sideburns, and beards.
1830-40	Styles remained the same but curls became looser.
1840-60	Curled or waved hair with side whiskers, sometimes to under the chin, became fashionable among some while other men wore their hair long over their ears and oiled around the face. Few wore beards, but side whiskers and moustaches were fashionable.
1860-70	Longer hair styles were brushed smoothly back from the face. Some hair was slightly waved and flattened on the crown. Shorter hairstyles had a slight fringe brushed onto the forehead. Long side whiskers were worn with full beards or drooping moustaches.
1870-80	Shorter hair styles were worn closer to the head. Most men wore short bushy beards with moustaches. Few were clean shaven until later in the decade.
1880-90	Three hair styles became popular. Many wore their hair brushed straight back from the forehead in a "Pompadour". Some wore it brushed forward from the back of the head. And the third style during those years included shorter side hair and center parts. Shorter side whiskers and long, drooping moustaches were popular. Mainly, older men wore beards or "mutton chops".
1890-1900	Men wore short hair and were usually clean shaven or only had moustaches. However, mutton chop whiskers were popular.
1900-05	Center parts came into style.
1905-10	Hair was worn shorter in the back and sides with side parts.
1910-20	Hair was brushed back from foreheads into a slight pompadour. Large moustaches were frequently waxed. Older men continued to wear beards.

1920-40	Smaller moustaches and fewer beards were worn. Most men were clean shaven.
1930-40	Smoothed, oiled hair styles were brushed straight back from the forehead with no parts.
1934 +	Permanent waves and neatly trimmed beards became fashionable.
1944-46	Hair was worn short on top and full on the sides.
1946	Height was added to hair in front.

Women's Hair Styles and Head Dressing

In the 1700's, women wore a great amount of makeup. Like men, women wore wigs, with the poorer women wearing horsehair wigs interwoven with natural hair.

Little decorative caps trimmed with ribbons, bows or lace were always worn during the first half of the century. Between 1740 and 1760, instead of caps; strings of pearls, ribbons, jewels or flowers were utilized to decorate hair. The usage of flowers, feathers, jewels and other ornaments became the most exaggerated circa 1775.

In the 1800's, many women wore long hair, held back in net bags. By the 1820's women sectioned their hair off with combs. But in the 1830's, hair decorations became much more elaborate with evening styles including plumes, flowers and coronets.

1700-10	Women wore exaggerated fontange (small linen caps with high pleated head-dress).
1710-20	Hair was pinned up under caps.
1700-20	Hair was worn in rolls and waves with loose ringlets on the shoulder. Sometimes curls were worn on top of the head with long curls hanging down behind the ears.
1730-50	Women wore a mass of small curls or ringlets called "Tete de mouton" (sheep's head). Sometimes false hair was added. Other women wore their hair long and simple.
1740-60	Hair was pulled back into a loose knot at the nape of the neck.

aft. 1765   The pompadour style became fashionable. Pads and artificial hair were used to give height at the top front of the head.

1775-80   By using frames, hair was given even more heigh.

1780-85   Hair had less height and more width. Many women wore chignons in back or knots on top of their heads.

1785-90   The style changed to loose vertical curls, with long tresses flowing down women's backs.

1790-1800 Hair became even simpler and some women even cut their hair short.

1800-10   Although some women still wore wigs of curls, chignons and braids, many women wore their hair short with close curls all over their heads. Others wore long hair pulled back in a net bag.

1815-20   Longer, more disheveled curls were fashionable.

1820-30   Many women wore puffs of curls, sometimes with oiled ringlets, at the sides and on the top of heads. Others wore their hair with a center part or their hair drawn across their forehead.

1830-40   Center parts became more widely used. Hair covered ears with loops, buns, curls or ringlets. Then another part from ear to ear divided the front from the top knot

1840-50   Hair styles included long simple rings at the sides with buns or complicated coils at the back of the head. A center part with hair drawn back covering cheeks led to a bun or bunches of long curls in the back of the head. Younger women wore dangling curls.

1850-60   Styles included a center part and hair pulled in broad loops on the sides into buns or loose chignons. Married women frequently wore lace hair coverings.

1860-70   Chignons were enclosed in net or chenille bags. Other women wore their hair flat on top with slight waves on the sides and gathered in a large looped coil in the back. Married women continued to wear lace or ribbons covering their hair.

1870-80   Hair was swept up, away from the face and sides. Sometimes women wore small fringe-type bangs on the forehead. Hair in the back was usually worn high in twists or rolls with corkscrew curls brought forward over the shoulder.

1880-90   Hair in front was worn closer to the head in Marcel waves with chignons or buns in back. Some women wore their hair shorter with fringed bangs and curls.

1890-95   Women wore their hair piled high on top.

1895-1900 The height of hair dropped toward the back.

In the 1900's hair styles and head dressings varied more from woman to woman.

1900-1905 Hair in the front of the head was dressed with pads in a pompadour style and swept back in a small bun.

1905-10   Waved hair went out of fashion and was replaced with loose "ball-shaped" hair.

1913-18   Hair was worn full, wrapped around the back of the head and high on top. A few women wore their hair short. False eyelashes were invented in 1916.

1919-30   The short "bob" cut close to the nape of the neck and flat on the sides became trendy. Some "bobs" were curly or had tight waves. The shingle cut was even shorter then men's hair.

1930-40   Women's hair was worn longer with waves on the forehead and small curls on the sides and back. Styles were more sculptured.

1937-40   Long page boys with rolled fringe bangs became common. Another style included piling all the hair on top of the head.

1940-50   Hair styles became simpler and more practical. Long hair was pinned up or rolled around the head. Other women wore pageboy hair styles or hair cut above the collar.

Clothing

Children's Clothing Styles

Year	Girls	Boys
1700-1740	bodice with tucked panel, front edge with lace, small mob cap	dressed like men of the time
1750-1770	bodice like adult, but without trim, sleeves with cuffs which ended at elbow, apron bib pinned onto bodice	Little boys - skirts and wide cuffs until out of diapers Older boys - pastel satin suits trimmed in braid had knee britches, white socks, large buckle shoes
1770-1790	high-waisted, ankle length simple dresses, 3/4 length sleeves, kerchiefs, ribbon sashes	skeleton suits (ankle-length loose trousers which buttoned onto a frilled shirt or belted jacket beginning at age 5.
1800-1810	simple muslin dresses with drawstring at neck, may have had wide sating sash or apron or smocks over pantalets (ruffled trousers) girls under 4	frilly blouses with wide collars, double breasted suits with wide lapels, long trousers, buckles on shoes with no tongues or pantaloons & jacket buttoned together to become 1 piece ankle length pants with front flap, low cut slippers
1810-1820	high-waisted, narrow sash	high waist, very wide collar edged in lace, long sleeves, high top, button shoes, pantaloons buttoned on blouse
1820-1830	empire sleeves full at top, drawstring ties at back sometimes skirts were short enough to show pantaloons below	vests, short double-breasted coats, long pantaloons, first sailor suits appeared
1830-1840	off-shoulder, wide-necked dresses	little boys - tunics with cords tied at waist over pantalets or dress

Year	Girls	Boys
1840-1850	off-shoulder, wide-necked dresses, pantalets under short (below knee) skirts	bowler hats, short jackets, shirts with ruffles & large collars, cravats, striped trousers
1850-1860	geometric hose, necklaces, wide shorter skirted dress & cloth boots	belts, Russian box-pleat tunics with matching bloomers, plaid or striped stockings
1860-1870	dressed like mothers, with looser collars, skirts with cloth jackets, pantalets, hoop skirts	round-cut jackets
1870-1880	"pique dresses" with bows, straw hats, boots and gloves	sailor suits
1880-1890	reefer jackets with large sailor collars, lace collars	short tight or baggy kneed britches & boots
1890-1900	brownie suits, overalls or pantaloons over pinafored skirts	Little Lord Fauntleroy - dark velvet suits with short pants and elaborate lace collars. Young boys - kilts, black or white stockings and shoes, straw hats
1900-1910	short dresses with belts worn at hips	rompers or short pants. Buster Brown (age 5-8) - short smock-like suit with bloomer pants worn to the knees with long stockings broad, white collar, large floppy broad brimmed sailor hats
1910-1930	applique work on simple dresses	short pants or knickers to just below the knee, long black cotton stockings
1930-1940	"Shirley Temple look" of short puffed sleeves and above knee length skirts, berets and wide brimmed hats, hand knitted cardigans, lace collars and cuffs on party dresses.	shorter pants for younger boys, knickers for age 8 up, sneakers, Eton Suits - stiff collars and long trousers, polo-necked sweaters

Year	Girls	Boys
1940-1950	high waist ruffled yokes & big collars, full petticoats	short and long pants, beginnings of blue jeans & T-shirts as casual wear

Men's Clothing Styles

Year	Vests/Coats	Pants	Hats	Other
1700	long, full-skirted with large cuffs		three corner, taller to crowned with brim	bleak colors, shirts with dropped shoulder line & open neck
1700-1720	velvet, collar-less, braid trim at buttons & cuffs, wide cuffs, sleeveless waistcoat	britches fastened at knee with a buckle or buttons	three corner or tri-corner	once-tied cravat hanging long over chest; square toed, low-heeled shoes
1720-1740 well-to-do	less or no braid, small stand-up collars, high pockets	knee britches	tri-corner with or without plume	cuff ruffled shirt, dark stockings, buckled shoes
1720-1740 poor	short, loose	loose knee britches	flat	collarless shirt
1740-1760	double breasted with lowered pocket flaps	knee britches, stockings	tri-corner hats with edging	big buckles & long tongue flaps on shoes
1760-1770	not as full & cuffs were slit & buttoned to wrist	knee britches, stockings	tri-corner	short waistcoats
1770-1800	knee length, rounded front corners back almost to the side seam, collarless, no cuffs, split sleeves fastened with buttons, split up back of coat, brocade jackets, wide lapels	banded knee britches, or longer & looser pants	a high crown straw hat, narrow & rolled brim	high boots or high-heeled shoes, ruffled/lacy shirt fronts & sleeve cuffs, black-buckled shoes, white stockings, knotted cravat

Year	Vests/Coats	Pants	Hats	Other
1800-1820	wide lapels, double-breasted cutaway, single/double-breasted tail coats with high collars, wide puffed shoulders; sleeves gather-ed in shoulder area, close-fitting from elbow; short vest with lapels, and pearl buttons.	moderate light, some velvet britches	soft, flared top hats	cravat wrapped high around neck twice with ends tied & tucked into vest, shirt front with frills, more drab & black colors, neck cloth tied in bow in front, narrow tie worn under collar, yarn stockings, functional shoes in black or brown leather or slippers
1820-1830	rounded lapels, double-breasted, rounded-tailed cutaways which went to just below the knees, fitted tightly at the waist and chest, and had shoulder padding, long sleeves; single-breasted, rounded lapels on vests	tapered to ankles, buttoned up to the knees or higher	conical & straight top hats	shirts tucked in, cravats wrapped around the neck & tied, patent leather boots with pointed toes
1830-1840	tight fighting, coat & sleeves, bodice to below the waist, had tails, notched lapels	long, high waisted trousers	top hats	false shirts or dickies, walking sticks, cravats tied in bows, some spurs, boots with spring heels

Year	Vests/Coats	Pants	Hats	Other
1840-1850	knee length, plaid or checked with stand-up collars in back & sleeves fitted narrow & cut high under the arm, embroidered lapels, brocade vests with wide lapels	loose at hips but tapered to ankles with front button flap closing	large & straw in South & Southwest	usually narrow ties tied in small bow but occasionally flamboyant ties
1850-1860	frock coat with, rounded lapels, striped double-breasted with notched collar vest (waistcoat), stand-up shirt collars and long jackets	jeans invented	top hat	stiff necktie & stiff upright shirt collars
1860-1870	became shorter & more fitted circa 1865, rounded or narrow lapels	baggy		smaller ties
1870-1880	coats were more fitted with double-breasted sack suit, wide lapels, velvet collars		bowler hats	patterned & colored shirts, wide ties with loose knots, walking sticks, turned-down, or collarless shirts
1880-1890	narrow lapels & sleeves, morning coat, high neck, short collar, hip length, buttons high on coat	striped trousers, some short britches, narrow pant legs	flat straw or top hat	tuxedos - a short, black coat with shiny satin lapels. White shirts , watch chains, bow ties
1890-1900	narrower, shorter coats with shirt cuffs exposed, black, also some three-piece lounging suits	striped	caps	hanging ties, white shirts for dress, colored shirts for work, short stiff collars

Year	Vests/Coats	Pants	Hats	Other
1900-1920	long formal frock, polo or morning coats. Sack Suit (shapeless, dartless jacket, with narrow shoulders, flap pockets, single rear vent, 3-4 buttons)	pleated at waist, tapered down the legs	bowler hats	button-down collars, pocket watches, more relaxed clothing
1920-1930	first sports jackets, natural shoulders, lounge suits with pointed lapels	cuffed trousers		spats

Women's Clothing Styles

Years	Dresses	Hats	Other
1700-1720	full, loose dresses with chemise sleeves, skirts show ankle, but with ankle-length petticoats, stripes popular in working class, trimmed aprons, some hooped skirts	hooded cloaks	pointed low-heeled shoes
1720-1740	sacque dress or front with train-like effect in back coming from shoulder, 3/4 sleeves or chemise sleeves underneath, diagonally fastened bodices, plain skirts	snug caps, like handkerchief with a few tucks	
1740-1770	chemise ruffles at neck & on sleeves, small double ruffles trim neck & bodice below-elbow sleeves, skirt shorter in front & longer in back, green & flower prints were popular, panniers (divided skirts) at hips formed by drawing up skirts in drapes, bodice hooks down front to a point, lightly laced waist	flat, circular hats, called skimmer hats held on with wide ribbons tied under the neck & veil-like bonnets. Older women still wore lappets on caps	drawstring bags with braids or tassels, kerchief falling at neckline & secured with large bow, handkerchiefs, muffs, parasols, tiny bouquets

Years	Dresses	Hats	Other
1770-1780	use of ribbons & lace, increased width in skirts, oval with side panniers embroidered or quilted, ankles visible	pearl ropes in hair, richly decorated, larger hats with ribbons & lace	pointed toed shoes with high curled heels
1780-1800	several yard long kerchiefs puffed out but still tied across bosom & tied or pinned in front or back with ribbons, trains from shoulders were pleated at the top, 3/4 length pointed sleeves, natural waistlines	large bonnets pulled on & puffed into tall full shapes, sometimes with satin bows	fingerless gloves(mitts), fur-trimmed coats, older / rural women - large triangle kerchiefs over shoulders & upper arms
1800-1810	high-waisted Greek tunics, low-necked bodices, puffed sleeves, large stiff ruffles at neck, straight or gathered skirts, eyelet or muslin	turbans	satin sashes used as belts
1810-1820	skirts decorated with frills & embroidery high-waisted, prints popular, large sleeves at upper arms	turbans, veils, large starched bonnets, or basket bonnets (high crowns & wide brims & ribbons)	shawls, kerchiefs around neck, long gloves, small 2-tier capes, pointed laced shoes
1820-1830	empire style with a little lower waist, A-line in front but flared in back, larger sleeve at top, longer sleeves, crisp ruffled "betsy" around the neck	bonnets & large hats	dickeys worn under low cut dresses, satin ribbon belts, white lace shawls, gloves
1830-1840	wide necklines & collars, wide sleeves at top but narrow below elbows, wide skirts at hems, waist lines in slightly high positions, tight bodices, shoulder lines dropped to upper arm, some hoop skirts a few inches off the floor	sheer lacy bonnets or wide, straw	pantalets, wide kerchiefs, belts

Years	Dresses	Hats	Other
1840-1850	floor length, bell-shaped skirts, narrow sleeves full at the bottom, plaids or checks popular, wide & low necklines, bodices straight to the waist sometimes shirred, pointed or boned in front, floor length skirts with some flounce around the hem,	bonnets flared in front, brims concealed faces	crinolines (vast amount of material draped over wicker or steel) or numer-ous petticoats, long chains, lockets, or ribbons around the neck, shawls of silk or lace, elbow length capes
1850-1860	one-piece dress styles, wider & more decorative skirts crinoline dresses covered by waist-length fitted coats, funnel or pagoda shaped sleeves, multiple layers of flounces, wider collars, boned bodice	more open lace bonnets or hats set back on the head & tied under the chin	shorter corsets, hooped skirts, crinolines over pantaloons or bloomers (long lacy pants protecting from indecency), parasols
1860-1870	low-necked in evening only, full hooped skirts especially in back, material in back looped up into folds or draped towards 1870, braid or stamped borders added to plain colored dresses, short-waisted bodices with long sloping shoulders, front fastening & small collars	pork pie hat poised on top, poke bonnets had side flaps which curled around & nearly covered the face, hats worn forward or on top of head	crinoline at widest & most material, wide belts with large buckles, parasols
1870-1880	bustle dresses with fitted sleeves, tight bodices, high necked, high-waisted, back-sweep silhouettes, tighter profiles	small hats tipped forward	more jewelry, black velvet ribbons with a broach in front were worn around the neck

Years	Dresses	Hats	Other
1880-1890	smaller more looser bustles, but still full or draped in back, bodices had high collars, tight sleeves, tight waists with emphasis on bust & abdomen. Two piece dresses with long sleeves became popular, a lot of ruffles & pleats	elaborate, high hats with flowers & ribbons & straw versions of poke bonnets worn by Quakers	brocade, velvet or silk evening slippers but buttoned or laced boots with heels during the day
1890-1900	bustles gone, leg of mutton sleeves (tremendously wide & puffed at top of sleeve), slight trains, exaggerated or long waisted, shirtwaist dresses	worn on top of head, lavishly adorned with wider brims	blouses & skirts popular, stripes were in fashion, looser corsets
1900-1910	long trailing skirts with sweeping lines, high collars, dresses long in front but even longer in back, tailor-made suits or shirtwaist dresses	large wide brimmed hats or big hats with feathers	kid or silk gloves, parasols, small drop earrings
1910-1920	narrow skirts with higher waistlines, split skirts, straight silhouettes	smaller hats	muffs, intense colors heavy capes
1920-1930	straight sack-like dresses, sleeveless or short sleeves, low waistlines & short skirts	deep crowned cloched hats worn low on the brow	wide belts, strands of pearls from chokers to long loops, long drop earrings
1930-1940	longer skirts, wide & padded suits & coats, some backless dresses, normally place waists	small hats, such as berets, sailors, pillbox & turbans	sunglasses, costume jewelry, open-toed shoes, wedge heels, ankle strap shoes

America's First Look into the Camera: Daguerreotype Portraits and Views 1839-1864 <lcweb2.loc.gov/ammem/daghtml/daghome.html> American Memory: Historical Collection for the National Digital Library. Prints and Photographs Division. Library of Congress. Dated 19 October 1998.

Asser, Joyce. *Historic Hairdressing*. New York: Pitman Publishing, 1966.

Ewing, Elizabeth. *History of Twentieth Century Fashion*. Revised and Updated by Alice Mackrell. Lanham, Maryland: Barnes & Noble Books, 1992.

Gagel, Diane V. *Windows on the Past: Identifying, Dating, & Preserving Photographs*. Bowie, Maryland: Heritage Books, Inc., 2000.

Gernsheim, Helmut. *The Origins of Photography*. New York: Thames and Hudson, 1982.

Hairstyle History. Online Costume Library. <www.costurmegallery.com/hairstyles.html> The Costume Gallery. <research.questions@costumegallery.com> Copyrighted 1997-2000.

Hansen, Henny Harald. *Costumes and Styles*. New York: E. P. Dutton & Company, 1972.

Moorshead. Halvor. Dating Old Photographs <www.familychronicle.com/dating.htm> Family Chronicle. Printout dated 18 June 2000.

Morris, Andrew J. 19th Century Photography for Genealogists <www.genealogy.org/~ajmorris/photo/history.htm> Copyrighted 1997.

"Reminiscent: From the Files of *The Romeo Observer* : Centennial Supplement". *The Romeo Observer*. Romeo, Michigan. 14 July 1966.

Rozzana, Dave. Dave Rozzana's Classy Image: Tips... for Dating Old Photographs. <www.classyimage.com> 1996-2000.

Simons, D. Brenton "New England Silhouettes: Profile Portraits ca. 1790-1850" *NEHGS Nexus*. Boston, Massachusetts: New England Historic Genealogical Society, Vol. IX No. 3&4 June-August 1992.

Smith, Pamela. *Collecting Vintage Fashion & Fabrics*. New York: Alliance Publishers, 1995.

Wagner, Christopher. "Boys Historical Clothing". <members.tripod.com/~hitclo>. Christopher Wagner, webmaster <histclo@lycosmail.com>

Willis, Ron and Maureen. Photography As a Tool in Genealogy. Willis Photo Lab <www.teleport.com/fgriffin/photos.txt> Mountain View, California. Printout dated 29 March 2000.

Worrell, Estelle Ansley. Early American Costume. Harrisburg, Pennsylvania: Stackpole, 1975.

Yarwood, Doreen. Fashion in the Western World 1500-1990. New York: Drama Book Publishers, 1992.

Diseases and Calamities

Those Old Time Diseases

A few things could be claimed as near certainties in Colonial America. Children died more often in summer, the elderly in winter. And epidemics wiped out large numbers of the population in relatively brief periods of time.

But sometimes the listed cause of death left more questions then answers. In 1900, Mrs. Samuel Story of Pickensville, Alabama, died of "paralysis" according to her obituary. Any number of diseases could be described under the listing "bone", "bowels", "digestion" "brain", or "lungs". "Digestion" could have referred to food poisoning, bleeding ulcer, stomach cancer, or any number of other problems.

In those days, even today's simplest of ailments could quickly become deadly. Through the years, supposed "diseases" that have been listed as cause of death have included "chills, "kidney infection", "measles", and "teething".

And then, of course, there were the diseases with those strange sounding names and curious spellings that are seldom, if ever, used today. As with proper names, spellings were not always considered important.

abepsia / ablepsy - blindness

acute mania - insanity

Addison's Disease - a serious debilitating disease with symptoms of weight loss, low blood pressure, gastrointestinal problems and brown pigmentation to skin

aglutition - incapable of swallowing

ague - a catch-all term for symptoms of fever, chills, twinge a cough or, sometimes, a nosebleed; which could have been a cold, influenza, or, sometimes even malaria.

air swellings - air or gas in intestines

American Plague - see "yellow fever"

anasarca - see "dropsy"

anchylosis - stiff joint

ancome - a boil

aphonia - laryngitis

aphtha - thrush

apoplexy - a stroke, and sometimes hysteria or epilepsy

asthma - asthma (Spanish)

bad blood - syphilis

barbers itch - ringworm

Barlow's Disease - see "infantile scurvy"

Barrel Fever - infirmity caused by intemperance

bilious - a disorder of the liver function, in particular, excess bile secretion, with headaches, upset stomachs, vomiting, and diarrhea. Symptoms of bilious fever usually included headaches, furred tongue, pain in the joints and, sometimes jaundice.

black death - Bubonic Plague or typhus. Between 1348 and 1349, it killed as many as 1/3 of the known world's population.

Black Fever - infection associated with a high temperature and dark red skin lesions

Black Jaundice - a bacterial infection of the liver carried by rats

black tongue - mineral deficiency which results in severe diarrhea, nervousness, blotching and peeling of the skin

black vomit - vomit of dark blood

Blackwater Fever - high temperature and dark urine

bladder in throat - see "diphtheria"

blood poisoning - septicemia

bloody flux - dysentery

Blue Disease - blue tinge to body (cyanosis)

bold hives - croup

bone hives - croup

brain fever - see "meningitis"

Bright's disease - serious kidney disease

bronchitis - serious inflammation of the bronchial tubes and upper portion of the lungs

Bronze John - see "yellow fever"

cachexy - malnourished

cacospysy - uneven pulse

calenture - see "yellow fever"

camp fever - see "typhus"

canine madness - rabies

cardilus - inflammation of the heart wall

catarrh - any illness involving a sore throat, cough, difficult breathing, and laryngitis

cerebritus - inflammation of the brain, thought to be caused by long "exposure to a vertical sun," the inordinate use of "ardent spirits", cold fright or injury. Symptoms included fever; flushed dry skin; delirium, blindness and deafness.

childbed fever - see "puerperal fever"

chilblains - swelling inflammation of the skin, especially the extremities, caused by exposure to cold. Although it could be acute or chronic, chilblains was less severe than frostbite.

chin cough - see "pertussis"

cholelithiasis - gall stones

cholera - any of several diseases marked by vomiting and severe gastrointestinal disturbance. In reality, cholera was an acute infectious bacterial disease eventually leading to collapse and frequently caused by drinking contaminated water. It thrived in filth and poverty; and spread rapidly, first appearing in America in 1832.

cholera infantum - disease of vomiting, diarrhea, fever, prostration, and collapse among infants. It mostly occurred during in cities during the summer and frequently was fatal.

cholera morbus - severe gastroenteritis characterized by gripping diarrhea, colic, vomiting; possibly leading to a quick death

chlorsis - anemia

chorea - nervous disorder

chronic - any disease of slow progress, long duration, or frequent return

clap - gonorrhea

colic - acute abdominal pains resulting from spasms generally attended by distension of the abdomen, primarily in infants

commotion - concussion

congestion of the brain - sunstroke.

congested brain - often associated with brain swelling

Congestive fever - malaria

consumption - tuberculosis, which was thought to be inherited at one time

corruption - infection

coryza - a cold

costiveness - constipation

coup de sang paralytic stroke (French)

cramp colic - appendicitis

cretinism - hypothyroidism

crop sickness - over-extended stomach

croup - inflammation of the larynx, especially in infants, with noticeable periods of difficult breathing, hoarse cough, and laryngitis

crusted tetter - impetigo

cyanosis - darkening of skin due to lack of oxygen

debility - loss of strength, feeble, weak

decrepitude - feeble

delirium tremens - hallucinations due to alcoholism

Diary Fever - see "yellow fever"

diphtheria - communicable disease of nose and throat; with fever, furred tongue, pain and frequently the enlargement of heart muscles

Dock fever - see "yellow fever"

domestic illness - mental breakdown

dropsy - congestive heart failure, edema; excessive buildup of clear fluid in body tissues or cavities

dropsy of the brain - encephalitis

dry bellyache - lead poisoning

dysentery - intestinal inflammation, abdominal pain, and passage of mucous and bloody stools. Dysentery might have been caused by bacteria, protozoa, or parasites passed through contaminated food or water. The first known outbreak in America occurred in 1607 in Virginia.

dyspepsia - indigestion; impairment to digestion caused by ulcer, gall bladder disease or inflamed colon

eclampsia / eclampsy - convulsions during labor

Egyptian Chlorosis - hookworm

encephalitis - swelling of the brain, sleeping sickness

enteric fever - see "typhoid fever"

enteritis - inflamed bowels

erysipelas - severe streptococcal inflammation of the skin; accompanied by sore limbs, sore throat and tenderness of glands

extravasated blood - ruptured blood vessel

falling sickness - epilepsy

fatty liver - cirrhosis

febrile - feverish

fieore tifoidea - typhoid fever (Spanish)

flux - excessive, abnormal discharge from the bowels resulting in dehydration

French disease - syphilis

French Pox - venereal disease

galloping consumption - pulmonary tuberculosis

gangrene - the decay of the tissue of a body part, usually a limb

gastric fever - probably "typhoid"

gathering - mass of pus

glandular fever - mononucleosis

gleet - see "catarrh"

goiters - a visible enlargement of the thyroid gland

gout - an overabundance of uric acid in the blood provoking arthritis-like symptoms

gravel - deposit of small calculous "stones" in the kidneys and bladder

Great Pox - syphilis

green sickness - anemia

grippe - acute communicable viral disease identical to or resembling influenza and sometimes causing death

Grocer's Itch - skin disease caused by mites usually found in flour or sugar

Hectical Complaint - recurring fever

hemophilia - inherited disorder passed by females to male offsprings characterized by excessive bleeding

hidropesia - dropsy (Spanish)

horrors - delirium

hospital fever - see "typhus"

hydrocephalic / "hydrocephalus" - an abnormal increase of fluid in the cranial cavity, appearing as an enlarged skull, especially the forehead; and deterioration of the brain

hydrophobia - see "rabies"

ictericia - jaundice (Spanish)

icterus - see "jaundice"

inanition - starvation

infantile paralysis - see "poliomyelitis"

infantile scurvy - acute scurvy brought about by malnutrition during infancy

intemperance - excessive drinking of intoxicating liquor, causing from cirrhosis of the liver to alcohol poisoning to an accident occurring under the influence of alcohol

intermittent fever - see "malaria"

jaundice - a disease with a yellowing of the skin, white of the eyes, body fluids, and tissue due to buildup of bile pigments in the blood

jail fever - see "typhus"

King's Evil - swelling of lymph glands; tuberculosis

Kruchusten - see "pertussis"

leprosy - a chronic disease causing nodules, loss of sensation, disfigurement and eventual paralysis

lingering - dying slowly, probably from a chronic disease

lockjaw - an early symptom of "tetanus", in which a spasm of the jaw muscles induces the jaw to shut in place or "lock"

long sickness - tuberculosis

long sickness - tuberculosis

lues - syphilis

lues venera - venereal disease

lumbago - back pain

lung fever - pneumonia

lung sickness - tuberculosis

mad dog disease - see "rabies"

malaria - an "ague" striking at intervals - with seemingly frequent relapses. It is a parasitic disease of red blood cells caused by infected mosquitos. In olden times, physicians frequently could not differentiate between malaria and other diseases which produced high fevers.

mania - insanity

marasmers - infant unable to absorb nutrition

membranous croup - hoarse cough, sometimes diphtheria

meningitis - inflammation of membranes of the brain or spinal chord

miasma - poisonous fumes, probably from decaying organic matter

milk leg - a painful swelling of a leg caused by an infection beginning after labor

milk pox - see "white pox"

milk sickness - disease from cow milk after cattle have eaten poisonous weeds mormal / morsal - gangrene

morphew - blisters caused by scurvy

mortification - infection

myelitis - inflammation of spine

nephritis / neuphritis - inflammation of kidneys

neuralgia - discomfort

nightsweats - excessive perspiring at night, occurs with pulmonary tuberculosis and other debilitating infirmities

nostalgia - homesickness

osmidrosis - perspiration with an order

palsy - full or partial paralysis, or uncontrollable tremor of a portion of the body

paroxysm- convulsion

pertussis - severe infectious disease with spasms of coughing until the breath is exhausted and ending with a laryngeal (whoop) cough

petechia fever - fever with spotting of skin

phthiriasis - lice

phthisis pulmonaris - see "consumption"

piles - hemorrhoids

plague - Bubonic Plague

pleurisy - an inflamed pleura (membrane lining of the thorax between the lungs and abdomen) characterized by fever, painful and difficult breathing, and a short dry cough

pneumonia - a disease including a cough, pains in the side and chest, and difficult breathing. Pneumonia was a particular problem of winter

podagra - gout

poliomyelitis - an acute infectious viral disease which attacked the spinal cord and brain. It was characterized by a high fever, paralysis, and atrophy of the muscles

Porphyra - any of several inherited disorders with symptoms of sensitivity to the sun, neuritis and manic depression

Pott's Disease - tuberculosis of the spine

pox - syphilis

Protein Disease - childhood kidney disease

puerperal - childbirth

puerperal fever - infection of the placental region following delivery. In serious cases the infection could pass through the uterine wall into the bloodstream

pulmonia - pneumonia (Spainish)

putrid fever - diphtheria or typhus

pyemia - form of blood poisoning

quinsy - inflamed throat with fever and swelling, strep throat, tonsillitis

rabies - a viral disease which attacked the brain and spinal cord

remitting fever - malaria

rickets - an insufficient absorption of calcium and phosphorus caused by inadequate vitamin D and sunlight. Rickets caused deformities when the condition struck during skeletal development.

rose cold - hay fever

rose rash - roseola

Royal Malady - see "Porphyra"

St. Anthony's Fire - see "erysipelas"

St. Vitus' Dance - nervous twitches, chorea

sangluneous crust - a scab

sarampion - measles (Spanish)

sciatica - rheumatism of the hips

scarlatina - see "scarlet fever"

scarlatine - scarlet fever (Spanish)

scarlet fever - a serious communicable streptococcal disease characterized by a skin rash, fever, tonsillitis and generalized toxemia. It frequently caused pulmonary, mastoid and brain abscesses and was most likely crippling or fatal.

screws - rheumatism

scrofula - tuberculosis of the lymph nodes.

scum pox - impetigo

scurvy - swollen knees, shrunken muscles, weakness, depressed spirits, spoiled teeth

septicemia - blood poisoning

ship fever - see "typhus"

sleeping sickness - see "encephalitis"

smallpox - severe, eruptive, contagious viral disease characterized by chills, high fever, back and head aches, and rash. Eruptions from smallpox caused scaring which remained after recovery.

softening of the brain - apoplexy / stroke

spasms - involuntary muscular contraction. The term "spasm" might have been assigned to any form of convulsions.

Spotted Fever - cerebro-spinal meningitis

Strangers Fever - see "yellow fever"

strangery - rupture

summer fever - see "cholera morbus"

summer diarrhea - see "summer complaint"

summer complaint - diarrhea caused by contaminated food. It was found particularly in children and was most prevalent in hot weather.

sweating sickness - an epidemic-type disease characterized by heavy sweating, high temperature, and early high mortality

teething (death by) - tooth infection and inflammation

tetanus - an acute infectious disease characterized by spasms in voluntary muscles and caused by bacteria passed into the bloodstream through a cut.

thrush - a parasitic fungal disease with white patches and ulcers on mucous membranes of the mouth

tos ferina - whooping cough (Spanish)

toux - cough (French)

toxemia - high blood pressure & seizures during pregnancy; eclampsia

tremors - trembling or shaking from physical weakness caused by any of a number of diseases

tuberculosis - a communicable disease brought about by infection with tubercle bacillus characterized by toxicity of the lungs. Indians were particularly hard hit with about 30% of all Indian deaths between 1911 and 1920 being due to tuberculosis.

Tumeur - tumor (French)

tussis convulsiva - see "pertussis"

typho-malarial fever - described by a physician in 1891 as consisting of chronic chills, soreness, "malarial poison", toxemia and occasional hemorrhages of the bowels continuing over a long period with a wasting away from high fever. If differed from typhoid in its absence of diarrhea and irregularity of fever.

typhoid fever - an infectious bacterial disease characterized by fever, headache, diarrhea and prostration. Temperatures sometimes rose to as high as 106-107 degrees.

typhus - a severe disease remarkable with its high fever, delirium, stupor, intense headaches, deep red rash, which was transmitted to man by lice uremia - blood in urine

variola - see "smallpox"

variole - smallpox (French)

venesection - bleeding

Viper's Dance - chorea, St. Vitus' Dance

viruelas - small pox (Spanish)

white death - tuberculosis of the lungs

white plague - see "white death"

white pox - a mild form of smallpox caused by a less virulent strain of the virus

white swelling - tuberculosis of the bone

whitlow - a boil

whooping cough - see "pertussis"

Wiel's Disease - see "Black Jaundice"

wind colic - pain in bowels; flatulent colic
winter fever - pneumonia, cholera morbus

winter itch - an itchiness brought on by extended exposure to cold dry air

worms - parasites. Hookworms originated in Africa, but were brought to America with slaves. Wormwood tea and oatmeal mixed with male ferns was a treatment for tapeworms.

yellow fever - a viral disease of warmer climates transmitted by mosquitoes and characterized by fever, prostration, jaundice, and occasional bleeding

yellow jacket - see "yellow fever"

Epidemics In America

Cases of a number of ancestors disappearing from records can frequently be traced to dying during an epidemic or moving away from an affected area. Some major epidemics which affected the United States are listed below:

1657	Boston	Measles
1687	Boston	Measles
1690	New York	Yellow Fever
1713	Boston	Measles
1729	Boston	Measles
1732-33	Worldwide	Influenza
1738	South Carolina	Smallpox
1739-40	Boston	Measles
1747	Connecticut, New York, Pennsylvania & South Carolina	Measles
1759	North America	Measles
1761	North America & West Indies	Influenza
1772	North America	Measles
1775	North America (especially New England)	Undetermined Epidemic
1775-76	Worldwide	Influenza
1781-82	Worldwide	Influenza
1783	Delaware	Bilious Disorder
1788	Philadelphia & New York	Measles
1793	Vermont	Influenza & Diphtheria or Typhus
1793	Virginia	Influenza
1793	Philadelphia	Yellow Fever
1793	Harrisburg & Middletown, Pennsylvania	Unexplained deaths
1794	Philadelphia	Yellow Fever
1796-97	Philadelphia	Yellow Fever
1798	Philadelphia	Yellow Fever
1803	New York	Yellow Fever
1820-23	United States	"fever"
1831-32	United States	Asiatic Cholera
1832	Major cities	Cholera
1833	Columbus, Ohio	Cholera
1834	New York	Cholera
1837	Philadelphia	Typhus
1841	United States, especially the South	Yellow Fever
1847	New Orleans	Yellow Fever
1847-48	Worldwide	Influenza
1848-49	North America	Cholera
1850	United States	Yellow Fever

1850-51	North America	Influenza
1851	Illinois, Great Plains, & Missouri	Cholera
1852	United States	Yellow Fever
1855	United States	Yellow Fever
1857-59	Worldwide	Influenza
1860-61	Pennsylvania	Smallpox
1865-73	Philadelphia, New York Boston, New Orleans, Baltimore, Memphis & Washington, D.C.	Recurring epidemics of Scarlet Fever, Yellow Fever, Smallpox, Typhus/Typhoid, or Cholera
1873-75	North America & Europe	Influenza
1878	New Orleans	Yellow Fever
1885	Plymouth, Pennsylvania	Typhoid
1886	Jacksonville, Florida	Yellow Fever
1918*	Worldwide	Influenza

* More people were hospitalized during World War I with influenza than wounds.

Important International Medical Events and Miracle Cures Having an Influence on Populations and Migrations

1347-1451 Bubonic Plague spreads through Europe
1348-1355 Plague in Egypt
1628   William Harvey discovers circulation of blood (England)
1665-1666 Great Plague of London
1732-1733 Worldwide influenza outbreak
1775-1776 Worldwide influenza outbreak
1781-1782 Worldwide influenza outbreak
1796   Dr. Edward Jenner develops smallpox vaccination (England)
1816   Rene Theophile Laennec invents stethoscope (France)
1826   Brugnatelli and Fontana discover active chemical salcin leading to the development of aspirin (Italy)
1826-1837 Cholera epidemic rages (Europe)
1846   First anesthetic use by a dentist
1847   Surgeon James Simpson first uses chloroform as anesthesia during childbirth (Scotland)
1853   Dr. Alexander wood devises hypodermic syringe (Scotland)
1857-1859 Worldwide influenza outbreak
1863   Mary Harris Thompson become first American female surgeon
1864   Pasteur discovers pasteurization process (France)
1865   Mendel issues findings on heredity

	Joseph Lister begins using carbolic acid as the first antiseptic used during surgery
1867	First gallstone operation
1873-1875	Influenza outbreak in Europe and America
1880	Chemist Louis Pasteur develops anti-cholera vaccine (France)
1881	Pasteur develops anthrax vaccine (France)
1885	Pasteur develops rabies vaccine (France)
1891	Emil von Behring, Shipasabure Kitazato, and Robert Koch discover anti-toxins used to treat diphtheria and tetanus
1899	First bottle of aspirin goes on sale
1901	Pathologist Karl Landstuna identifies blood groups leafing to matching of donor and recipient blood (Austria)
1903	Invention of Electrocardiograph (Holland)
1918-1919	Worldwide Influenza
1922	Pasteur Institute develops vaccine for Tuberculosis first used on schoolchildren (France)
1928	Discovery of the antibiotic penicillin by Alexander Fleming
1953	Dr. Jonas Salk develops polio vaccine (USA)
1960	Bacteriologist John F. Enders develops measles vaccine (USA)
	Dr. Thomas Weller develops Rubella (German Measles) vaccine (USA)

Disasters in the United States

Some ancestors disappeared during a major disaster, either because the ancestors died or moved away. Disasters occurring in the United States which could have led to such a disappearance include -

1805	Fire	Detroit, Michigan
1811	Earthquake	New Madrid, Missouri
1812	Earthquake	New Madrid, Missouri (the quake was so strong that it caused church bells to ring in New York)
	Earthquake/ Tsunami	Santa Barbara, California
1840	Tornado	Natchez, Mississippi (317 died)
1857	Earthquake	Fort Tejon, California
1863	Draft riots	New York City (1200 died)
1871	Forest Fire	Wisconsin (1182 died)
	Fire	Chicago, Illinois (250 died)
1872	Earthquake	Owens Valley, California
1876	Theater Fire	Brooklyn, New York (295 died)
1888	Blizzard	Northeast US (500+ died)
1889	Flood	Johnstown, Pennsylvania (2209 died)
1892	Earthquake	Imperial Valley, California

1894	Forest Fire	Minnesota (413 died)
1899	Earthquake	Cape Yakataga, Alaska
1900	Hurricane	Galveston, Texas (6000+ died)
1903	Theater Fire	Chicago, Illinois (602 died)
1906	Earthquake	San Francisco, California
	Hurricane	Southeast Florida
1907	Mine Disaster	Monongah, West Virginia (361 died)
1913	Mine Disaster	Dawson, New Mexico (263 died)
1919	Hurricane	Florida and Texas
1925	Tornado	Indiana, Illinois, and Missouri (689 died)
1928	Hurricane	Lake Okeechobee, Florida area (1836 died)
	Mine Disaster	Mather, Pennsylvania (195 died)
1930's	Dust Bowl	Southwestern Great Plains
1935	Hurricane	Florida Keys
1936	Tornado	Georgia and Mississippi (455 died)
1938	Hurricane	New England
1942	Fire	Cocoanut Grove, Boston (491 died)

World's Worst Disasters

1333-1337	China	Famine	6 million died
1556	China	Earthquake	830 thousand
1642	China	Flood	300 thousand
1669-1670	India	Famine	3 million
1703	Japan	Earthquake	200 thousand
1737	India	Earthquake	300 thousand
1769-1770	India	Famine	3 million
1838	India	Famine	800 thousand
1846-1847	Ireland	Famine	1 million
1857	Japan	Earthquake/Fire	107 thousand
1876	India	Tsunami	215 thousand
1876-1878	India	Famine	6 million
1876-1879	China	Famine	9.5-13 million
1881	Indochina	Typhoon	300 thousand
1887	China	Flood	900 thousand
1896-1897	India	Famine	6 million
1914-1924	Russia	Famine	25 million
1920	China	Earthquake	180 thousand
1921-23	USSR	Famine	1 million +
1928-1929	China	Famine	3 million
1939	China	Flood	3.7 million
1932-1934	USSR	Famine	5 million
1936	China	Famine	5 million
1939	China	Flood/Famine	10 million

Sometimes an ancestor disappears for a census. Sometimes a young male suddenly appears to have died. And sometimes the reason for those disappearances is war or other military action.

Below is a list of the military actions the United States has been involved in and the years of its direct involvement.

1636-1637	Pequot War
1664	British taking of Amsterdam(NY) from Dutch
1675-1676	King Phillip's War
1680	Pueblo uprising against the Spanish
1689-1697	King William's War
1704	French and Indians destruction of Deerfield, Massachusetts
1754-1763	French and Indian War
1763	Pontiac's War in the Northwest Territory
1770	Boston Massacre
1774	Naval battle against British off coast of Rhode Island
1775-1783	Revolutionary War
1786-1787	Shay's Rebellion
1789	US Army established
1794	Whiskey Rebellion in Pennsylvania
1794	General Anthony Wayne's Battle of Fallen Timbers, Northwest Territory
1797	XYZ Affair - undeclared naval conflict begun with French interference of American shipping
1801-1805	War with North African Barbary pirates (Tripoli)
1811	Harrison's defeat of Shawnee "Prophet" at Tippecanoe
1812-1815	War of 1812
1831	Nat Turner's slave uprising
1832	Black Hawk War
1836	Siege at the Alamo
1838	Conflict over New Brunswick/Maine border
1846-1848	Mexican-American War
1861	Apache declaration of war on US
1861-1865	Civil War
1863	Draft riots of New York City
1869-1878	Two hundred major battles between US Army and Indians
1876	Custer's Last Stand
1890	Battle of Wounded Knee
1898	Spanish-American War
1898	Expedition against Ojibwa in Minnesota
1899-1902	Philippine Insurrection
1914	American occupation of Vera Cruz
1916-1917	Mexican Border Campaign

1917-1918	World War I
1941-1945	World War II
1950-1953	Korean War
1965-1973	Vietnam War
1983	Grenada Invasion
1989	Panama Invasion
1990	Persian Gulf War
2001	War on terriorism

Major Revolutionary War Events and Battles

October 26, 1774	Minute Men are established
April 19, 1775	Revolutionary War begins with the Battles of Concord and Lexington
May 10, 1775	Americans take British held Ft. Ticonderoga in New York
June 14, 1775	Continental Army is established
November 13, 1775	Americans take Montreal
July 4, 1776	The United States declare independence from Britain
August 27, 1776	British win the Battle of Long Island
December 25, 1776	Washington and his troops cross the Delaware River to Trenton
May 4, 1778	Treaty of Alliance with France is ratified by the Continental Congress
December 29, 1778	Battle of Savannah
January 29, 1779	Battle of Augusta
May 12, 1780	British win at the Battle of Charleston
January 17, 1781	Americans win at the Battle of Cowpens
October 19, 1781	Americans and French defeat British in the Battle of Yorktown

Foreign Military and Armed Engagements (Ending with World War I)

Many of these military actions may have eventually brought ancestors to the United States as refuges.

1519-1520	Spanish defeat Aztecs and seize Mexico
1526	Turks (Ottomans) take over Hungary
1546-1566	Schmalkaldic War in Germany
1562-1568	Wars of Religion - Catholic League vs Protestant Huguenots (France)
1572	Dutch revolt against Spanish rule
1585	Floating mines used by Dutch
1588	British defeat Spanish Armada
1605	Gunpowder Plot (England)

1618	Thirty Years War begins in Prague
1636-1637	Pequot War
1638-1746	Scottish Civil Wars
1642-1649	English Civil War
1655	Jamaica seized from Spain by the British
1664	British defeat Dutch in New Amsterdam (New York City)
1687	Venetians besiege Athens
1689-1697	King William's War
1701	War of Spanish Succession
1702-1713	Queen Anne's War
1744-1748	King George's War
1740-1748	War of Austrian Succession (France vs. Austria)
1745	Jacobite Rebellion (Scotland)
1756-1763	Seven Years War
1759	British defeat France at Quebec
1768-1774	Russo-Turkish War
1775-1783	American Revolution
1789	Paris mob storm Bastille
1789-1799	French Revolution
1791-1803	Haitian Revolution
1792	Franco-Prussian War
1796	Beginning of Napoleonic Wars
1798	Irish Rebellion
1800-1815	Napoleonic Wars
1812	Napoleon enters Moscow and finds it burning and the people gone
1815	Napoleon defeat at Waterloo
1818	Argentine forces defeat the Spanish, winning independence for Chile
1821	Greek War of Independence from Turkey begins
1826	Turkish-Egyptian forces defeat Greeks
1827	Greece is freed when Russian, French and British forces defeat Turks and Egyptians
1831	French Foreign Legion is established
1833	Breech-loading bolt-action rifle designed by Dryse
1837	Canadians revolt against British attempts to unite Upper and Lower Canada
1839-1842	Chinese Opium War
1845-1851	Irish Famine
1846	US declares war on Mexico
1848	Austrians capture Milan
1848	Revolution in Vienna
1848	Revolution in Paris
1848-1849	German Peasant Wars
1851-1864	Chinese Rebellion

1853	Turkey declares war on Russia
1853-1856	Crimean War between France and Great Britain
1858	French occupy Saigon
1861	English launch first ironclad
1862	Richard Gatling invents 5 barrel gun which fires 700 rounds per minute
1863	French capture Mexico City
1866	Prussia invades Austria
1867	Alfred Noble invents dynamite
1870	British put down the Red River Rebellion in West Canada
1870	Franco-Prussian War
1876	Execution of members of terrorist Molly Maguires
1880-1881	First Boer War
1884	Hiram Maxim invents the fully automatic machine gun
1886	Haymarket Massacre
1894-1895	Sino-Japanese War
1895	Turks attempt to exterminate Christian Armenians
1896	Defeat of Italy's invasion of Ethiopia
1899-1902	Boer War between Great Britain and Dutch settlers in South Africa
1900	Boxer Rebellion in China
1904	Russo-Japanese War
1910	Italo-Turkish War
1910-1920	Mexican Revolution
1914-1918	World War I
1917-1921	Russian Revolution
1935-1936	Italo-Ethiopian War
1936-1939	Spanish Civil War
1939-1945	World War II
1946-	Israel-Arab Conflicts
1971	India-Pakistan War
1979-1989	Soviet occupation of Afghanistan
1980-1988	Iran-Iraq War
1982	Falkland Islands War

Topic Sources and Additional Reading

Burrows, Daniel, comp. Car Chart. <www.genrecords.com/library/war.htm> Printout dated 12 July 2000.

Epidemics and Military Battles <www.ento.bt.edu/IHS/militaryEpedemics.html> Based on slide presentation by Dr. Tim Mack. Printout dated 26 July 2000.

Gormley, Myra Vanderpool. *Family Diseases: Are You at Risk?* Baltimore: Genealogical Publishing Company, 1989.

Household Physician. Buffalo, New York: Brown-Flynn Publishing Company, 1926.

Jacobson, Judy. *Genealogist's Refresher Course.* 2nd ed. Baltimore: Clearfield Company, 1996.

Iowa Genealogical Society. Outdated Medical Terminology. <www. digiserv.com/igs/med.htm>. Printed out 24 July 2000.

Werle, Susan Farrell. "Medical Terms for Genealogists" *The Genealogical Helper.* Everton Publishers, July-August 1988. p. 11

Courthouses

The number of times an ancestor's name appears in records increases proportionately to decreases in population. So courthouses are outstanding sources, especially for farther removed or early ancestors.

Problems to Expect Working in a Courthouse

Patience is important when researching in a courthouse, particularly the small county courthouse.

- First, counties were formed from portions of other or parent counties and boundaries changed. So, it may be necessary to check the records of two or three counties for one area.
- That also applies when families lived on the border of a county. They might have owned land in both counties. Or land records might appear in one county, marriage records in the other.
- Counties also have changed names. Everton's *Handy Book for Genealogists* and other books like it list all counties along with their original and / or parent county's name.
- County officials are frequently unfamiliar with the older records. Many courthouse workers are underpaid and overworked. They have little experience or interest in helping the genealogist.
- Many early records lack indexes. Luckily, however, land records are almost always indexed.
- However, those people indexing the records also were trying to decipher names that were illegible, and unfamiliar. Check out any similar names. The indexer may not have copied the name correctly.
- Older records may have been banished to the courthouse basement, the local museum or the public library. It may take some detection work to find where needed records can be found.
- Courthouse fires occurred in almost epidemic proportions, especially in the South, so large portions of some records have been destroyed.
- Early handwritten records on old fragile paper can be hard to read.
- Small town courthouses are packed and staff are run ragged on court days. Avoid going on those days.
- Birth and death certificates were not issued until at least the 1880's and many times they are held at the state, rather then the county level.
- Courthouses close on most Federal three-day holidays.
- Some probate districts, as in Vermont, do not coincide with it counties.

- Signatures do not change drastically.
- Couples who filed for divorce did not always divorce. And couples that divorced may have continued to remain together.
    1   One couple in the 1800's divorced because the children from his first marriage wanted to inherit everything. But for some reason, the ex-wife remained in the home.
    2   A more modern couple divorced for income tax purposes, but the family unit remained unchanged in any way.
    3   Divorced couples have been known to remarry.
- Conviction or commitment to an asylum did not mean guilt.
    1   A woman found guilty of killing her child may have been a victim herself in days that Sudden Death Syndrome or Crib Death was unknown.
    2   Salem was not the only town to arrest people who were innocent. Two men brought to trial in Mississippi in the early 1800's for killing two children by hexing their father were found innocent of murder.
    3   Commitment papers for a 52-year-old mother of thirteen children who was sent to a mental institution in the 1800's reported symptoms indicating she merely suffered from menopause and fatigue.

Types of County Courthouse Records Which Could Be Useful to Genealogists

Despite the problems working in courthouses, the wealth of information available is unparalleled. Records fall into a number of different categories.

Family	divorces	guardianships	adoptions
	bankruptcies	marriages	probates
	name changes	births	deaths
	dower releases	welfare records	lunacy hearings
Land	deeds	land abstracts	county maps
	mortgages	land grants	bounty warrants
	property taxes	land disputes	seizures for taxes
	section maps		
Criminal	indictments	jury lists	warrants
	witness lists	judgements	pardons
	coroner's reports	probation	trial transcripts
Institutions	poor farms	hospitals	orphanages
	old folk's homes	schools	asylums

veterans' homes	jails	public health offices
Other	voter registrations	tax lists	military service
	livestock brands	naturalizations	financial disputes
	business licenses,	apprenticeships	poor taxes
	medical licenses	newspapers	oaths of loyalty
	powers of attorney	slave ownership	passport
	statues/plaques	clerk's minutes	applications

Types of County Courts

Court is the place where justice is administered by a judge and jury, or just a judge and clerk. Local courts come with a variety of names and duties, depending upon the state. Some of the most frequently used are

civil	chancery	district
circuit	family	criminal
equity	probate	common pleas
justice	small claims	orphans'*
superior	debtors	conciliation

*Orphans' Court may also include children "bound out" to learn a trade.

Two Most Under-Used County Records and Why They Are Important

The Superintendent of Schools lists of educable children are frequently compiled census which usually give
    a list of all school aged children in the family,
    ages of children,
    names of parents or guardians,
    race of family,
    area of county (by community or township) where family lives.

Land Abstracts show the history of a piece of land and its neighboring land, making it easier for the genealogist to determine
    when and if land passes to the owner's children,
    if the land is divided among the owner's children,
    who has authority to sell the land at the owner's death (usually the name of the executor),
    which family members marry neighbors,
    if family members settle near each other.

Information Which Might Be Found in Records

Probate Records

Probate records are much more than just the will. In fact, there may be probate records even when there was no will. If a person dies leaving a valid will, he died "testate". Without a will, he died "intestate."

But either way, probate records should include estate inventories and sales, legal notices, claims against the estate, and guardianship papers for minor children.

The will is found in bound will books. Other records can be found by going to the probate indexes, which give the court case numbers. Those documents are filed in "packets" which are usually folded and filed in envelopes.

Although all probate records do not have the same information, things that might be discovered are listed below. But remember, if a relationship is not spelled out in a will, it cannot be assumed. It also is possible to have someone declared legally dead when they have only been missing for from five to seven years.

legal name of deceased
name of spouse
children and their spouses
other relatives and in-laws
approximate date of death
names of minor children
guardians appointed for minors
the "black sheep" of the family

close friends
land owned
financial worth
hint to occupation
appraisers of the estate
those with claims against estate
widow's next husband's name

Birth Records

legal name
father's name
mother's name
date of birth

place of birth
if multiple birth (twins/triplets)
date of birth

Marriage Records

bride's maiden name
groom's name
parents of couple
date of marriage
place of marriage

religious affiliation
witnesses (usually relatives)
bondsmen (usually relatives)
ages of couples
minister

Tax Records

Tax records only indicate a person owned land in a particular place, not that he ever lived on the land. But they are an indication of

financial standing
time period person lived in area

property owned
fluxuations in finances

Land Records

Land records are usually indexed by Grantor (seller) and Grantee (buyer) and then by the first letter of the surname. The book and page number of the deed are also given. Once the deed, abstract and other land records are found, information in them can include

legal name of owner
location of land
name of spouse
siblings' names
division of estate among heirs
cost of property
arrival in area
departure from area
local churches and cemeteries
neighbors' names

if literate
witnesses
release of dower rights
financial stability
amount of land sold
other co-owners of the land
legal age
generation sequence
liens and loans

Topic Sources and Additional Reading

Carlberg, Nancy Ellen. *Overcoming Dead Ends*. Anaheim: Carlberg Press, 1991.

Eichholz, Alice, ed. *Ancestry's Red Book: American State, Country and Town Source*. Salt Lake City: Ancestry, 1992.

Jacobson, Judy. *Genealogist's Refresher Course*. 2nd ed. Baltimore: Clearfield Company, 1996.

Nicholson, Mary Ann "'Where There's a Will...' (Some Curious Mid-Atlantic Probate Records)" *NEHGS Nexus*. Boston: New England Historic Genealogical Society, October-November 1991. Vol. Viii No. 5.

Probate Record UK: Legal Records Information 23: Where to Look for a Will or Grant of Administration <www.pro.gov.uk/leaflets/ri2241.htm> Public Records Office. The National Archives. Crown Copyrighted 1999.

Public Records Online <websearch.about.com/internet/websearch/library/howto/ht_public_records.htm> About, The Human Internet. Copyrighted 2000.

Vital Records Information: United States <vitalrec.com> Dated 28 June 1996.

Land Records

While usually land records are found on the county level, the Federal and state governments also have their share. Bounty lands were given for military service and Homestead Acts opened huge areas of land to settlers.

Information Available in Land Records

That information can easily be transferred into useable information for the genealogist, as shown below.

Legal name of owner	The legal name, including middle name or initial, is more likely to appear on this kind of document than a nickname. Other land held under the same name may be owned by the same person, or by a father or son (Sr. or Jr.) or other relation of this person.
Location of land	Plotting out written land descriptions sounds like just a waste of time. But frequently it can be a useful tool for the genealogist. In fact, it can <ul><li>distinguish between two people with the same or very similar names</li><li>place the ancestral home,</li><li>place the family cemetery,</li><li>differentiate between purchased and inherited land,</li><li>uncover family members, in-laws and friends in the area,</li><li>determine whether the land was inherited or purchased.</li></ul>
Name of spouse	Usually land was put in the name of both husband and wife. But if the wife's name does not appear, that does not mean the man was single or a widower.
Siblings' names	Often, siblings inherit or purchase land together. They act as witnesses for each other and sell land to one another. They may appear in other important papers involving family members.
Division of estate	If land is being divided among heirs following the death of the owner, it should be apparent in the

last deed in a person's name. In the index, the grantor might be listed as "the estate of..."

Cost of property	Property going to someone "for love and affection" versus $1000 is probably going to a relative. The cost and terms of a sale also indicate the wealth of the purchaser
Arrival in area	The first deed in a man's name pretty well indicates his reaching the age of maturity or his arrival in the area. Ancestral migration to the area also can be unearthed by tracing the surname back through land records.
Departure from area	The last property sold by a person usually indicates his death or departure from the county. But notice the date of the selling of the land. It does not have to be the same as the date the sale is recorded in the courthouse.
Neighbor's names	Neighbors are frequently friends, in-laws, or family members who inherited land or moved into the area with the researched ancestor .
Reason for land sale	A sheriff's deed indicates that land was seized for taxes to satisfy a legal judgement. A sale by an executor denotes that the land was sold following the death of the owner.
If literate	If the deed is signed with an "X" or other mark, the person is probably illiterate.
Witnesses	Witnesses to important events of life are frequently immediate family members, in-laws or close friends. Usually they can be expected to live within five miles of the land owner.
Release of dower	Even if a wife is not on the deed, her release of dower rights may be included when the land is sold.
Financial stability	Land sold by the county for back taxes does not indicate financial stability on the part of the original owner. The terms of the sale can also indicate financial means.

Amount of land	If more land was sold then was purchased, perhaps some of the land was received through inheritance or land grant. If more land was purchased than was sold, what happened to that additional land?
Land's co-owners	"Et al." and "et ux" indicate others co-own the land with the individual actually listed as the owner. They may be family members.
Legal age	Most land could not be in the name of anyone under 18 years of age, and sometimes 21. Minors sold land through their legal guardians.
Generation sequence	Records for land handed down through a family can show direct line of decent as well as any genealogy.
Liens and loans	Financial conditions of the family can be discerned through the taking and payment of mortgages.
Local churches	Platt maps can show the location of local churches and cemeteries which might have been the sites of family baptisms, marriages and burials.

Land Surveying

There were two systems of land surveying most commonly used in the United States to sub-divide land into distinguishable parcels.

Surveying System	Definition	Example
Rectangular System	Used in the Midwest and West, this system used grids of ranges and townships surveyed from baselines running east and west and meridians running north and south. Each square in the grid was divided into 36 sections.	"NE 1/2 Sec. 9, Range 15 West, Township 2 South"

Surveying System	Definition	Example
Metes and Bounds System	Boundary lines were described using physical features such as water and boulders or man-made markers. This system was used prior to the rectangular system.	"Beginning at the ash tree follow Deer Creek south to Dan Lees' land, thence due west 260 poles, thence 20 degrees "

Rectangular Survey System

The rectangular survey system was established as an orderly way to survey and sell land by the 1785 Land Ordinance. Area descriptions based on the Rectangular System are based on a section like the one below.

One Mile × One Mile

Half Section **320 acres**	
1/4 Section **160 acres**	**1/8 Section** **80 acres**
	1/16 Section **40 acres**

Legal descriptions were based on the rectangular system begin with the smallest unit. A section like the one below might have had a parcel of land described as "SE1/4 SE 1/4".

N 1/2 of Section **320 acres**	
SW 1/2 of Section **160 acres**	**N 1/2 of SE 1/4** **80 acres**
	SE1/4 of SE1/4 **40 acres**

Land and Survey Terms

abeyance - of undetermined ownership

abode - a dwelling

abstract - summary of successive conveyances

abstract company - private agency which compiles histories of ownership of pieces of property

accession number - one of two Bureau of Land Management codes used to identify a land patent by state, volume and page number

acre - land measurement equal to 43,560 square feet. Or, the term may be used to mean no more than a parcel of land of no referenced size.

acres - accumulative acreage expressed in BLM records to nearest thousandths

Aliquot parts - notations use to describe subdivision of a section of land in retangular survey system. Halves are divided by N, S, E, or W (south ½ of section 12), quarters by NW, SW, NE, or SE (southeast 1/4 of section 12). A section equals 640 acres, a ½ section equals 320 acres.

appraisal - value of property as determined by authorized person

assessment - official listing of property to be taxed and its value

assignee - person to whom court turns over property

assignor - person who signs over property to another

backsyde - back yard and outbuildings

Bargain & Sale - property transferred on a cash basis

baseline - true east to west survey line

bill of sale - formal transfer of title of property

BLM serial number - Bureau of Land Management identifier number

bounty certificate - document giving land to those who served in the military in a war bounty land warrant - a right to land granted for military service

caballeria - land given by Spain to horse soldiers (Spanish)

cadastral - survey or map showing ownership of land for tax purposes

call - a landmark or measurement referred to in a survey, such as "maple tree next to Deer Creek"

chain - sixty-six feet in length

chain carrier - surveyor's assistant who moves the survey chain

condition / conditional line - agreed upon line between two pieces of property that have not been surveyed

congreción - settlement (Spanish)

conveyance - transfer of real property

conveyor - settler (grantor)

copyhold - lease, a title to land written in manor court rolls in an effort to protect the tenant. The tenant held a copy.

corner - the beginning and ending of each survey line

credit entry files - land sold on credit before 1820

curtesy - life tenancy of land; future claim a husband has to his wife's real property upon the live birth of a child to them

declination - deviation between magnetic north and true north

deed - legal, written conveyance of real estate

deed of partition - deed for those holding land jointly

dehesa - common pasture ground (Spanish)

demesne - land reserved exclusively for the lord of the manor, separate from land used by tenants.

demise - transfer of property

donation certificate - document giving 640 acres to anyone who participated in Mexican War

donor - giver of bestowed lands

dower widows right - right to life interest in 1/3 of husband's estate

ejido - pueblo commons used for new residents, recreation and livestock (Spanish)

encroachment - an extension of a piece of property

escheat - land deeded to the state by default in the original 13 colonies

estancia - livestock ranch (Spanish)

et al. - and others

et ux - and wife

fee simple - absolute ownership of land

Feet of Fines - records of judgements concerning property ownership

feoffment - transferal of land ownership

finca - small farm (Spanish)

first station (see point of beginning)

"for love and affection" - used in land deed to denote no money is being exchanged. Its use does not necessarily mean blood relationship between grantor and grantee.

freeholder - owner of land by fee simple, and citizen of town

gore - piece of land which causes a gap between or overlap of adjacent properties

grant - to transfer property deed

grantee - purchaser

grantor - seller

hacienda - privately owned estate (Spanish)

headright patent - a charter giving acreage to a settler who can pay his passage and be self-sufficient upon arrival

hereditament - property transferred by line of descent

homestead - gain title to public land

Homestead Law - 1862 law allotting land to those without any land of their own, for just the cost of filing.

hovel - open shed or outbuilding usually used for storing grain or animals

joint tenancy - ownership of land by two or more persons

jointure - settlement of property to a woman in lieu of her dower rights

labor - cultivated field (Spanish)

Land Entry Papers - documents filed in connection with entry onto public land, such as bounty land warrants, payments, homestead applications

land grant - conveyance of real estate by a government entity

Land Ordinance of 1785 - law providing for the survey and auction of public land

land patent - conveyance of real estate from federal government to persons

land script - a certificate the holder can use to obtain public land

lands and tenements - real property

leban - territory (French)

lien - having a proprietary interest in land

meander - twists of a survey line within a stream

merced de tierra - land grant (Spanish)

meridian - north to south survey line running from pole to pole

messuage - dwelling with lands and buildings

mortgage - agreement using land as security for a debt

muniment - evidence defending the title of property

non grant land transfer - land paid for rather then granted by the government

notarial records - French land records kept in the New World by notaries

out - ten chains in length

patent - conveyance of title to land from a government to an individual

patentee - person receiving a land title from the government

peonia - land given by Spain to foot soldiers for pasture and garden space (Spanish)

peppercorn rent - nominal rent required to acknowledge property has been passed

plat - drawing or map of a piece of land showing owners and neighbors

plat book - book of maps indicating location of land

primogeniture - the right of the first born male to inherit

plaza - town square (Spanish)

point of beginning - starting place of a survey

Preemption Application - application for someone who had already settled on land

private land claim - land owned by persons having grants from foreign sovereigns

proprietor - received land from the crown

propio - royal lands which were rented (Spanish)

public domain land states - thirty states established through purchase or treaties of war

public lands - land titled to the government

quicksett - hedge or thicket

quit claim deed - conveys all rights of ownership of land from seller to buyer

quit-rent - rent on land

rancho (small private farm (Spanish)

range - imaginary lines running six miles apart from north to south

schepen kennis 0 mortgage (Dutch)

section - 640 acres or a one square mile piece of land

small holding claim - legal continuous proprietorship of southwestern public lands for a minimum of twenty years. These were metes and bounds tracts.

solar - house lot (Spanish)

sollars - attic

state-land states - original thirteen colonies and additional states which controlled their own public land

suerte - agricultural lot (Spanish)

survey date - date of official approval of Federal land survey plat

tenement - land and buildings

terreno - tract of land (Spanish)

terres - estate (French)

Title Transfer Authority - treaty or congressional act which transfers public land to private ownership

township - a six square mile parcel of land under a rectangular system of survey

tract book - land history/description arranged by township and range giving acreage, owner, purchase price, date and type of sale. A tract was 24 square miles made up of 16 townships of 6 square miles each.

US Reservation - provision retaining some rights or title to land, such as a right of way.

vacant public lands - public domain land, primarily in the Western states, still titled to the Federal government and set aside for a specific purpose

warrantee name - name on document of receiver of a military warrant

warranty deed - deed conveying land with covenants against encumbrances

Homestead and Bounty Lands

Revolutionary War Bounty Lands

Bounty land was government land which was donated to reward volunteer service and to induce men to join the military. For instance, Revolutionary War Veterans were given unsettled land as reward for their patriotic service.

No. of Acres	Military Rank
100	Private and non-commissioned officers
150	Ensign
200	Lieutenant
300	Captain
400	Major
450	Lieutenant Colonel
500	Colonel
850	Brigadier General
1100	General

States Which Gave Additional Land to War Veterans

Georgia (Revolutionary War)   Pennsylvania (Revolutionary)
Maryland (Revolutionary)   South Carolina (Revolutionary)
Massachusetts (Revolutionary)   Texas (Mexican War)
New York (Revolutionary)   Virginia (Revolutionary)
North Carolina (Revolutionary)

Homestead-type Acts

Cash Entry Act of 1820 - offered public lands for $1.25 per acre for a minimum of 80 acres. District land offices initially offered the land through public auction.

Homestead Act of 1862 - tendered 160 acres of land to the head of any family or any citizen over the age of 21. Residency and improvement of the land were required. After 6 months, the homesteader could purchase the land for $1.25 per acre. After five years the homesteader could apply for the title for $15.00.

Topic Sources and Additional Reading

Analyzing Deeds for Useful Clues. <www.bcgcertification.org/skbld955. html> Online. Reprint from On Board. Newsletter of the Board for Certification of Genealogists. Vol. 1. No. 2 (May 1995). Mike St. Clair, Webmaster <St-Clair @bcgcertification.org> Copyrighted 1995.

Bureau of Land Management, Eastern General Land Office. "Early Public Land Laws". <www.blm.gov>. Printout dated 19 May 1999.

Bureau of Land management, Eastern General Land Office. "GLO Terms and Field definitions". <www.glorecords.blm.gov/help/glossary.asp> Printout dated 15 May 2000

Holsclaw, Berdie Monk. "'Beginning at the Black Oak...' Reconstructing Your Ancestor's Neighborhood with Plat Maps." *Unlock Your Heritage... With Creative Problem Solving: Conference Syllabus.* The Federation of Genealogical Societies & The Dallas Genealogical Society 3-6 September 1997 p 219-222. Richardson, Texas: The Federation, 1997.

Hone, E. Wade Land & Property Research in the United States. Salt Lake City: Ancestry, 1997.

Larson, Frances. *The Genealogist's Dictionary.* N.p. 1986.

Official Federal Land Patent Records Site <www.glorecords.blm.gov> Bureau of Land Management. US Department of the Interior. 29 February 2000.

Raney, Don. "Research in the Texas Land Records" *Unlock Your Heritage... With Creative Problem Solving: Conference Syllabus.* The Federation of Genealogical Societies & The Dallas Genealogical Society 3-6 September 1997 p 223-226. Richardson, Texas: The Federation, 1997.

"Skill Building: Analyzing Deeds for Useful Clues." *On Board: Newsletter of the BCG.* Board of Certification of Genealogists. Vol. 1 No. 1. January 1995.

Thoyts, Emma Elizabeth. *The Key to the Family Deed Chest: How to Decipher and Study Old Documents: Being a Guide to the Reading of*

Ancient Manuscripts. Reprint. 1903. Ann Arbor, Michigan: Gryphon Books, 1971.

United States Department of the Interior - Bureau of Land Management. The Official Federal Land Patent Records Site <www.glorecords.blm.gov/default.asp?> Last modified February 29, 2000

Law

Two Sides of the Law

The law mirrors a society's values. In colonial America, Common Law was the system used in the English colonies: Civil Law was the system practiced in the French and Spanish colonies. When the American system of law was developed, it was divided into two parts. Criminal cases were considered crimes against the state. These cases were divided into
- misdemeanors (minor offences)
- felonies (major offences)

Civil Cases involved disputes between one or more persons against another party. They might have included
- land or boundary disputes
- divorces
- adoption
- financial disputes

Legal Terms

Legal documents have used long, meandering sentences and stilted language for centuries. Consequently, some legal writings seem to be ambiguous, with words unfamiliar to the lay person. Some terms are found with different spellings in those vintage records, while other terms are outdated. Many are in Latin, while yet other terms have slightly changed meanings from what was initially intended in old documents.

a consitius - of counsel

a menso et thoro - separation of couple, but not a divorce; literally, separation "from table and bed"

a posteriori - by reason of what follows

ab initio - from the beginning

abacea - executor of estate (Spanish)

abate - reduction

abatement- making less or a decrease

abettor - person who aids

abstract - summary of essential facts of a document

accola - immigrates to till land

acquittance - notice of discharge of debt

acta - document (Spanish)

action - a court proceeding

ad colligin dum - summary to date

ad interim - in the meantime

ad litero - in this case only

ad quod damnum - sheriff's writ to determine damages and take action

administration - settlement of an estate

administration de bonis non - disposal of goods after estate administrator has also died

administrator - court appointee who settles the business affairs of a deceased, minor or incompetent person

administrator's bond - bond posted to insure the proper discharge of an administrator's duties

administratrix - female administrator

advocate - champion of a cause

affiant - person making an affidavit

affidavit - a written statement sworn to and signed in front of a court officer

affinitas - related through marriage

aiding and abetting - being present or doing something to aid a person in the breaking of the law

albacea - executor of estate (Spanish)

alias - formerly or otherwise known as...

alien - one born in a foreign country

almshouse - poor house

annuity - yearly payment of specific sum of money

annus - year

ante - before

appearer - deponent (Dutch)

appellant - one who takes an appeal

appellee - party against who appeal is made

appurtenances - rights and duties connected to use of manorial land, such as grazing rights and payment of fines to the lord of the manor

artificial person - a non-human entity, such as a corporation

assignee - person to whom an assignment is made

assumpsit - implied promise to perform or pay for something

asylum - place of refuge or confinement

attest - to declare something is true

award - decision of arbitrators

banns - announcement of pending marriage

base tenant - one obligated to perform inferior services

behoff / behoofe - to benefit

bench warrant - warrant order by judge mandating immediate seizure or arrest.

beneficiary - person entitled to receive profit

bequest - specific property left in a will

bienes de difunto - holdings of legal heirs (Spanish)

Blue Laws - laws restricting commercial / business activities on sunday

bon - good, sufficient

bona - goods

bona fide - in good faith

bond - a written promise to repay

bondsman - person acting for or giving surety for others

borough - incorporated town

bound - obliged to serve another in payment of a debt

burgher excise - tax on liquor for home use

cannon - church law

canons of descent - principles dictating transmission of property from ancestor to heir

capitation tax - head tax

carte blanche - authority to do anything relating to an affair

census - routine official count of a population

certiorari - see writ to...

chancellor - presiding judge in a chancery court

chancery court - court dealing with family matters

charter - terms of an old deed or contract

chattel - any property except real estate

circuit court - traveling court or criminal court

civil action - case in which one party sues another to enforce a private right or redress a wrong

civil court - court which decides disputes between people as individuals, partnerships or corporations civil lawsuit - legal case between two or more parties

civitate - city of...

codicil - a subsequent addition to a will

common law - man and woman living together as a married couple without legal action. Once established, the marriages become of public concern.

common pleas - court hearing plea between individuals, as opposed to a plea between an individual and the government.

Compegtent - qualified and capable of discharging a duty

convey - transfer property

co-parcenary - joint inheritance

corporeal property - as can be seen...

corporeal hereditaments - inheritable material items

corum - quorum

county court - court handling business of county government

court leet - manorial court

court of record - the court which keeps a permanent record of proceedings of a case

criminal - act against the best interest of society.

criminal lawsuit - case in which the state sues one or more parties to redress a public wrong

cui - of whom, of what place

cum testo annexo - with will annexed

cruateur - guardian (French)

curtesy right - possession of real estate for life of survivor in a marriage

de bonis non de bonis non adminestratis - of the goods not yet administered

decem - ten

decedent - deceased person

Declaration of Intention - a sworn statement by someone indicating the goal of becoming a citizen

decree - order of a court

dedimus - commission of a private individual to carry out a court order

de facto - arising from

defendant - person being sued or charged with a crime

deforciant - person who prevents another from inheriting an estate

de jure - by law

demise - to will or lease property for a life or a term of years

demense - parts of the land that the lord kept for himself

denization - giving an alien the rights of a citizen

department - county (French)

deponent - one who gives written or oral testimony

deposition - written testimony by a witness for use in court

devise - to give by will, to bequeath

devisee - person who receives a gift in a will

devisor - person who wills land to another

divorce a mensaet thoro - "divorce from bed and board" (legal separation)

divorce a vincuo matrimonii - "divorce from the bonds of matrimony;" full divorce docket - calendar of court cases kept by a clerk of the court

donee - person who receives a gift

dower - widow's life interest in one-third of the lands and buildings owned by her husband

dowager - widow endowed

eadem - same

eam - she

ecclescia - church

ejus - he

ejusdem - of the same

eleemosynary institution - charity organization, such as a poor house or an orphanage

encouragement and restraint of marriage - concept that children born out of wedlock should be considered legitimate if parents eventually marry

enumeration - the tallying of persons for a census

eodem die - same place or day

ergo - I

escheat - property which reverts to the state when no heir exists

est - is

estate - the whole of a person's possessions at time of death

et - and

et al. - and others

et ux / uxor - and wife

etiam - also, again

ex - from

executor - person named in will to carry out the provisions

executrix - female executor

exhumación - exhumed body (Spanish)

extant - existing

eygenpandem - seizure containing proprietary rights

extract - copy of all or a portion of a record

fee simple - an inheritance without condition or restriction

freehold - person receiving civil political rights

filiam - daughter

filium - son

final papers - petition for citizenship

firmo - I sign (Spanish)

first papers - declaration of intention to become a citizen

glebe - land belonging to a church or assigned to a minister

grant entail - conveyance of a limited estate of inheritance

guardian - court appointee who supervises property and rights of someone, such as a minor, who is incapable of handling their own affairs

habeas corpus - writ seeking a speedy trail or a speedy release of an illegally detained person

head tax - tax on people

hearth tax - tax on fireplaces in force between 1662 and1689

heir - person who is entitled to inherit

hereditament - property tramitted by right of descent

hiatus - opening or break

holographic will - will written entirely by the hand of the person who signs it

huc - here

hujus - of this

hujusidem - of this month and year

immens - to be near

imminens - immediate

impeachment - attempt to show a person is unworthy of belief

impositum - the name bestowed

impots - taxation (French)

impressment - seizing of people or property for public use

imprimis - in the first place

impuesto - tax (Spanish)

incorporeal - immaterial in nature

incorporeal property - property which cannot be seen, but of which there is ownership, such as a copyright

indenture - contract entered into by two or more people in which a person is bound over services

infant - a minor

infantum - a child

infra - below

inmate - person who lives in the same house or lives in an institution

inprimis - in the first place

inqus - repeated or maintained

instrument - formal document

instestado - person who died intestate (Spanish)

intestate - dying without a valid will

inventory - detailed list of goods in an estate

joint will - two or more person create a single will

jointure - settlement of an estate or property upon a woman in lieu of dower rights

judge advocate - legal officer who acts as prosecutor during a military trial

juizo de orgaos - orphans' court records (Spanish)

jur - sworn

jurisdiction - the right to speak

lay subsidy - tax on moveable property

legacy - property bequeathed in a will

legal notice - newspaper advertisement notifying the public of a legal action

lessee - holder of an estate under lease

lessor - person who grants a lease

letter of attorney - document appoint an agent

letters of administration - court action authorizing administration of an estate of a person who died without a valid will

letters testamentary - documents issued by probate court to the executor after probate of a will

livery of seizin - delivery of lands, tenements and hereditaments to entitled person

loco - to place or establish

locus - place

manumission - written act to free slaves

mark - substitute for a signature

marriage bond - document guarantying there are no moral impediments to an intended marriage

meet - suitable

mensis - month

messuage - dwelling house with adjacent land and buildings

mineur - minor (French)

moiety - one-half

Moot Hall - manor court

mortis - death

mulierem - woman

natum - born

naturalize - grant of full citizenship

non compos mentis - of unsound mind

notary - person authorized to draw up and attest to contracts and wills

novem - nine

now wife - term implying a former (or ex) wife

nuber huc adventis - recently arrived in this place

nuncupative will - oral will recorded later

oath of abjuration - statement renouncing former allegiance

ob - before, in front of

obit - died

octo - eight

ordinary - probate judge or a tavern

partition - division of ownership of property by two or more persons

paucis hebdomadibus - in a few weeks

peace warrant - warrant for arrest ordered by a Justice of the Peace

per - for

per stripes - division of an intestate estate in which children of an heir who has died receive only that which the heir was entitled

per se - by itself

per stirpes - division of an estate so that children are treated as a group rather than individually

personal property - property other than land, such as livestock, jewelry, slaves

petit - small (French)

piéces - documents (French)

pleitos - court action (Spanish)

posthumous - after death

prae - in front, before

praecende - preceding

pridie / priede - previous day

primogeniture - right of first born to inherit in full

probate - official dispersal of property in an estate

procuratorem - in behalf of

prothonotary - chief notary

proximo - the next month

quarta - four

qui - who

quinque - five

quit-rent - rent of land

registres d'etat - civil registry of birth, marriage and death (French)

reglamento - regulations (Spanish)

replevin - common law action to obtain what plaintiff claims as his property

return of marriage - requirement that the person performing a marriage return the endorsed license to the county recorder within a proscribed period

revocation of a will - annulment of a will

scire facias - and it is ordered that...

seizin - possession of real property

septum - seven

sex - six

shopps - any house or building where goods are produced to be sold

sine die - indefinitely

squashed - suppressed

statu quo - as things are

stirk / sterke / styrke - between one and two years old

suit - proceeding during which one party prosecutes another

supra - above

surrogate - officer charged with probate of a will

tenement - possession of land and buildings

tertius - third person

testament - disposition of property by will

testamento - will (Spanish)

testate - leaving a valid will

testator - person leaving a valid will

testatrix - female leaving a valid will

thoro - marriage or union

transientibus - in transit

tres - three

tribus mensibus - three months

tutela - guardianship (Spanish)

tuteur - guardian (French)

tutor - guardian

ultimo - last

unus - one

uxor - wife

venire - a summoning to jury duty

vero - certainly

vincinitate - neighboring area

viz't - to wit

will - legal document stating a person's wishes for dispersal of his or her property after death

witness - person who signs or makes his mark on a document attesting to correctness of the information in the document.

writ - mandate issued by a court

writ of certiorari - a court writ directing a lower court to certify or send up the record of a cause

Topic Sources and Additional Reading

Drake, Paul. *What Did They Mean By That?: A Dictionary of Historical Terms for Genealogists.* Bowie, Maryland: Heritage Books, 1994.

Duhaime, Lloyd. Timetable of World Legal History. <wwlia.org/hist.htm> LAW Museum. Worldwide Legal Information Association. Copyrighted 1994-1998.

Fitzhugh, Terrich V.H. *The Dictionary of Genealogy.* London: A&C Black, 1994.

Larson, Frances. *The Genealogist's Dictionary.* N.p. 1986.

'Lectric Law Library Reference Room <www.lectlaw.com/ref.html> 'Lectric Law Library <staff@lectlaw.com> Revised May 1999.

Legal Terminology Etc. As Found in Original Records and on Microfilm. Salt Lake City: Kay Publishing Company, 1961.

Nicholson, Mary Ann "'Where There's a Will...' (Some Curious Mid-Atlantic Probate Records)" *NEHGS Nexus.* Boston, Massachusetts: New England Historic Genealogical Society, October-November 1991. Vol. viii No. 5.

North, S.N.D. (comp.) *Marriage Laws in the United States, 1887-1906.* Conway, Arkansas: Arkansas Research, 1993.

Deciphering Documents

Changes in letter formation over the years have made early American documents difficult to read. Additionally, exposure to lights and the elements, age and quality of paper and ink all have affected the ease of reading old records.

Nevertheless, as Kay Kirkham wrote, some problems were "due neither to lack paper, pen nor lack of training." Instead many were due simply to the schoolmaster's technique.

Generally government clerks and official scribes had good penmanship and wrote as they had been taught, with a more formal hand. It was the writing of the poorly educated and the foreign born that could cause a bigger problem. Their handwriting was a less careful, less mechanical style.

But even those with legible handwriting had difficulty. Standardized spelling really did not begin until after Noah Webster's 1783 dictionary was published. Unusual abbreviations were used, even for names. Since the uneducated could not tell others how to spell their names, their names might be spelled phonetically. A lot was plain guess work.

How to Decipher Handwriting in Old Documents

In older documents, capitals "I" and "J" and capitals "U" and "V" were frequently used interchangeably. Similarly, lowercase "s" and "f" could be interchanged. Many times when there was a double "s", the first appear as a backward, lower case "f" and the second as a normal "s".

So the names Isaac and Joshua would appear to begin with the same letter. And they would also appear to have "f" in them. Hence, Isaac could have appeared to be "Jafaac".

Letter	What a letter could look like in a document
A/a	usually easy to decipher.
B/b	usually easy to decipher.
C/c	can appear like an open-topped "O" with a crown or a closed top "O" with a large loop at the top. The small "c" frequently appears to be a printed "r".
D/d	occasionally takes on the appearance of an "8" or a cursive "I". The little "d" has just an upward stroke or a loop above instead of the final downward stroke.
E/e	can look like a "C" with a small "z" or "2" just inside or overlapping the downstroke. The "e" might be confused with "c" or "o".

Letter	What a letter could look like in a document
F/f/ff	cursive capital can look like "T". The small "f" is frequently just a sloping slash with a hook on the upper right. The "ff" might be used in surnames like "ffrench" from the 1600's-1800's. It is also used instead of "ss".
G/g	usually identifiable, but sometimes appearing as a backwards, sideways "C" or a "C" with a diagonal line through it. The "g" frequently looks like a "y" with a cross at the top.
H/h	appears as an "S" with a loop at the top and with a tail running down and to the right of the letter. Or it can look like a large, decorative "C". The lower case sometimes appears more as a cursive capital "E". The small "h" can look like a fish hook.
I/i & J/j	interchangeable into the 1800's, the lower case sometimes looks like a small cursive "y".
K/k	sometimes resembles a cursive "R". The lower case looks like a capital "B" or a printed "f" being assaulted by a "z".
L/l	downward stroke twists more to the right, making the capital look like the symbol for the British pound or a cursive capital "S" or "T". A small "l" is usually easily decipherable.
M/m	usually easy to decipher.
N/n	usually easy to decipher.
O/o	may have a perpendicular line or two parallel diagonal lines. The "o" is easily decipherable.
P/p	heavy downward stroke crossed by a line which goes into a loop or semicircle on the right.
Q/q	resembles a "2" or a printed "Q" with a diagonal line through it. The small "q" can look like a cursive "y".
R/r	a "P" crossed at the center. Lower case can be just a stroke to the right, ending with a loop. It also sometimes appeared to be an "n".
S/s	usually ornate, the "S" looks like a cursive "L". It can have a diagonal line through it. The lower case can appear to be a cursive "p" or a backwards, lower case "f".
T/t/tt	an "F" or a "C" beginning with a large loop or arc at the top, sometimes with a diagonal line, sometimes resembling a cursive "L" or an "8". A "tt" might appear as a double "s".

Letter	What a letter could look like in a document
U/u&V/v	more square ends in the capitals. The "u" can have a diagonal upward stroke ending with a small cup-like shape. The upper stroke of the "v" tends to disappear when connected to other letters.
W/w	lower case may appear to be "nv".
X/x	resembles a lower case, printed "e".
Y/y	easily deciphered. Occasionally the capital "Y" can look like a cursive "P". Both the capital and small forms can appear to be closed at the top.
Z/z	lower case "z" has a long loop below the line.

Hints for Deciphering Records

1. Three consonants seldom appear together in a word.
2. Words have at least one vowel.
3. Sentences have nouns and verbs.
4. Read slowly and carefully. Make sure what you are reading makes sense.
5. Spell out each word letter by letter.
6. Most spelling in old documents was done phonetically.
7. If a word can't be deciphered immediately, go on with the rest of the sentence. Sometimes getting the general sense of a sentence will lead to deciphering a single word.
8. Find other letters and words in the document which can be read and use them to help figure out the letters which are difficult to read.
9. Make a photocopy of an ancestor's signature to determine if it is the same person who signed other records.
10. Letters which can be easily confused include -

        m n w uv   ao
        R P   ei
        Q O   hk
        F T   gyjz
        C G E   ys ip
        I J G   d cl el
11. Check for cursive handwriting errors, such as
    • Uncrossed "t" appearing to be an "l"
    • Undotted "i" being read as an "e"
    • Sloppy "r" looking like a "u" or "n"
12. Look for foreign language alphabet differences, such as
    å   ā   æ   ç   é   ï   ô   ø   œ   ź

Bolton, Charles Knowles "Colonial Handwriting". *The Essex Antiquarian.* Salem, Massachusetts. Vol. 1 p. 175. 1897.

Deciphering German Handwriting. <genweb.net/~inripley/decipher.html> GenWeb.net. Printout dated 06 June 2000.

Drake, Paul. *What Did They Mean By That?: A Dictionary of Historical Terms for Genealogists.* Bowie, Maryland: Heritage Books, 1994.

Examples of Letters of the 17th Century Found in Parish Records <www.rootsweb.com/~genepool/oldalpha.htm> Kindred Keepsakes. Joanne Todd Rabun, Webmaster. <rabun@ix.netcom.com> Established 02 January 1997.

Kirkham, E. Kay. *How to Read the Handwriting and Records of Early America: The Reading and Interpretation of the Handwriting, Symbols and Abbreviations, Legal Terminology etc. As Found in Original Records and on Microfilm.* Salt Lake City: Kay Publishing Company, 1961.

Old Handwriting Samples <www.rotsweb.com/~ote/writing.htm> Olive Tree Enterprises. Updated 03 January 1998. Copyrighted 1996-2000.

Thoyts, Emma Elizabeth. *The Key to the Family Deed Chest: How to Decipher and Study Old Documents: Being a Guide to the Reading of Ancient Manuscripts.* Reprint. 1903. Ann Arbor, Michigan: Gryphon Books, 1971.

Graveyards

Finding the Cemetery

Although many travelers in the old west were simply buried alongside the trail with a wooden cross that has long since disappeared, most ancestors were buried in church, town, privately-owned or corporate-owned, or family burial grounds. The place of burial for an ancestor can frequently be found through one of the following:

Obituary	Family plots
Cemetery closest to residence	Church records
Will	Published cemetery records
Township records	Memories of older relatives
Death certificate	Land deeds
Place of burial of relative	Old letters
Funeral home records	US Dept of Veterans Affairs

Other aspects to consider include the following
- When did the person die? What local cemeteries were in existence at that time?
- What was the person's economic background? Sad but true, social status could determine the cemetery or even the placement of a grave in a cemetery.
- How long was the person married to a surviving spouse? A young wife who died in childbirth might have been buried in her parents' plot.

Interpreting the Cemetery

The cemetery itself can provide a genealogy with unexpected data. Obviously a church cemetery indicates the religion of those buried there. But think of the information learned by discovering an ancestor is buried in "Small Pox Cemetery" in Massachusetts.
1. Record the location of the grave and all names of family members in the family plot. Frequently placement of tombstones indicates relationship. Also record family names adjacent to the family plot.
2. Check the entire graveyard. Families were not always buried together.
3. Study the stones for fraternal emblems or occupational carved icon symbols and epitaphs.
4. Look inside the church. Following English traditions, early Anglican Churches in Colonial America sometimes buried their dead within the church. The closer the grave to the alter, the higher the social standing was.

173

5.	Check graveyards in neighboring towns. Families were usually buried on their own land or in cemeteries of local churches and towns.
6.	Check for markers in the graveyard for common dates. Epidemics killed large numbers of people in a short period.
7.	Look at cemetery records or early cemetery inventories for information on possibly vandalized or lost markers.

Pinpointing Grave Sites

Grave Markers

Finding the cemetery does not necessarily guaranty finding the grave. For some reason, in 1853, the people of Worcester, Massachusetts decided to turn the markers of 300 graves of early settlers face down. Other cemeteries have been vandalized by uncaring people and man-made pollution has caused peeling and scaling of surfaces.

Mother Nature has rivaled humans with her assault on graveyards. Rain, snow, humidity and sun have slowly eroded layers of stone making them illegible. Brush and brambles cover them and the ground swallows them. Floods, tornados and hurricanes move and sometimes destroy them.

However, there were ways in which graves were marked in Colonial America which improve chances of finding one.
•	Single post of wood / post and rail markers
•	Fieldstone boulders
•	Slabs or wolf stones (large flat horizontal stone)
•	Standing tomb or table stone (elevated off the ground and walled or pillared on all sides)
•	Family vault tombs (built to avoid body snatching and neglect of burying grounds)
•	Upright marker

Ways to Find Unmarked Graves

Some graves were never marked. Others were marked with bio-degradable markers. Some were carved wood or wood with the epitaph written on them. More recently, funeral homes left small markers at the grave. But they were easily removed or ruined by the elements. Still other graves were marked with stones which have since worn down, broken, or toppled.
1.	Land is sometimes sunken. When a wooden coffin has deteriorated and the earth has settled, a depression is left.

2. Swollen ground or a mound might indicate a burial. Graves were seldom trampled down after burial.
3. Periwinkle and Vinca were occasionally used as groundcover over grave sites.
4. There is a machine which takes soundings and helps locate unmarked graves.
5. Cedar trees thought to be the "tree of life" were frequently planted in cemeteries.
6. Cement, brick or concrete block foundations around cemeteries or family plots may have outlived the tombstones.

Look for unmarked graves in late fall or winter, when foliage is thin and signs of unmarked graves are easier to find. Also check if there is a cemetery association which keeps records.

Epitaphs

Tombstones are sometimes the only surviving record of a person's death. And frequently a lot more information can be found on them then just basic birth and death dates. Of course, symbols such as the Star of David or a Cross would indicate the Jewish or Christian religions, respectively. Emblems for the American Legion or the Masons indicate membership in organizations which might have records regarding the deceased. Crests or coats of arms can also appear.

In Mayfield, Kentucky, Henry Wooldridge erected statues of his mother, three sisters, four brothers, two grandnieces; a hunting dog, a deer, a fox; and himself astride a horse around his tomb. Although only Wooldridge is buried in the vault, consider the information given through the statues.

A former railroad man buried in Union Cemetery in Ohio has a caboose-shaped tombstone. Across the United States, a number of early pioneers have had log cabin -shaped tombstones erected in their honor. But the most information comes from the words.

Information Which Might Be Found on a Tombstone	Examples
Place of birth or residence	• *From Bolivar, Tennessee:* Here lies... old E.P. (Ezekiel Polk)... Pennsylvania born. Carolina bred. In Tennessee died on his bed. • *From Starkville, Mississippi:* Arunah Bardwell, M.D. a native of Mass. a resident of N.C. for 20 years and of Oktibbeha County for the last five

Information Which Might Be Found on a Tombstone	Examples
Cause of death	• *From Grinstead, England*: He lived, And died, By suicide • *From Pepperell, Massachusetts*: Neh'h Hobart's death was caused by falling back-wards, on a stick, as he was loading wood. Nobody present, but his grandson, who lived with him... his death remarcable!(sic) • *From Albany, New York*: Harry Edsel Smith, Born 1903-Died 1942, Looked up the elevator shaft to see if the car was on the way down. It was.
Occupation	• *From Starkville, Mississippi*: Our Pastor Rev. T.G. Sellars • *From Death Valley, California*: Here lies the body of poor Aunt Charlotte. Born a virgin, died a harlot. • *From New York City:* In memory of Thial Clark, the jeweler
Relationships / Relatives	• *From Milford, Massachusetts*: Erected by Patrick McGarry to the memory of his Father & Mother... • *From Moultrie, Georgia*: Here lies the father of twenty-nine • *From Charleston, South Carolina*: Sarah Anna, daughter of Capt. William and Harriet Brown and wife of Robert L. Baker
Education	• *From Flamorganshire, Wales*: In memory of Edward Jenkins D.D... He was educated at Jesus College Oxford...
Sex	• *From Giles County, Tennessee*: Thomas Marietta Abernathy dau of James Polk
Accusation of Murder	• *From Pelham, Massachusetts:* Warren Gibbs died by arsenic poison Mar. 23, 1860... Think my friends when this you see, how my wife hath dealt by me. She in some oyster did prepare some poison for my lot and share... Before she my wife became, Mary Fulton was her name.

Information Which Might Be Found on a Tombstone	Examples
Military service	• *From Starkville, Mississippi:* Jas. W. Howard 1842-1912, CSA 1861-1865, Columbus Rifleman Co. • *From Island of Skyros, Greece:* Here Lies... Sub-Lieutenant in the English Navy Who died for the Deliverance of Constantinople from the Turks
What was important to the family	• *From New Hampshire:* To the memory of Amos Fortune who was born free in Africa, a slave in America he purchased liberty professed Christianity, lived reputably & died hopefully
Politics	• *From Hamblin County, Tennessee:* Julia Bales Noe Callaway, devoted Christian, Mother, Civic Worker and Leader in Republican politics • *From Elgin, Minnesota:* Family of Robert R. Hallenbeck, Maude C. Evans His wife, Vern R., Keith H., Their sons, None of us ever voted for Roosevelt or Truman
Social Comment on the person's life	• *From Danvers, Massachusetts:* Rebecca Nurse, Accused of Witchcraft She declared,"I am innocent and God will clear my innocency" Once acquitted yet falsely condemned, She suffered death July 19, 1692 • *From Falkirk, England:* At rest beneath this slab of stone, Lies stingy Jimmy Wyatt, He died one morning just at ten, And save a dinner by it.
Religion	• *From Flamorganshire, Wales:* Harriet Fowler... received communion in the Episcopal church at age 14.

Information Which Might Be Found on a Tombstone	Examples
Social Standing	• *From Shelter Island, New York:* Nathaniel Sylvester, First Resident Proprietor of Manor of Shelter Island, under Grant of Charles II • *From Colma, California: for Joshua Norton* Norton I, Emperor of the United States and Protector of Mexico
Misc. Information	• *From Woburn, Massachusetts:* Sacred to the memory of J. Bates, his widow, aged 24, lives at 7 Elm Street... Has every qualification for a good wife and yearns to be comforted. • *From Staten Island, New York:* John Young... Those who knew him best deplored him most. • *From Giles County, Tennessee:* James Polk Abernathy Grandmaster I.O.F.F of Tennessee Member original KKK

Terms of Death

Aetatis / A.E. AE - of the age (Latin)

Anno Domini / A.D. - In the year of our Lord (Latin)

anthropomorphic, discoid / head and shoulders-style marker - wooden or stone marker whose shape has human qualities such as a round head and neck, and a solid rectangular body

back-dated tombstone - marker carved or purchased after the date of death inscribed on the stone

bier - frame stand or carrier on which a coffin is laid before burial

box / chest tomb - above ground, box-like monument

breast stone - horizontal marker laid over body

burial ground - term for a graveyard which predated "cemetery" catacomb - underground cemetery comprising of tunnels and recesses for tombs

catafalque - decorated, elevated structure used for displaying or carrying a corpse

cemetery - term derived from the Greek *Koimeterion* for "sleeping place" used for a graveyard beginning in the 19th century

cenotaph - memorial erected to honor a person buried elsewhere

cerecloth - sheet or cloth bag dipped in wax, pitch or alum for waterproofing and used for wrapping the dead

chamber tomb - monument used for subsequent burials, made with corridor and side chambers

coffin - pre-casket lidded burial container, from the Greek kophinos

columbarium - building with hundreds of niches for urns holding cremated remains

corpse - dead body coming from the Latin for "body"

cremains - end results of a crematorium

crematorium - facility where dead bodies are reduced to carbon, steam and other particles

crypt - see "chamber tomb"

documented gravestone - a gravestone whose carver identified by initials, name, account book, receipt

effigy - image of a person, as a monument

embalming - technique of preserving a corpse to prevent decay

entlerrado - burial (Spanish)

epitaph - originally a funeral oration, later the tombstone inscription honoring a deceased person

Fecit - carved by... (Latin)

foot stone - small stone marking the foot of a grave

funèbre - funeral (French)

granite - coarse-grained igneous quartz rock

grave - excavation in the earth for burial of a dead body

grave boards - flat boards extended between two wooden posts, used to indicate early graves

hatchment - funeral board decorated with arms

head stone - upright stone marking the head of a grave

hearse - vehicle used to a dead person for burial

iconography - ornamental symbols on tombstones

interment - interring / burying of dead

ledger stone - large, smooth stone covering a grave

lich -body (Old English)

lichen - fungus and algae living on tombstones

lichgate/lychgate - roofed gateway to a churchyard originally where the bier was placed

marble - a smooth limestone rock capable of taking high polish

mausoleum - a stately, above-ground tomb named for Mausolus, King of Caria whose wife's tomb became one of the Seven Wonders of the World.

memento mort - "remember that you must die"

mis enterre - buried (French)

monument - memorial structure

mortalem - mortal

M.S. - Sacred to the memory of...; Memoriae Sacrum (Latin)

naked - unshrouded corpse in a unlined coffin, usually a member of a poor family

necropolis - large cemetery of an ancient city

Obit. (OB, Obt.) - he/she died

requiescat in pace (RIP) - may he/she rest in peace (Latin)

sarcophagus - stone coffin

sepulcher - a burial place, usually a stone coffin bearing inscriptions; from "spulcrum" (Latin)

sepulcro - grave (Spanish)

sepultura - burial (Spanish)

tomb - the vault or chamber for a corpse

vault - underground tomb from "uoluere" (Latin)referring to curving roof of some structures

wake - a watch over a dead body before burial

Woollen Act - to support the wool industry. This 1660 British law required the wrapping of corpses and lining of coffins with wool.

Topic Sources and Additional Reading

Azis-Sax, Joel G.,comp. The Epitaph Browser <www.alsirat.com/epitaphs/index.html>. Copyright 1997-1999

Cemeteries of the US: A Guide to Contact Information for US Cemeteries and Their Records. Detroit: Gale Research, 1994.

Cemetery Records of Oktibbeha County, Mississippi. Starkville, Mississippi: Oktibbehad County Genealogical Society, 1969.

CGN Cemetery Do's and Don't's <members.aol.com/ctgravenet/dosdonts. htm> Connecticut Gravestone Network. Updated 3 May 1998. Copyrighted 1997-1999.

George, Dianna Hume and Malcom A. Nelson. "Resurrecting the Epitaph" *Markers: The Annual Journal of the Association for Gravestone Studies.* Worcester, Massachusetts: AGS Publication, Vol. 1 1979/80 p. 85 .

Hey, David, ed. *The Oxford Companion to Local and Family History*. New York: Oxford University Press, 1996.

Hughes, Mark "Forward" to Reamy, Martha and William. *Index To the Roll of Honor*. Baltimore: Genealogical Publishing Company, 1995.

Jacobson, Judy. *Genealogist's Refresher Course*. 2nd ed. Baltimore: Clearfield Company, 1996.

Kestenbaum, Lawrence. Links to Resources on Cemetery History and Preservation. <www.potifos.com/cemeteries.html> Created 1996. Updated 21 July 2000.

Larson, Frances. The Genealogist's Dictionary. N.p. 1986

Miller, Richard E. *Gone But Not Forgotten: Genealogy and Grave Hunting*. New Haven: In-Time Publications, n.d.

National Yellow Book of Funeral Directors. Youngstown, Ohio: Nomis Publications, 1996.

Pike, Robert E. *Laughter & Tears*. Eatontown, New Jersey: H-H Press, 1974.

Schafer, Louis S. *Tombstones of Your Ancestors*. Bowie, Maryland: Heritage Books, 1991.

Williams, Melvin. Mystery, History, and ... an Ancient Graveyard" *Markers: The Annual Journal of the Association for Gravestone Studies*. Worcester, Massachusetts: AGS Publication, Volume 1 1979/80 p. 1670.

Measurements

A Quick History of Measurements

Length was one of the earliest types of measurement and was usually determined by a body part. An early Egyptian "cubit" was equal to the length of the arm from the finger tip to the elbow. By 2500 BC, it was standardized to a black marble square at which time

1 cubit = approximately 52 cm.

1 cubit = 28 digits (finger width)

The mile came from the Romans whose "Mille" stood for "one thousand paces" of five feet each. Eventually,

1 mile = 8 (220 yard) furlongs

The standardizing of English measurements did not begin until the 1200's. And gallons for various liquids were not standardized in England until 1824. Since then, the standard has been

1 gallon US = 231 cubic inches

1 gallon English = 277 cubic inches

The French adopted the metric system in 1799. A meter was defined as "one ten-millionth part of a quarter of the earth's circumference."

Measurement Prefixes

mega (M)	1 million	deci (d)	a tenth
kilo (K)	1 thousand	centi (c)	a hundredth
hecto (h)	1 hundred	milli (m)	a thousandth
deca (da)	ten	micro (*mu*)	a millionth

Measurement Terms Found in Old Records

acre - any of a variety of units of area, sometimes vague and sometimes equaling

160 square rods
10 square chains
5645.4 square varas
4840 square yards
43560 square feet

are -   100 square meters
119.6 square yards

arpent - similar to an acre.
1 side of an arpent = 191.994 feet

183

1 square arpent = 0.84625 acre
1 square Missouri arpent = 0.8507 acres / 192.5 sq. feet

barleycorn - an old unit of measuring length equaling 1/3 inch

chain - invented by Edmund Gunter. In Virginia, chains one-half the standard length are sometimes found.

1 mile	=	80 chains
1 chain	=	66 feet long with 100 links
		23.76 varas
		4 rods/poles/perches
		1/80 mile
		22 yards
		66 feet

degree - 1/360th of the distance around a circle
    60 minutes

furlong - 10 chains
    1006 links
    40 rods / poles / perches
    1/8 mile
    237 varas
    664 feet

hectare - 10,000 square meters
    2.471 acres

hide - Old English measurement equaling 120 acres

hundred weight - British unit equal to 100 pounds (a.k.a. short hundred weight) to 112 pounds (a.k.a. long hundred weight)

labor - unit of measurement used in Mexico and Texas
    2788 feet square
    177.136 acres

league - 13,889 feet square
    4428.4 acres

link - 1/100th of a chain

1 link	=	7.92 inches
1 rod	=	25 links

metes and bounds - survey based on measurements such as chains, perches; and boundary markers such as stakes and trees

mile - distance measurement of Roman origin
8 (220 yard) furlongs
1760 yards
5280 feet
1609 kilometers
320 rods / poles / perches
80 chains
1901 varas

minute - land description equaling 1/60th of a degree

moiety - one-half

nautical mile - a navigational measurement
1 nautical mile = 160th degree of longitude

pace - 2.5 feet

perche - 1 rod / pole

pole - 1 rod / perche

rectangular survey - adopted in 1785. Used in public lands west of the Appalachian Mountains, it was used on longitude and latitude (meridians and baselines). Land is described in range, township, sections, quarter sections.

rod - also called a pole or perche

1 rod	=	16.5 feet
1 rod	=	1/4 chain
1 rod	=	25 links
1 rod	=	5.5 yards
320 rods	=	1 mile

rood - unit equal to 1/4 acre

stone - British unit of weight equal to 14 pounds, or 6.3 kilograms

tolvel - measurement, holding half a bushel

vara - varying measurement used in parts of the United States originally settled by Spain

Foreign Measurements Found in American Land Records

Spanish Measurements Used in North America

Texas had been controlled by Spain for 300 years when Mexico became independent in 1821. That was also the year that Stephen F. Austin led the first group of Anglos into Spanish Texas. Because of their Spanish background, in 1836 all of Texas, the Southwestern United States and Florida measurements were based on the "vara". However, Florida's was larger than the Texas and Southwestern vara.

As used in Texas and the Southwest

1 cordel	=	50 varas
1 fanega	=	1.59 acres 6400 varas square
1 fundo legal	=	1200 varas square 250 acres 1440 square varas
1 labor	=	1000 sq. feet 177.1 acres 0.53 sq. miles 1 million square varas
1 league (legua)	=	5000 varas 25 labors 100 cordeles 4428.4 acres (Texas) 4439 acres (California) 2.63 sq. miles
1 suerte	=	200 x 200 vara agricultural lot
1 criadero de grando mayor	=	1/4 sitio de granado mayor
1 vara	=	33.5 inches / 2.78 feet
36 varas	=	100 feet
1 sitio de granado menor	=	3333 1/3 varas square

```
1 sitio de granado    =    1 sitio
mayor                      5000 varas square
                           41 caballereas
                           4428 acres

1 suerte de tierra    =    1/4 caballerea
                           552 x 276 varas
```

French Measurements Used in North America

The French had strongholds in Louisiana, the Northwest Territory, and Canada. Consequently, French terms of measurement can be found in old documents in any of those areas, including Michigan and Ohio.

```
1 perche      =    19.188 feet
1 arpent      =    .84 acres
27.5 arpent   =    1 US mile
```

Russian Measurements Used in North America

Because of the Russian presence in Alaska and Canadian Northwest, Russian measurements have found their way into old North American documents.

```
1 verst            =    0.663 mile
1 kosaya sazhen    =    2.71 yards
1 arshin           =    2.33
1 Old Russian ft.  =    0.999 American foot
1 Old Russian in.  =    0.999 American inch
```

Metric

```
10 millimeters    =    1 centimeter
10 centimeters    =    1 decimeter
10 decimeters     =    1 meter
10 meters         =    1 decameter
10 decameters     =    1 hectometer
10 hectometers    =    1 kilometer
1000 meters       =    1 kilometer
```

U.S. System of Measurement

```
Length    1 inch       =    0.0833 feet
          12 inches    =    1 foot
          3 feet       =    1 yard
          22 yards     =    1 chain
```

	8 furlongs	=	1 mile
	5280 feet	=	1 mile
	1760 yards	=	1 mile
Area	144 sq. Inches	=	1 sq. foot
	9 sq. feet	=	1 sq. yard
	30.5 sq. yards	=	1 sq. rod
	1 sq. rod	=	272.25 sq. feet
	16 sq. rods	=	1 sq. chain
	43,560 sq. feet	=	1 acre
	4840 sq. yard	=	1 acre
	640 acres	=	1 sq. mile
	1 sq. mile	=	1 section
	36 sq. mile	=	1 township
	6 miles square	=	1 township

Conversion

To Meters

To convert to meters take the number of the measurement below and multiply by the appropriate factor. For instance, 3 feet equals 3 times .3048 (.9144).

Centimeters	x	0.01
chains	x	20.1168
cubits	x	0.048
fathoms	x	1.8288
feet	x	0.3048
furlongs	x	201.168
inches	x	0.0254
leagues	x	4000 to 5000
links	x	0.201
miles (US)	x	1609.34
miles (nautical)	x	1852
poles/rods	x	5.0292
yards	x	0.9144

From Meters

To convert from meters, take the number of meters and multiply by the appropriate factor.

1 meter	=	3.2808 feet
1 meter	=	1.0936 yards

1 sq. meter	=	10.764 sq. feet
1 sq. meter	=	1.196 sq. yards
1 hectare	=	2.471 acres
1 sq. kilometer	=	.386 miles

Topic Sources and Additional Reading

Dictionary of Units. <www.ex.ac.uk/cimt/dictunit/dictunit.htm> University of Exeter. Center for Innovation in Mathematics Teaching. Frank Tapson, Webmaster. <F.Tapson@ex.ac.uk> Printout dated 13 December 1999.

Fitzhugh, Terrich V.H. *The Dictionary of Genealogy.* London: A&C Black, 1994.

Larson, Frances. *The Genealogist's Dictionary.* N.p. 1986.

"Length Conversion". Measurement Units Translation. <www.virtualginza.com/lencon.htm>. Printout dated 24 July 2000.

Raney, Don. "Research in the Texas Land Records" *Unlock Your Heritage... With Creative Problem Solving: Conference Syllabus.* The Federation of Genealogical Societies & The Dallas Genealogical Society 3-6 September 1997 p 223-226. Richardson, Texas: The Federation, 1997.

Christian Time

Christian chronology was first used in 525 by monk Dionysis Exiguus, who fixed Christ's birth as the Roman year 753. For canonical time, the Catholic Church divided a day into seven parts.

Matins / Lauds	Midnight - 6 a.m.
Prime	6 a.m. - 9 a.m.
Tierce	9 a.m. - Noon
Sext	Noon - 2 p.m.
Nones	2 p.m. - 4 p.m.
Vespers	4 p.m. - 7 p.m.
Completorium / Complin	7 p.m. - Midnight

Calendars

Types of Calendars

There are two basic types of calendars - lunar and solar. The lunar is based on phases of the moon, with months going from new moon to new moon, making each month approximately twenty-eight days long. These calendars are used by religious and ethnic groups, such as Islamic, Judaic and oriental groups.

The solar type of calendar is based on the sun's relationship to the earth - solstices and equinoxes - and divides a year into twelve equal months. Since the Roman era, most westerners have used solar based calendars.

Julian Calendar

In 45 B.C., Sosigenes, a Greek mathematician and astronomer, devised a calendar for Rome which was the basis for our present calendar. Named after Julius Caesar, the Julian Calendar attempted to correct earlier calendar errors by assigning one additional (leap) day to every fourth year.

Gregorian Calendar

By studying the equinoxes, it became evident that, in reality, the error discovered prior to the Julian Calendar actually had required an adding of only 7 days every 900 years rather than 25 days every 100 years.

So in an attempt to off-set the Julian Calendar's over-correction, The Gregorian Calendar which omitted ten days beginning on October

4th, 1582, was released during Pope Gregory XIII's reign. It was based on the 6th century work of Bede, an Anglo Saxon monk. The day of October 5th, 1582; became October 15th.

Actually the use of January 1 as the first day of the New Year was adopted slowly. The first to use it was Venice (1556); then Germany (1544); Spain, Portugal (1582) and Catholic Netherlands (1583); Prussia, Denmark and Sweden (1559); France (1564); Lorraine (1579); Protestant Netherlands (1701); Scotland (1600); Tuscany (1721); and Russia (1725). But although these countries used January as the first month of the year, they did not all make the change to include leap years.

Protestant Version of the Gregorian Calendar

Even though Roman Catholic nations adopted the new calendar immediately, England and the other Protestant nations did not adopt it until 1752. So by the time Protestant countries finally adopted the calendar, eleven rather than ten days had to be skipped. And so, September 3rd, 1752 became September 14th.

The English legislation also shortened the previous year. Prior to that time, each new legal and ecclesiastical year began on March 25th. But because of the legislation, 1752 began with what would have been on January 1, 1751 instead of March 25, 1752. So when an event took place in a Protestant country in a January, February or March prior to 1752, the double-year date (i.e. February 3, 1682/3) has frequently been used in books to indicate both the old and new calendar. And any reference to "New Years Day" prior to 1752 referred to March 25th in Britain and its colonies.

To figure a date before 1752, eleven days need to be subtracted and, for events occurring between January 1 and March 25, one year needs to be added. Anything that occurred on January 21, 1740 under the old calendar, would be dated January 10, 1741 under the new one.

When using dates in books and newspapers from before the adoption of the Gregorian calendar, it is important for the researcher to know if the author/editor of the book has already translated the old style to the new; or if the dates given were as they appeared in the original document.

Quaker Calendar

The Quakers did not use names for their days or months. In the Gregorian Calendar they were primarily named for pagan gods. Instead, Quakers wrote dates as "16th da 4th mo 1750" or "4 mo 16 da 1750".

But like other American colonists, Quakers were still using the old Julian Calendar until 1752. So like those using that calendar, many days from prior to 1752 are given with two years, such as "1750/1751." And the "4th mo" was not April because the Julian year at the time began with March. So prior to 1752 in the Quaker Calendar, the "4th mo" was June.

And when a Quaker date is written in a family history as April 16, 1750, a genealogist needs to be cautious. Did the author transcribe correctly? Or was the date supposed to read June 16, 1750?

French Revolution or Republican Calendar

Adopted during the French Revolution and lasting until January, 1806, this calendar began at midnight on the autumn equinox, September 22, 1792. Supposedly based on scientific principals rather than religion, it included twelve months of thirty days, with five additional festival days - celebrating Genius, Labor, Opinion, Virtue and Rewards - at the end. There was a leap year every four years.

Months were divided into three "decades" instead of weeks. Each day in each decade was numbered. Nivose ("Snowy Month") ran from December 21 to January 19. So Nivose Decadi II Tridi was the third day of the second decade of the month of Nivose (January 2).

Although the calendar was used for only a short period of time, it was used in areas that fell under French control before 1805, such as Louisiana and Quebec.

Jewish Calendar

A month of the Jewish calendar has always started on or near the new moon. Based on both lunar and solar cycles, it included twelve alternating 29 and 30 day months, making up a 354 day year.

Because that was 11 1/4 days short of a solar year, periodically a 13th month named Adar II has been added. Adar II has been added in 19 year intervals in the 3rd, 6th, 8th, 11th, 14th, 17th and 19th years.

The first year of the Jewish calendar was 3761/60 B.C. and was believed to be the year of creation. The first month of the Jewish calendar is Tishri and the first day of the New Year is Rosh-Ha-Shanah.

Year of Reign

Occasionally a document will be dated by the year of the reign of a king or Queen. For instance, in Britain a record may be dated -

"the 2nd day of June in the fifth year of the reign of Her Majesty Ann".

H.R.H. Anne ruled England from March 8, 1702 to August 1, 1714. So the fifth year of her rule began in March of 1707.

Zodiac

Sometimes dates have been recorded using Zodiac signs. Especially true among Pennsylvania Germans, their dates may have been actually based on moon signs rather then sun signs, making them inaccurate by as much as several months.

Miscellaneous

September may sometimes be found written as "7ber", with "sept" standing for the number 7 and not to be confused with the present month numbers in which July is the 7th month. Likewise, October may be found written as "8ber", not to be confused with August, the 8th month of the year of the present calendar.

When Was He Born?

Tombstones and church records frequently record date of death along with the exact age at death. Following are some examples for determining what the date of birth might be. Dates still need to be verified using other records, since leap years and errors in records make these formulas only useful for determining probable dates of birth.

Easy
Using the Gregorian Calendar
Example died on May 7, 1862 at age 40 years 2 months and 2 days

	year	1862	month	05 (May)	day	07
minus	age	40		02		02
answer		1822		03 (March)		05

So the probable date of birth was March 5, 1822.

Medium
Georgian Calendar
Died July 25, 1844 at age 60 years, 5 months, and 28 days

	year	1844	month	07 (July)	day	25
minus	age	60		05		28
answer				?		?

Obviously, the above cannot be subtracted as it stands. When the number of days at death is larger than the number of days in the death date, days from the previous month must be carried over to the days column.

So, in this problem, one month is subtracted from July (7), making it June (6) and the 30 days of June are added to the days column.

	year	1844	month	07 (July) - 1 month = 06	day	25 + 30 days = 55
minus	age	60		05		28
answer		1784		01 (January)		27

So the probable date of birth was January 27, 1784.

Hard

Julian Calendar in the New World
Died January 16, 1753 at age of 23 years 3 months and 27 days

	year	1753	month	01 (January)	day	16
minus	age	23		03		27
answer		?		?		?

As with the problem above, this cannot be subtracted as it stands. First, January needs to be converted to December, changing the year to 1752 and adding the 31 days in December to the date of death.

	year	1753 - 1 year 1752	month	01 (January) - 1 month = 12 (Dec.)	day	16 + 31 days = 47
minus	age	23		03		27
answer		1729		09 (Sept.)		20

So the probable date of birth (Georgian Calendar) was September 20, 1729. However, since the Julian Calendar was in use in North America in 1729, this time the date of birth should be translated from the Georgian date. The Julian Calendar equivalent would be September 9, 1729.

It should also be remembered that if the year was prior to 1752, January 1 through March 24 belonged in the previous year. So a child who was born on March 23, 1750 and died March 26, 1751 lived for only 3 days. Similarly, someone born on March 23, 1740 who died May 25, 1770 lived 29 years 2 months and 2 days, not the expected 30 years 2 months and 2 days.

Today, double dating is used for the days January 1 to March 24 in years prior to 1752. The above birth date would be written March 23, 1740/41.

A Couple of Things to Remember When Reading Dates

- While Americans generally write dates with the month first, day second and year last, other countries put the day first followed by the month. So 01/02/47 could be January 2, 1947 or February 1, 1947. To determine which system is being used, look at other dates in the record. Any number over 12 (as in months in the year) in one of the first two places would indicate the day position. For instance, 30/11/62 could only mean the November 30, 1962.

- The dates of marriage banns are not the wedding dates.

- Burials seldom occur on the day of death.

- Days disappeared making English and American birth, death and marriage dates prior to 1751 confusing. Eleven days between September 3 and September 14 were completely eliminated. Those calendar changes have made the dating system probably one of the most difficult things for a researcher to understand; but also probably the most important. In order to make sure dates are correct, a researcher needs to understand calendar changes that have taken place. There are sites on the internet which will convert dates, making it unnecessary for researchers to do complicated computations.

Approximating a Date

An exact date of birth, marriage or death may never be found. In those instances, "between" and "circa" dates may have to be accepted. There are some formulas which can at least narrow down the time span for those "between" dates.

Date Needed	Known	Period of Time in Which the Event Occurred
Birth	Age at specific event	Period between (date - age plus 5 years) and (date - age minus 5 years)
Birth	Marriage date	Period between (date - 16 years) and (date - 40 years)
Birth (Female)	Birth of children	Period between (birth of first child - 16 years) and (birth of last child - 50 years)

Date Needed	Known	Period of Time in Which the Event Occurred
Birth (Male)	Birth of children	Period between (birth of first child - 16 years) and (birth of last child - 70 years)
Marriage	Age at specific event	Period between (age at birth as calculated above + 15 years) and (age of birth + 40 years)
Marriage	Birth of children	Period between (birth date of first child - 1 year) and (birth of last child - 34 years)
Death		Period between (date of birth + 90 years) and (last date known to be alive)

Topic Sources and Additional Reading

Bisbee, M.J. "Formula 8870". *Genealogical Helper*. Everton Publishing. March 1976. p. 80-81.

Calendar Zone. <www.calendarzone.com> Janice Mclean, Webmaster. Established 19 January 1999.

Carlberg, Nancy Ellen. *Overcoming Dead Ends*. Anaheim: Carlberg Press, 1991.

Chase, Theodore and Laurel K. Gabel. *Gravestone Chronicles: Some Eighteenth-Century New England Carvers and their Work*. Boston: New England Historic Genealogical Society, 1997.

Jacobson, Judy. *Genealogist's Refresher Course*. 2nd ed. Baltimore: Clearfield Company, 1996.

Portwood Group. Did you know? The Amazing Disappearing Days. <www.portwoodgroup.com/dynamaz.htm> Baton Rouge, Louisiana: Portwood International, Copyright dated 2000.

Smith, Kenneth L. *A Practical Guide Dating Systems for Genealogists*. Ohio: Kenneth L. Smith, Columbus, 1983.

Western - Chinese Calendar Converter. <www.mandarintools.com/calconv.html> Erick Peterson, Webmaster <erik@mandarintools.com> Printout dated 24 July 2000.

Time Line for Money
as It Relates to the United States

1619	Tobacco is used as currency in Virginia.
1621	Act against usury limiting interest charged in England to 8% is passed.
1637	Wampum (type of shell) is used as currency equaling up to one shilling in Massachusetts.
1643	Massachusetts raises value of wampum to two pounds.
1652-1684	John Hull unofficially mints three pence, six pence and pine-tree shillings in Massachusetts.
1659	First check is issued by London goldsmith to Mr. Delboe for four hundred pounds.
1661	Wampum is outlawed as legal tender in New England.
1664	Workers building the citadel in New York are paid in wampum equal to five thousand Dutch gilders.
1681	First public bills of credit are issued for a temporary period.
1690	Massachusetts Bay Colony issues paper money.
1694	Bank of England is founded.
1704	Goldsmith's notes are made legally negotiable to bearer.
1708	Britain designates the maximum rate of exchange for Spanish peso or the dollar to be six shillings.
1715	The colonies are beginning to coin their own currency, besides using tobacco; wampum; and coins from Britain, Spain and Portugal. North Carolina has seventeen various forms of money.
1727	Certificates guaranteeing quantity and quality of tobacco replaces the leaf itself as legal tender in Virginia.
1729	Benjamin Franklin receives a contract for printing the third issue of notes for the Pennsylvania Land Bank.
1733	Maryland issues paper money.
1741	British Parliament declares Boston Land Bank unlawful.
1752	British outlaw New England colonies issuances of bills of credit.
1760	Factory to manufacture wampum opens in New Jersey, causing tremendous inflation.
1764	British ban the issuance of paper money by American colonies
1770	Rhode Island's paper money becomes worthless through major inflation.
1775	Colonists issue paper currency backed by the prospect of tax revenues to finance the American Revolution.
1780	Bank of Pennsylvania is founded.
1782	Bank of North America opens.

1784	Bank of New York and Bank of Massachusetts open.
1785	The Continental Congress designates the "dollar", based on one hundred cents, to be used as the unit of money for the new country.
1786	US Confederation Congress passes the Mint Act which allows for the minting a few tons of copper coins.
1789	US Constitution gives Congress power to create money.
1790	US has four banks.
1791	Bank of the United States is chartered and authorized to issue paper money.
1792	The US Mint is established.
1793	The country begins to mint the "dollar".
1797	Spanish dollars receive indefinite legal tender status.
1799	Income tax introduced by William Pitt.
1800	US has twenty-nine banks.
1806	Because newly minted coins begin to vanish from circulation, Thomas Jefferson temporarily discontinues the minting of silver coins.
1809	Ohio issues five, ten and twenty dollar warrants as currency.
1816	The Second Bank of the United States was given a twenty year charter.
1824	A clearing system is developed in Boston.
1834	The US Coinage Act reduces the value of silver compared to gold.
1837	States are given the right to issue paper money. US banking crisis leads to a depression.
1840	US organizes a separate US Treasury.
1850	Britain begins to invest in the US.
1853	Amount of silver in half-dollars, quarters and dimes is reduced.
1857	Foreign coins are no longer legal currency.
1860	Cotton constitutes nearly 58% of US exports.
1861	Congress assesses tax on incomes over $800 per year, making it the first US income tax.
1862	US Treasury starts issuing "Greenbacks" as legal tender except for payment of duties or interest of government securities. They are engraved and printed by private banknote companies. Western Union Telegraph brings about Pony Express bankruptcy.
1863	The Treasury seal is included on US currency to make counterfeiting more difficult.
1864	US wheat reaches $4 a bushel. A 2% tax rate is placed on state bank notes.
1865	"Greenbacks" lose ½ their worth and the government begins to withdraw them from circulation.

Confederate money drops in value to $1.76 per $100.
Gold certificates against gold and bullion deposits are issued by the Treasury.
The US Secret Service is established to control counterfeiting.

1866	After a 10% tax rate is applied to state bank notes, national bank notes back by federal securities become the primary forms of currency.
1868	US wheat drops in value to 67 cents a bushel.
1877	Treasury's Bureau of Engraving and Printing begins to print all US currency.
1878	Silver Certificates are issued in exchange for silver dollars.
1893	Financial panic erupts.
1907	Financial panic erupts.
1910	Bureau of Engraving and Printing takes on all production of currency.
1913	The Federal Reserve Act creates the Federal Reserve System to regulate money and credit. It was authorized to issue Federal Reserve Notes, currently the only form of US currency.
1929	Currency is standardized in appearance and is reduced in size.
1929	The Wall Street Crash brings financial panic and bank failures.
1930's	Great Depression
1933	Franklin Roosevelt introduces The New Deal as a strategy for economic relief.
1955	Congress passes a bill to include the inscription "In God We Trust" on all currency.
1957	The first money bearing the words "In God We Trust" begins to appear.
1970's	Severe inflation spread throughout all the western countries.
1971	Huge balance of payment deficits made devaluation of the US currency necessary.
1980's	Although inflation in the US slowed, trade deficits grew.
1987	A massive stock market plunge on October 19 became known as "Black Monday".
1990	A security thread and micro-printing are added to money to prevent counterfeiting.

Consumer Price Index Conversion Factors

The chart below can be used to determine value of dollars in a certain year. Divide the number of dollars of a certain year by the conversion factor given below for that year. The result will be the worth of that sum compared to 1996 amounts. For instance, an inheritance of $1000 received in 1810 would be equivalent to $10,000 in 1996 (1000 divided by .10)

1996 1.00	1930 .106	1860 .06
1990 .832	1920 .127	1850 .05
1980 .525	1910 .06	1840 .06
1970 .247	1900 .05	1830 .07
1960 .189	1890 .06	1820 .09
1950 .154	1880 .06	1810 .10
1940 .089	1870 .08	1800 .11

Value of the British Pound Sterling

In Years Prior to the Settlement in the New World

The value of the British Pound Sterling dropped drastically between the 1400's and the 1600's, adding to financial woes to the populace.

1601	1 Pound
1560	1.033
1543	1.163
1527	1.378
1464	1.550
1412	1.937

Number of Dollars Equaling One Pound 1800-1996

When determining the rate of exchange in dollars of an item reported in British pounds, multiply the factor below by the number of dollars. For instance, in 1860, five British pounds would have been equivalent to $24.40 (4.88 times 5) in the United States.

1800	4.544	1870	5.847	1940	4.032
1810	4.322	1880	4.895	1950	2.577
1820	4.583	1890	4.897	1960	2.817
1830	4.867	1900	4.902	1970	2.41
1840	4.833	1910	4.878	1980	2.439
1850	4.922	1920	3.953	1990	1.965
1860	4.88	1930	4.878		

Value of a British Pound Sterling c. 1775

1 British pound	equaled	20s (20 shillings)
1 British shilling	equaled	12d (12 pence)
1 British pound	equaled	240 pence in Britain

1 British pound	equaled	320 pence in Massachusetts
1 British pound	equaled	400 pence in Pennsylvania
1 British pound	equaled	427 pence in New York
1 British pound	equaled	1 French livre

Value of One Spanish Dollar

Before the United States produced its first dollar, the Spanish dollar was widely used in Spanish held areas of North America, such as Florida and the Southwestern United States.

1690	4s 6d*	British Sterling
1705	7s	British Sterling
c. 1760	4s 6d	British Sterling
	6s	Massachusetts
	7s 6d	Pennsylvania
	8s	New York

* "s" is the British sign for "shilling" and "d" is the sign for "pence"

Value of Halifax Currency in 1780

Halifax (Canada) currency was widely used in British controlled areas of the North America and areas bordering Canada.

Halifax Currency	equaled	75% - 80% British Pound Sterling
New York Currency	equaled	60% Halifax Currency

Money Glossary

beaver value - beaver pelts used as money

cent - lowest valued coin minted in the United States. The cent was first minted in 1792 with the head of Washington on one side and a thirteen link chain on the other.

commodity money - form of bartering which came about due to scarcity of money

country pay - use of natural commodities, such as wheat or tobacco, as currency

currency - money which is in circulation

dollar - US official unit of money equal to 100 cents. It came from the Germanic "Thaler" was a large 1400's silver Austrian coin. Later Scandinavia adopted the "daler" and the Dutch adopted the "daalder". The Spanish version was widely used in the New World.

Dukaton of zilveren rijder (Ducatoon - silverrider) - a Dutch coin equaled 6 shillings in Massachusetts in 1642

farthing - former British coin equal to 1/4 penny

greenbacks - paper money, which was not immediately redeemable in gold or silver, issued by the US treasury in the 1860's

heavy money - hard cash as opposed to using wampum, beaver or wheat for trade

leewendaalder (lion dollar) - a Dutch coin equaled to 3 guilder which was produced between 1575 and 1713. In 1701 Massachusetts, 1 lion dollar equaled 4 shillings 6 pence.

loan script - certificates backed by land, issued to repay loans made to government. These were especially popular in Texas.

mill - only official US coin that has never been minted. It equals one-tenth of one cent and was designated by Congress in 1786.

pence - British penny

rijksdaalder (rixdollar) - a Dutch coin equaled to 5 shillings in 1642 Massachusetts

sales script - land script sold directly to raise money

sewant - wampum used in place of hard cash

Spanish dollar - direct predecessor to American dollar. One Spanish dollar equaled eight reales.

trade tokens - brass or copper tokens issued when there was a shortage of coins

wampum - a shell used as currancy

Derks, Scott, editor. *The Value of a Dollar: Prices and Incomes in the United States: 1860-1999.* Lakeville, Connecticut: Grey House Publishing, 1999.

Fitzhugh, Terrich V.H. *The Dictionary of Genealogy.* London: A&C Black, 1994.

Global Financial Data. Global Financial Data: For Your Financial Data Needs from 1264 to 2000. California: <www.globalfinddata.com> Dated 2000.

Historic British Coinage. <www.colbybos.demon.co.uk/measures/coinage.html> John and Sandy Colby. <Webmaster@colbybos.demon.co.uk> Updated 01 January 1999.

Jordan, Louis. "Colonial Currency" <www.coins.nd.edu/ColCurrancy/index. html> A Project of the Robert H. Gore, Jr. Numismatic Endowment. University of Notre Dame. Department of Special Collection. <rarebook.1@ nd.edu> Printout dated 12 June 1999.

Larson, Frances. *The Genealogist's Dictionary.* N.p. 1986.

Universal Currency Converter. <www.xe.net/ucc> Xenon Laboratories. Copyrighted 1995-2000.

US Inflation Calculator <www.westegg.com/inflation> S. Morgan Friedman, Webmaster. <morgan@westegg.com> Updated 19 January 2000.

Museums

Where to Look in the Museum

Genealogical information can be hiding just about anywhere in any type of historical museum. Museums are dedicated to the African-American, the Chinese-American and others. The Melugeon Heritage Association preserves artifacts and histories of the Mulugeon people.

Other historical museums honor early settlers. The Seaport Museum in Galveston, Texas, has a database of immigrants entering the United States through Galveston. Meanwhile, San Francisco has the National Maritime Museum and the Society of California Pioneers Museum. The Temple Collection at the Los Angeles County Museum contains information about the area's early Spanish Missions.

Some museums are dedicated to occupations, like country doctors and vaudeville artists. And even though the Buffalo Bill Historical Center in Cody, Wyoming, is primarily dedicated to one individual, its research library specializes in all Western history.

While all these historical museums can have information valuable to the genealogist, the best source is probably a local history museum in the area where ancestors lived. It is amazing what people will donate. Just a few places family information might be found there include -

Account books
Bible class pictures
Birth announcements
Books
Cemetery records
Church records
Church yearbooks
Class reunion books
Club minutes
Correspondence
County maps
County records
DAR materials
Diaries (even of neighbors)
Diplomas
Doctor's records
Family albums
Family Bibles
Genealogies
Geologic survey maps (indicating
    cemeteries and churches)
Grade school pictures
House histories
Hotel registers

Maps
Mementos
Membership lists
Newspaper clippings
Newspapers
Old trunks
Oral histories
Organization and club yearbooks
Photo albums
Pictures of homes and
    businesses
Pictures of persons
Postal records
Recital programs
Reference library
Report cards
Rosters of soldiers
School records
School programs
School yearbooks
Scrapbooks
Servicemen's albums
Store ledgers
Survey records

Teachers' contracts   Video histories
Veterans pictures   Wedding invitations

What to Look for in a Museum

- Migration routes into the area
- Names of soldiers and their companies
- Lists of public officials or ministers
- Pictures of homes, towns, schools and churches through the years
- Epidemics and calamities in the area
- Names of area churches and membership lists
- Papers indicating ownership of land through the years
- Area land sales
- Community organizations and membership lists
- Names of local newspapers through the years

Topic Sources and Additional Reading

American Vaudeville Museum <www.vaudeville.org> American Museum of Vaudeville. Copyrighted 2000.

Buffalo Bill Historical Center <www.bbhc.org/index_flashversion.html> Devendra Shrikhande, Webmaster. <dvendras@bbhc.org%20> Printout dated 06 August 2000.

Country Doctor Museum Site. <www.drmuseum.net/index.html> Arkansas Country Doctor Museum. Updated 07 May 1999.

Jacobson, Judy. *Genealogist's Refresher Course.* 2nd ed. Baltimore: Clearfield Company, 1996.

National Maritime Museum <www.maritime.org> National Maritime Museum Association. <info@maritime.org> Updated 03 August 2000.

National Afro-American Museum & Cultural Center <www.ohiohistory.org/ places/afroam> The Ohio Historical Society. Update 03 March 2000.

San Diego Chinese Historical Museum <www.sandiego-online.com/forums/Chinese/htmls.museum.htm> Chinese Historical Society of Greater San Diego and Baja California. <sdchmus@earthlink. net> Printout dated 06 August 2000.

Society of California Pioneers <www.californiapioneers.org/museum.html> Susan Haas, Registrar. <pioneers@wenet.net> Copyrighted 1996-1997.

Occupations

America's Earliest Professionals

A large number of early immigrants to the New World were what would be called "professionals" today. But as time went on, an enormous percentage of immigrants changed to what would be called "blue-collared workers" today. Few professionals arrived in the 1800's. The 1855 immigrants who stated their profession made up the following percentages.

PROFESSION	IMMIGRANTS
Merchants	13.00%
Farmers	30.60%
Laborers	37.50%
Mechanics	13.20%
Teachers	.03%
Clergy	.13%
Lawyer	.19%
Physician	.22%

Less Obvious Occupations of Old

Unfortunately, many of the occupations are no longer named the same, or in many cases, no longer exist. Spellings were not consistent. So even when an ancestor's occupation has been discovered by a researcher, it is not always evident his job was.

In addition, there were overlapping professions. For the first settlers in the New World workers skills went more towards survival. Carpenters might find themselves making caskets, coopers making furniture. A colonial blacksmith might use his skills making guns. Shipbuilders needed to be joiners.

Colonial women might have worked for any number of reasons. Some arrived in the New World as indentured servants. Daughters and wives helped with the family business. Upon the death of her husband, a widow might need to take over their husband's business in order to feed her family. However, most women who worked were relegated to becoming milliners, dressmakers or domestics.

accouter - person who supplied food provisions, usually for ships

accipitrary - falconer

accomptant - accountant

accoucheur / accoucheuse - medical practitioner who

specialized in women - childbirth, in particular

ackerman / acreman - ploughman

actuary - person who kept public business accounts

advertisement conveyancer - sandwich board man

advocate - a lawyer

advocate depute - Scottish public prosecutor

aeronaut - balloonist or trapeze artist

affeeror - assessor, especially in manorial courts

agister - official of the Royal Forests

agricultor - farmer (Spanish)

alblastere - crossbow man

alchemist - chemist who claimed to turn metals into gold

ale-conner / ale founder - tester of quality of ale served in public houses

ale draper - seller of ale

ale tunner - person who filled the ale casks in the brewery

ale wife - female innkeeper

all spice - grocer

almoner - person who dispensed contributions to the poor on behalf of the parish

almsman - person who received alms (charity)

ananuensis - secretary

alnager - official who examined and approved the quality of woolen products

amanuense/amanuensis - clerk, secretary or stenographer

ambler - person who broke horses for the Royal Stable

amen man - the parish clerk

anchor smith - person who made anchors

anchoress - female hermit or religious recluse

anchorite - male hermit or religious recluse

anilepman - tenant of the manor

ankle beater - young person who drove cattle to market

annatto maker - person who manufactured dyes for paint or printing

annuitant - pensioner

apiarian - beekeeper

apothecary - dispenser of drugs who sometimes acted as a family doctor apparitor - authority who summoned witnesses to ecclesiastical courts

apprentice - person bound by legal agreement to a skilled laborer to learn a trade

aproneer - London shopkeeper

apron man - mechanic

aquariusewar - waterman

aquavita seller - seller of alcohol

arcediano - archdeacon (Spanish)

archiator - physician

arkwright - skilled craftsman who manufactured wooden chests

armiger - squire who carried a knight's armor

armorer - individual in the colonies who repaired assembled and tested the militia's guns

armourer - individual who made suits of armor, or made and repaired guns

artificer - skilled mechanic

artisan - tradesman skilled in a manual craft

ashman - dustman

asesor - legal advisor (Spanish)

assay master - person who ascertained the percentage of gold or silver to go into coins

assayer - person who ascertained the percentage of a metal in ore

assistant marshall - census taker prior to 1880

astronomer - person who studied the stars and planets to help mariners navigate

aurifaber - goldsmith

avenator - hay and forage merchant

axeman - worker in logging camps who felled the trees

backster - baker

back'us boy - kitchen servant

badger - licensed pauper who could only work an assigned area (badgering) or an itinerant food trader

badgy fiddler - boy trumpeter in the military

bagman - traveling salesman

bangiokeeper - individual in charge of a brothel or bath house

bailie / bailee - officer of the sheriff, a land steward, a Scottish magistrate, or the person who upheld fishing rights

bairman / bareman - pauper

balister - archer

baller - measurer of balls of clay for a potter

bal maiden - female mine worker who worked on the surface

bang beggar - parish officer who determined length of a stranger's stay

banker - trench digger

banksman - person in charge of cages at the pit head of a mine

bard - poet or minstrel

barkeeper - tollkeeper

barker - tanner

barrister - lawyer

bartoner - the person in charge of a monastic farm

basil worker - person who worked with goat and sheep skins

bathing machine proprietor - operator of changing huts used by bathers at the beach

batman - a servant to army officers

battledore maker - made beaters used to clean dust off of clothes and rugs

baxter - baker

beadle / bedell - parish officer who kept order; town crier

bearer - carrier of coal to the bottom of the pit shaft

beater - person who cleaned and thickened material

beaver - felt hat maker

bêcher - field worker (French)

bedman / bedsman / beadsman - man paid to pray for the soul or spiritual welfare of others, sexton

bedral - minor Scottish church official

belhoste - tavern keeper

bedwevere - individual who wove quilts and made webbing for bed frames

beeskepmaker - person who made bee hives

bellter/billiter - bell maker

bellman - town crier or person who collected the mail

bellow farmer - caretaker of church organ

belly builder - builder of piano interiors

bender - leather cutter

berger - shepherd (French)

besswarden - animal caretaker for the parish

besom maker - broom maker

biddy - Irish female servant

bird boy - person hired to scare birds away from crops

birlyman - Scottish parish arbiter

bladesmith - knife and sword maker

blaxter - bleacher of cloth or paper

blemmere - plumber

blentonist - water diviner

blindsman - person in the post office who worked with mis-addressed mail

bloodman - a blood letter who used leeches as a curative

bloomer - producer of iron from ore, a smithy

bluestocking - female writer

bluffer - innkeeper

boardman - truant officer

boardwright - carpenter

boatswain - ship officer in charge of sails and rigging

bobber - a person who helped unload fishing boats

bodeys - maker of ladies bodices

bodger - maker of wooden chair legs

boilermaker - metal worker

boll - person who took care of power looms

bolter - meal sifter

bondager - bonded female farm worker

bondman - individual bonded to learn a skill or trade

boniface - innkeeper

bonne maid - female servant (French)

bookman - student

boonmaster - road surveyor

bookholder - theater prompter

boot catcher - person who helped inn guests remove their boots

boot closer - stitcher of upper portions of boots

boothman - corn merchant

borler - maker of cheap coarse clothing

botcher - tailor or cobbler

bottiler / bottler - maker of leather containers for liquids

bottle boy - pharmacist assistant

bottomer - worker in mine pits who removed ore

bowdler - iron worker

bowker - yarn bleacher

bowler - bowl and dish maker

bowlman - dealer in crockery

bowlminder - person in charge of vats washing raw wool

bowyer / bower - makers of bows for arrows

bozzler - constable

brabener - weaver

brachygrapher - shorthand writer

braider - maker of cord

brailler - maker of girdles

brasiler - dyer

brassier - farm laborer (French)

brazier - brass worker

brewster - female brewer

brightsmith - metal worker

broom squire - broom maker

brotherer / browderer / broderer - embroiderer

brouwer - brewer (Dutch)

brownsmith - copper or brass worker

buckler - buckle maker

buckle tongue maker - maker of metal points that go into the holes of a belt

buck washer - laundress

buddleboy - maintainer of vats used to wash ore in lead mines

buffalo soldier - black soldier in the US Army in the American West

bullwhacker - oxen driver

bumboat man - seller of goods when a ship docked

bummer - deserter

bummaree - deliverer of fish from the wholesaler to the retailer

bunter - female collector or rags and bones

burgess - borough representative

burgomaster - mayor

burler - clothing inspector

burnisher - metal shiner

bury man - grave digger

bushel maker - cooper

busheler - tailor's helper

buss maker - gun maker

busker - hair dresser

butner - button maker

butter carver - imprinter of butter pats

butty - negotiator and supplier of labor to mining companies

cabman - driver of a small horse drawn passenger vehicle

cad - individual who fed and watered horses at coach stops

caddie - errand boy

caddy butcher - butcher dealing in horse meat

cadger - beggar

cafender - carpenter

caffler - collector of rags and bones

cainer - maker of walking sticks

caird - tinker

calender - recorder of documents

cambist - banker

cambric maker - manufacturer of fine linen or cotton

camerist - lady's maid

camister - minister

campanologist - bell ringer

candler - candle maker

candy man - bailiff

canter - beggar or religious speaker

canvasser - maker of canvas

capper - maker of working class caps

carder - operator of carding machine used to prepare wool and cotton for weaving

cardroomer - worker in a mill's carding room

carman / charman - transporter of goods

carner - granary keeper

carnifex - butcher

carpentarius - carpenter

cartomancer - a fortune teller, using cards

cartwright - maker of carts

cashmarie - fish seller at inland markets

castrator - a gelder

catagman - a cottager

catchpole / catchpoll - bailiff

catechist - teacher of religion

caudillo - military leader (Spanish)

causewayer - repairer of roads

ceiler - person who put in ceilings

cellar man - laborer who looked after the alcoholic beverages in public houses and warehouses cemmer - individual who combed yarn before it was woven

chaff cutte - person who made chaff by cutting straw

chaisemaker - craftsman who made two and four-wheeled carriages

chaloner - blanket maker

chamberlain - steward in charge of the household for nobility

chambermaid - female servant who takes care of bedroom areas

chamber master - a shoemaker who worked out of his home

chancellery - chancellor

chandler - provisioned ships or maker of candles

chapeler - hat maker and seller

chapman / copeman / ceapman - itinerant pedlar, dealer in small items

chart master - negotiator of contracts and supplier of labor in mines

chaser - engraver

chaunter - street entertainer

chiffonier - wig maker

childbed linen warehouse keeper - one who leased out bed linen to use during childbirth

chinglor - roof tiler

chip - shipwright

chippers laborer - assistant shipwright

chirographer - writer or copier

clapman - town crier

clarke - cleric or scribe

class man - unemployed labourer

claviger - servant

clayman / cleyman - person who worked in clay pits or coated buildings with clay

clipper - person who attached coal carts to rope used to drag the carts

clogger - clog maker

closer - finisher of fingers on glover

cloth lapper - worker who removed cloth from the carding machine

clouter - nail or shoe maker

clower - nail maker

coal higgler - person who sold coal from a cart

coalmeter - measurer of coal

coal whipper - person who unloaded coal from ships

coast surveyor/waiter - customs officer

cobbler - repairer of shoes

cobleman - one who fished from a flat bottomed boat

cock feeder - person who cared for fighting cock

cod placer - person who put containers of pottery into a kiln

coiner - worker at the Mint

collar maker - person who made horse collars

collier - coal dealer

colourator / colorator - dye worker

colour man - mixer of dyes for textiles

colporteur - book seller

compositor - typesetter in print shop

conder / conner - person who gave directions to ship steersman or fishermen

coney catcher - rabbit catcher

coniger / conygrye - rabbit warren

cooper - repairer of wooden barrels and casks

copeman - dealer in goods

coper - horse dealer

copperbeater - coppersmith

coppice keeper - one who takes care of small wood

coracle maker - person who make small round fishing boats

cornet - commissioned office in the calvalry

cordwainer / corviner / cordiner - worker with leather / shoemaker

corviser / corvisor / coveyser - shoemaker

costermonger - fruit and vegetable vender

coteler / cotyler - individual who made and repaired knives

cottager / cottar / cotter / cottier - agricultural laborer who lived on the land owner's farm

coucher - person who worked with making paper

countour - rates collector

couper - cattle and horse dealer

courtier - owner and driver of horse and cart

cow leech - animal doctor

coward - cattle herder

crapper - worker in a slate quarry

crate man - door-to-door earthenware salesman

crayman - driver of cart carrying heavy loads

crimp - crew finder for ships

crofter - owner of a small farm

croker - saffron grower

crookmaker - individual who made shepherd's crooks and walking sticks

cropper - person who grew crops

crowner - coroner

cuirassier - mounted soldier

culler - person who grades animals for slaughter or who gelds male animals

cupper - individual who applied cups for drawing blood

cura - clergyman (Spanish)

currier - tanner or horse groomer

curistor - Chancery Court clerk

custos - warden or guardian

cutler - maker of knives and swords

daguerreotype artist - photographer using the Daguerreotype style of pictures

danter - female manager of winding room of silk mill

dataller / dayman / daytaleman - employed by the day

decoyman - decoyed waterfowl and animals

decretist - individual knowledgeable in decrees

delver - ditch digger

departer - metal refiner

deputy - safety officer for the pit crew in a mine

devil - printer's errand boy or apprentice

deviller - operator of the machine that tore rags in the textile industry

dexter - dyer

dikeman / dykeman - hedger or ditcher

dipper - glazer of pottery

disher - maker of dishes and bowls

distributor - parish oracle who looked after needs of those in the workhouse or poorhouse

docker - stevedore

doffer - worker who took empty bobbins out of spinning wheels

dog killer - parish worker who killed dogs found running loose

domo - director of household activities of a home

donkey boy / donkey man - driver

of passenger carriage

doubler - operator of machine which twisted strands of fiber

dowser / diviner - person who professed to be able to locate underground water using a forked stick

dragman - fisherman who used a drag line

dragsman - driver of a small stage or public carriage

drapery painter - artist hired by another artist to paint the clothing on the subject

draper - seller of sewing needs and material

drawboy - weaver's assistant

drayman - driver of a cart

dresser - person who prepared clothing for a nobleman or acted as a surgeon's assistant

drift maker - maker of drift nets for fishermen

dripping man - seller of meat drippings

drover - person who took stock to market

drummer - traveling salesman

dry salter - person who salted meats

dry stane dyker - dry stone waller

dry stone waller - builder of stone walls

duffer - peddler

dustman/dustbin man - garbage man

dyker - stonemason

earth stopper - person employed to block the entrance to a fox's den before a hunt

échevin - alderman / magistrate (French)

eggler - egg dealer

ellerman / elliman - seller of oil for lamps

employé - clerk (French)

engine tenter - individual who tended machines in mills

equerry - person responsible for the royal horses

episcopus - bishop

ewe here - shepherd

exchequer - revenue collector

eyer - maker of eyes in sewing needles

faber - smith

factor - merchant's agent for transacting business

fagetter - seller of firewood

faker - photographic assistant

farandman - traveling merchant

farrier - shoe smith or doctor for horses and oxen

fear-nothing maker - weaver

feather-beater - cleanser of feathers

featherman - seller of feathers and plumes

feather-wife - female who prepared feathers

fellmonger - dealer of hides and skins

felter - worker in the hatting industry

fermier - farmer (French)

feroner - ironmonger

festitian - typical mis-spelling of physician

fettler - machine cleaner or needle maker

fewster - maker of saddle trees

fewterer - keeper of hunting dogs

feydur beater - feather beater

fine drawer - tailor specializing in invisible mending

fiscere - fisherman

fitter - joiner

flasher - specialized worker in glass industry

flatman - navigator of flat-bottomed boat

flax dresser - preparer of flax for spinning

flesher - butcher in a tannery

fletcher - maker of bows and arrows

flint knapper - chipper of stone flints for flintlock guns

floater / floatman - vagrant

flower - archer

flusherman - cleaner of water mains

flycoachman - driver of one-horse carriage

flying stationer - broadsides seller

flyman - driver of light hired-out carriage or theatre stage hand

foister / foisterer - joiner

foot-boy/man - livery attendant

foot straightener - person who assemble clock dials

forgeman - blacksmith or coach smith

forger - blacksmith

forgeron - smith (French)

forkner - falconer

fossetmaker - maker of ale cask faucets

fower - street cleaner

framar - farmer

frame spinner - laborer working on a loom

frobisher / furbisher - metal polisher

fustian weaver - corduroy maker

gaffer - foreman

gaffman - iron worker

gamester - gambler or prostitute

gardien - herdsman (French)

garthman - yardman

gater - watchman

gatherer - glassworker

gatward - goat keeper

gauger - customs official

gaunter - glover

gaveller - usurer or a female harvest worker

gelder - castrator of animals

gilder - applier of gold leaf

gimler - machinist

ginerr - joiner

girdler - leather worker

glassman / glazier - maker and seller of glassware

goaler - jailer

gorzeman - broom seller

grandjero - farmer (Spanish)

graver - sculptor or engraver

greave/grieve - bailiff, foreman

grecher - grocer

green smith - Individual who works with copper

guilder - maker of gold or silver coins

guinea pig - day worker whose fee was a guinea

gummer - person who refurbished old saws

gyp - servant attending to undergraduate college students

haberdasher - dealer in small articles, in particular hats and caps

hacker - wood cutter

hair weaver - weaver of cloth from horsehair

hammerman - smith

handseller - street peddler

harlot - beggar or male servant or promiscuous woman

harper - performer of the harp

hatcher - flax cleaner

hausknect - house servant (German)

hawker - itinerant street vendor

hayward / hedge looker - hedge inspector for the parish

heald knitter - operator of machine which made jersey type fabric

hellier / hillard / hillier - tiler of roofs

henchman / hensman - horse groomer

hewer - miner

higgler - itinerant dealer who haggles over prices

hind - farm laborer

hobbler - individual hired to tow boats

hod - bricklayer's laborer

hoggard - pig drover

holloware worker - pottery worker

hooker - reaper

hooper - maker of barrel hoops

horner - maker of spoons, combs or musical instruments out of horns

horse capper - seller of worthless horses

horse leech - horse doctor/farrier

horse marine - barges pulled by men rather than horses

hosier - retailer of stockings and socks

hosteller - innkeeper

hostler - individual who took care of horse at inns

housewright - builder of houses

hoyman - carrier of goods by water

huckster - street vendor, hawker

huissher - usher

hurdleman - hedge maker

hurriers - girls employed by mines

husbandman - tenant farmer

hush shop keeper - beer brewer without a license

indentured servant - person who sold himself to pay off a debt. They could be sold to someone else for the period of time still left on the contract.

iron smith - iron worker

jack-smith - cotton worker

jagger - fish peddler

jakes-farmer - cleaner of cesspools

jerquer - custom officer

job coachman - hired coach driver

jobling gardener - gardener hired by the job

jobmaster joiner - supplier of coaches and drivers for hire

joiner - craftsman who pieces wood together to form floors, window and door frames and furniture

journeyman - craftsman hired by the day who had completed an apprenticeship but wasn't yet a master

jouster - female fish vendor who traveled from town to town

kedger - fisherman

keeker - weigh man at mine

keeler - bargeman

keller - salt keeper

kellogg - slaughter man

kempster - wool comber

kiddier - skinner

kilner - lime burner

kisser - armour maker

knacker - seller in old or dead animals, harness and saddle maker

knappers - maker of flints for flintlock weapons

kneller / knuller - chimney sweep

knocker up - person hired to waken those working the early shift at factories

labrador - farmer (Spanish)

laceman - seller of lace

lace-master/mistress - person who hired lace workers

lagger - sailor

landsman - seaman on first voyage

landwaiter - customs officer

lardner - official in charge of pig food

laster - customs officer

laster - shoemaker

lath renderer - plaster's assistant

lattener - skilled metal worker

lavender - washerwoman

layer - employee in paper mill

layman / leyman - worker with metal

leavelooker - food examiner

leech - physician

legger - canal boatman

leightonward - gardener

lighterman - boatman

liner / lyner - flax dresser

linkerman/boy - person who hired out to carry a torch and guide people through the streets at night

lister / litster - cloth dyer

litterman - horse groomer

loblolly boy - errand boy

long song seller - street vendor of song sheets

lorimer / loiner - maker of spurs, bits and harnesses

lotseller - street seller

lumper - dock worker

lum swooper - chimney sweep

lyndraeyer - rope maker (Dutch)

maderer - garlic vendor

mail guard - armed guard

maker-up - garment assembler

malemaker / maler - traveling bag maker

malster - malted beverage maker

mantle forewoman - skilled dressmaker

mantua maker - dressmaker

marchant - merchant (French)

mashmaker - maker of mash vats

master - grade of skilled worker

master lumper - contractor of laborers

mawer - mower

mayer - physician

melder - corn miller

mercator - merchant

milestone inspector - vagrant

milliner - dressmaker who both sold custom made and ready-made

millwright - individual who built mills

molitor - miller

mondayman - landowner who paid rent working someone else's land on Mondays

moulder - assistant pottery moulder

mule spinner - spinner on a machine which produced a fine thread narrow weaver - weaver of ribbons and tapes

napier - individual in charge of table linen in a manor

neatherd - cow herder

necessary woman - servant who emptied chamber pots

necker - box maker

negidor - alderman (Spanish)

netter - net maker

nightsoilman / nightman - emptier of ashpits, cesspools, and outhouses

nightwalker - night watchman

nipper - wagoner's assistant

noon tender - guard for goods while regular workers were at lunch

notario - notary (Spanish)

notary - person officially authorized to draw up or attest to legal documents

occupier - tradesman

olitor - kitchen gardener

operario - laborer (Spanish)

osier peeler - person who peeled wood bark to be used in making baskets

osler - bird catcher

outrider - mounted attendant riding before or behind a carriage

outworker - person who carried out their job at home

overlooker - mill superintendent

owler - smuggler

packman - itinerant peddler

pad maker - worker who made small measuring

padre - priest (Spanish)

palingman - fishmonger

palister - park keeper

pannifex - worker in the cloth trade

pansmith - person who make or repaired pans

paperer - person who inserted needles in paper to ready them for sale

pargeter - ornamental plasterer

paritor - church officer who executed orders of magistrates and justices in court

parker - keeper of hunting or game park

parochus - rector or pastor

passage keeper - cleaner of passages and alleys

pavious - layer of paving stones

pedascule - schoolmaster

peeler - policeman

peever - pepper seller

pelterer - worker with animal skins

perchemear - parchment maker

peruke maker - wig maker

peter man - fisherman

petty chapman - pedlar

philosophical instrument maker - maker of scientific instruments

picker - shuttle caster

piecener / piecer - child who worked in a spinning mill piecing together broken threads

pigmaker - pottery worker

pigman - crockery seller

pikeman - miller's helper

piker - vagrant

pinder - pound keeper

pinner - pin maker

pistor - baker

pit brow lass - female laborer at surface of mines

plaisterer - plasterer

playderer - plaid maker

pleacher / plaicher / plasher - hedge layer

plumassier - seller of plumes and ornamental feathers

pointer - worker who sharpened needles

pointmaker - maker of lace tips

pointsman - railway worker

pole lathe turner - craftsman in woodwork

poller / powler - barber

ponderator - inspector of weights and measures

pony driver - child in charge of pit pony which pulled coal tubs underground

porcher - pig keeper

post boy - guard who traveled on mail coach

postillion - person who changed horses on long distance coaches

poster - quarry worker

potato badger - potato seller

pot burner - person who put a pot in a furnace

potter carrier - pharmacist/ chemist

poulterer - poultry trader

poynter - lace maker

preceptress - school mistress

presbitero - priest (Spanish)

pricker - horseman

publican - tax collector or innkeeper

pugger - worker who stomped on clay for brick manufacturer

pumbum worker - plumber

putter - hauler of mine tubs

quarrel picker - glazier

quarrier - stone cutter

quister - person who bleached things

qwylwryghte - wheelwright

rademaeker - wheelwright (Dutch)

raffman - dealer in rubbish

ragman - collector and seller of old rags and clothes

rag and bone man - person who carted away old rubbish

redemptioner - indentured person who sold himself as a servant for a specific period of time in order to pay a debt - usually passage fare to America

redsmith - goldsmith

reed maker - manufacturer of pipes for musical instruments

reeler - operator of machine which wound yarn onto a bobbin

riddler - wool stapler

riftere - reaper

ripper / rippier - seller of fresh water fish at market

rockman - individual who place charges in quarries

rockgetter - rocksalt miner

rolleyway man - custodian of roads in mines

roll turner - carder of wool or cotton

roper - rope and net maker

rower - builder of small wagon wheels

rubbisher / rubbler - sorter of small stones in a quarry

runner - individual who worked for a magistrate

saddler - saddle and harness maker

salt boiler - person who obtained salt by boiling water

salter - dealer in salt

sarcinet weaver - silk weaver

saw doctor - saw repairer

sawyer - log or wood cutter

225

scaleraker / scavenger - street cleaner

scavelman - person who cleared ditches and waterways

schout - court officer (Dutch)

scotch draper / scotchman - door-to-door salesman

scripture reader - employee of clergy. They went from house to house reading the Bible.

scrivener - individual who wrote legal documents

scutcher - flax beater

scullery maid - female servant who did lowly jobs

scullion - male servant who did lowly jobs

semi lorer - maker of leather thongs

sempstress - seamstress

seneschal - senior steward in a Manor

server - shoemaker or tailor

servus - servant

sett maker - maker of paving stones

sewer rat - bricklayer specializing in sewers and tunnels

sexton - gravedigger

shear grinder - sharpener of shears and scissors

shearman - cutter of cloth or metal

shepster - sheep shearer

shipsmith - blacksmith specializing in nautical items

shot firer - person in charge of blasting in mines and quarries

showmaker - shoemaker

shrager - tree trimmer and pruner

shriever - sheriff

shuffler - a farm yardsman

shunter - person who moved stock around rail yards

sidesman - assistant to the churchwarden

silker - individual who sewed fabric ends together to keep them from separating

skeeper / skelper - maker and seller of beehives

skipmaster - person who made skips used in mines and quarries to move men to the surface

slapper - preparer of clay for a potter

slater - slate roof tiler

slop seller - basket vendor

slopper out - person who cleaned dirty vessels

slubber - worker who operated the machine which prepared cotton for spinning

smith - person who worked with metal

smugsmith - smuggler

snobscat - shoe repair

snuffer maker - maker of candle snuffers

sojourner clothier - a traveling clothes salesman

souter - shoemaker

spallier - person who did menial jobs in a tin works

spenhauer - carpenter (German)

splitter - person who split things by hand

spooner - spoon maker

spurrier - spur maker

statist - politician

staymaker - corset maker

stenterer - worker who operated cloth finishing machinery

stevedore - dock worker

stilliard maker - scales maker

stock maker - rifle or shotgun

stock maker

stockiner / stockinger - stocking maker

stoneman / stonewarden - surveyor of highways

stone picker - hand who removed stones from a field before planting

stravaiger - vagrant

straw joiner - roof thatcher

streaker - individual who prepared a body for burial

street orderly/boy - street cleaner

stretcher - stretcher of fabrics in textile mills

striker - blacksmith's helper

stripper - employee who removed rubbish from carding machines in the wool industry

sucksmith - ploughshare maker

sutler - seller of food, drink and supplies to troops in the field or garrison

swailer / swealer - corn miller

sweep - chimney sweep

swell maker - maker of shallow baskets

sytherator - harpist

tackler - foreman of power loom

weavers

tallow chandler - candle maker and seller

tallyman / tallyfellow - seller of goods on installment

taper weaver - candle wick maker

tapster - bartender in public houses

tapiter / tapicer - weaver of worsted cloth

tarrier / terrier - caretaker of hunting terriers

tasker - thresher

tavernier - tavern owner (French)

teamer / teamster - person who took care of a team of horses

teemer - worker who emptied grain from a cart

tejedor - weaver (Spanish)

tenter / tenterer - worker who stretched material on a machine while it was drying

textor - weaver

thirdborough - underconstable

throwster - person who twisted strands of fiber into yarn

tickney man - individual who sold earthenware from town to town

tidesman / tide waiter - customs inspector

tiemaker - wooden railway tie maker

tiltmaker - awning and canopy maker

times ironer - servant who ironed the newspaper

tinctor - dyer

tinker - traveling salesman and repairer of pots and pans

tinmen / tin sanders / tin duster - finisher of tinplate

tinner - tin miner

tin pickler - worker who put sheets of tin into acid

tinsmith - tin worker

tipper - person who put tips on arrows

tippler - individual who kept an ale house

tipstaff - court officer

tirewoman - a milliner or hairdresser

tixor - weaver

todhunter - parish employee who hunted foxes

toe rag - dock worker who carried corn

toller / tolman - toll collector

tonsor - barber

tool helver - maker of tool handles

touch holer - worker in gun manufacturing industry

toyman - seller of toys

trabajador - laborer (Spanish)

trader - purchaser and seller of mechandise for profit

trammer - young mine worker

tranqueter - hoop maker

trapper - young person who opened and shut door in mines

treenail maker - maker of long wooden pins used in shipbuilding

trepanger - person who used a circular saw

trimmer - individual who moved coal around in a ship to ready it for sea

tripper - dancer

troacher - peddler

trolley carter - operator of mine tubs

troner - weighing official in markets

trouchman / trunchman-interpreter

trugger - maker of long shallow baskets

tubedrawer - tube maker

tubman - miner who filled the tubs

tunist - instrument tuner

turner - lathe operator

turning boy - weaver's assistant

turnkey - jail keeper

turnspit - operator of spit handle

tweenie / tweeny - maid who worked "between stairs" helping cooks and housemaids

twister / twisterer - operator of machine which twisted yarn and threads together

twist hand - lace machine operator

ulnager - inspector of woolen goods

upholder - quilt and mattress maker

upright worker - chimney sweep

valuator - appraiser of objects

vassal - lowest servant

vendue - auctioneer (Dutch)

verderer - official in charge of the royal forest

verger - priest's assistant

verge maker - maker of watch and clock spindles

verrier - glazier

viewer - manager of a mine

villein - person who paid for use of manorial land

vinter - wine merchant

virginal player - musician with an instrument similar to a harpsichord

vulcan - blacksmith

wabster - weaver

wailer - remover of impurities from coal

wainwright - wagon builder

wait / wakeman - night watchman

walker - clothes cleaner

waller - brick or stone wall builder

wantcatcher - mole catcher

warder - jailer

warper - preparer of the warp for a loom

warrener - rabbit and other small game breeder

wasteman - inspector in a mine who checked and maintained old gas workings

water bailiff - river policeman who is empowered to search ships for contraband

water gilder - water fowl trapper

water leader/leder/loder - seller of fresh drinking water

waterman - worker with or on boats

wattle hurdle maker - maker of fence from wattle which was used to keep sheep in

waver - weaver

waymaker - builder of roads

way man - surveyor of roads

way warden - highway overseer

weatherspy - astrologer

webster - weaver

weever - weaver (Dutch)

wellmaster - individual whose responsibility was to ensure clean water for the village

well sinker - well digger

well wright - maker of winding equipment used in wells

wet glover - leather glove maker

wet nurse - woman hired to suckle the child of another

wetter - employee who dampened paper in a print shop

wharfinger - person in charge of a wharf

wheeler - wheel maker

wherryman - person in charge of a small light row boat

whig - horse driver

whipperin - manager of the hounds during a hunt

whitcher - person who built wagon wheels

whitear - hide cleaner

whit cooper - tin barrel maker

white limer - -plasterer

white wing - street sweeper

whitener / whitester / whitster - cloth bleacher

whitesmith - tinsmith

whittawer - saddle and harness maker

willow plaiter - basket maker

windster - silk winder

woodbreaker - maker of wooden water casks

woodranger/woodward - individual in charge of the forest

woolen billy piecer - person in woolen mills who pieced together broken yarn

wool man / wool sorter / stapler - sorter of wool into different grades

wool stapler - merchant who buys, grades and sells wool

woolsted man - seller of wool clothing

wool winder - person who made balls of wool to sell

wright - skilled worker

wyrtha - laborer

xylographer - illustration printer who used wooden blocks

yatman - gate keeper

yearman - person with a yearly contract to work

yeoman - freeholder farmer or a ships officer

zoographer - classifier of animals

Topic Sources and Additional Reading

Culling, Joyce. Occupation Descriptions. The Langham Genealogy Page. <www.onthenet.com.au/~tonylang/occupa.htm> Printout dated 24 July 2000.

Deceased American Physician Records. <www.ngsgenealogy.org/library/content/ama-info.html> National Genealogical Society. Copyrighted 1998.

Fitzhugh, Terrich V.H. *The Dictionary of Genealogy.* London: A&C Black, 1994.

Hey, David, ed. *The Oxford Companion to Local and Family History.* New York: Oxford University Press, 1996.

Jacobson, Judy. *Genealogist's Refresher Course.* 2nd ed. Baltimore: Clearfield Company, 1996.

Lacombe, John, Jr. List of [Old] Occupations (So Grandma was a fish fag, eh?). <cpcug.org/user/jlacombe/terms.html> Updated 15 May 2000. Copyrighted 1996-2000

Larson, Frances. *The Genealogist's Dictionary.* N.p. 1986

Stevens, Bernadine S. *Colonial American Crafts People.* New York: Franklin Watts, 1993.

Tylcoat, Dave and Sue Tylcoat. Glossary <ourworld.compuserve.com/homepages/dave-tylcoat> Printout dated 13 September 1999

West Virginia Coal Miners. <www.rootsweb.com/~wvcoal> US GenWeb. Copyrighted January 1999.

Early Immigrant Groups

To understand your ancestors, learn their history. What was going on in their home country to make them move? How did they interact with other ethnic groups before and after their move? What laws had negative and positive effects on them?

Acadians - descendants of French settlers who went to Nova Scotia in the early 1600's. In 1755, the British ousted them and they scattered. Large numbers of them ended up in New England and Louisiana.

Africans - captured primarily by other Africans and exchanged for goods by white traders who transported them via ships to Europe and the New World. Although they came from all along the 3000 mile west African coast, the slave trade began in Nigeria as early as the 15th century. By 1715, 39 percent of the Black slaves lived in Virginia. The numbers continued to grow until the abolition of slavery in Britain and America in the mid to late 1800's.

Amish - strict Swiss Mennonite sect which broke from the Southern German Anabaptists-Mennonites sometime between 1639-1697. They followed Jakob Amman who supported "shunning" those excommunicated from the sect. These pacifists settled in America in the 1700's.

Basques - from an area which straddles Spain and France where the Bay of Biscay meets the Pyrenees. The French Basques were known as Navarrese and many of them settled in the San Francisco, California area. Spanish Basques were known as Vizcayans and settled in Reno, Nevada They entered the New World with French and Spanish adventurers. More arrived after the 1850's when the French Revolution, Napoleonic Wars and Spanish uprisings had a negative effect. Ten thousand of these agricultural people were in the American West by 1895.

Black Dutch - any number of groups of people. The term was frequently used in a disparaging manner for working class people of small stature and dark coloring in the mid-1800's. Although their appearance was more similar to Native Americans and immigrants from the Mediterranean and Middle East regions, among those identified as Black Dutch have been
* Spaniards who ventured first to Holland and then emigrated with the Dutch,
* Melungeons,

- Emigrants from the Black Forest of Germany,
- Creek or Cherokee Indians,
- Descendants of those West Indians under Dutch control
- Portuguese and Spanish Jews who married Dutch Protestants as a way to escape the Inquisition,
- Members of religious groups, such as the Amish, who wore primarily black clothing,
- Mixed descendants of Dutch and Blacks or Indians,
- Descendants of Dutch born when The Netherlands was occupied by Spain.

Bruderhofs of the Hutterite Brethren - see "Hutterite Brethren"

Cajuns of Louisiana - descendants of Acadians who ended up going to Louisiana after their ouster from Nova Scotia.

Convenanters - 17th century Scots who were committed to keep the covenants of Presbyterianism as the exclusive religion of Scotland and make Parliament supreme over the Scottish and English monarchs. Between 1557 and 1688, Covenanters were frequently persecuted.

Creole - French form of the Spanish "Criolle". A Creole was a native of Spanish America or the West Indies who was descended from one person of pure French or Spanish ancestry and another of West Indian or European/ Native American mixed ancestry.

Czechs - middle Europeans persecuted for their religion. Beginning in 1624, Protestant Czechs were oppressed and their clergy were banished. Catholic priests were the only ones allowed to perform marriages and christenings. The State controlled Catholic Church even maintained the Jewish records. Eventually, many Czechs settled in Texas and Oklahoma.

Dunkards - fifty-nine families belonging to the Church of the Brethren who established their first Dunkard Church in Germantown, Pennsylvania in 1719. In 1729, Dunkard founder Alexander Mack brought another large group to Pennsylvania. Several groups, including Seventh Day Baptists and Brethren in Christ, were offshoots of the Dunkards.

German Baptists - non-conformist sect of Dunkards who were especially opposed to higher education. They were also known as the "Old German Baptist Brethren."

Gypsies - called themselves "Romanus". They were descendants of tribes from India which fled from Alexander the Great. After settling in the Middle East they moved to Europe in the 1400's where they suffered constant persecution. Since Gypsy slaves were legal in Europe until 1856, the first probably came to the New World with French settlers to Louisiana. When free, the Gypsies followed a nomadic life in America.

Haugeanists - evangelical Lutheran dissenters.

Hessian - German mercenaries who fought for the British during the American Revolution were supplied by Frederick II (1720-1785). They originated in the state of Hesse, in west central Germany. After the revolution, many remained in the United States.

Hibernia - an ancient name for Ireland

Huguenot - adherents of a Swiss political movement and Protestants who fled religious persecution in France in the 16th and 17th centuries. Many went to Prussia, England, Ireland, the German Palatinate and/or the French West Indies before coming to America.

Hutterite Brethren (Bruderhofs of the Hutterite Brethren) - communal group organized in the 16th century. Their leader, Jacob Hutter, was burned at the stake during their persecution in Moravia. After being expelled from Austria, the group went to Rumania and Russia. But in 1874, a group joined a group of Russian Mennonites going to the United States and generally settled in the South Dakota region. Because of their non-resistance stance, many went to Canada during World War II.

Irish - By 1703, the Irish had braved invasion by the Scots, the Rebellion of 1641, Cromwell, the Treaty of Limerick, the Penal Laws and the Test Act. Cromwell deported Irish to the Colonies, but others came on their own, driven by religious and economic conditions at home. In the years 1717-18, 1725-29, 1740-41 and 1754-55, drought and famine drove even more Irish west. While another influx began in 1783, just the potato famine of 1846-47 brought 1.5 million Irish to American. Then, by 1890, another 4 million had left Ireland.

Loyalists (Tories) - colonists who sided with the British during the American Revolutionary War. Many were beaten for their loyalty to the crown and had their land confiscated. Tories hiked west along the St. Lawrence and the Niagara River into what would become Southern Ontario and along both sides other Detroit River. Others trudged North to Canada's Maritime Provinces. And a few remained behind in the United States

Mennonite - Swiss followers of Protestant Menno Simons. They arrived in America by way of Alsace, England and Russia. They settled in Pennsylvania and were conscientious objectors.

Moravian - A Protestant group organized by followers of Jan Huss in the 1400's in Bohemia and Moravia which went on to Germany, Poland and England. Although the first group in the United States arrived in Pennsylvania in 1734, the first settlement was in Georgia. They wore simple clothes and served as missionaries among the Indians.

Palatines - German Protestants living on the West Bank of the Rhine River. They were devastated by the Thirty Years War, local religious wars, the War of Spanish Succession and were persecuted by France. Then, the winter of 1708 was so bad, the sea along the coast actually froze. Fruit trees and grape vines were destroyed. And all along, the Palatines were being hit with heavy taxes. So thousands fled to London in mid-1709. Nearly 800 families went to Ireland. But the 3000 Palatinates who landed in New York in 1710 became the largest single group of immigrants to arrive in America during the colonial period. Still others went to North Carolina and Virginia. However, the majority, believing the reputation of fairness of William Penn, ended up settling in Pennsylvania.

Pennsylvania Dutch - Germans and some Swiss who were Moravians, Mennonites, Amish or Dunkards. Despite the name, they were not Dutch. Theories of the origin of the group's name include
• 	the use of the German name for German, "Deutsche"
• 	the emigration of many German through Dutch ports.
The group settled primarily in southeastern Pennsylvania.

Puritans - English Protestant dissenters who were characterized as rigidly moral and who advocated reforms in the Church of England.

Quaker (Society of Friends) - a religious group formed in England, they went to the Americas as early as 1656, with the majority settling in Pennsylvania and Rhode Island. In 1661, they held their first annual meeting in Rhode Island. They opposed war and refused to swear in legal matters. Easy to use records are available for this denomination which include birth, death, marriage, business and disciplinary records.

Schwenkfelders - followers of Casper Schwenkfeld who emigrated from Silesia to Pennsylvania in 1733, after being persecuted by Charles VI. Some members eventually migrated to Canada.

Scotch-Irish - lowland Scottish Presbyterians who were sent by the British to Ireland to act as a buffer between them and the Irish. When life became difficult in Ireland, the Scotch-Irish moved to the frontiers of America. They were also known as Ulstermen and Ulster Scots.

Shakers - Puritanical non-conformists who believed totally abstaining from sex was the core of man's spiritual redemption. Led by Ann Lee, they began their first American Colony in 1774.

Tasks - Christians from southern Albania who were escaping starvation and unemployment, aggravated by the Austro-Hungarian and Ottoman Empires. The first Tasks to arrive in America were single men or married men who intended to return to their families with their American earnings. However, most stayed, with many bringing their families from Albania to join them.

Walloon - French dialect Flemish who lived in southern and southeastern Belgium who were led by Cornelius May of Flanders, Holland to America in 1624. They established Fort Orange, which was to become Albany, New York.

Wends - descendants from Slavic tribes. The Wends, also referred to as "Sorbs", were nearly annihilated by the 1800's. Remaining Wends were occupying a small area along the Spree River when Prussians began to require them to speak German, Germanize their names, become part of the state-regulated church and receive less pay for equal work. Then laws initiated in 1832 appropriated their property. While some Wends went to Australia in 1854, over 500 of them went to Texas to search for religious freedom and the right to speak their own language. The trip was arduous with a cholera epidemic causing a three week quarantine of their ship in Ireland. Upon arrival in Galveston, Texas, many contracted Yellow Fever. But when the survivors finally reached Lee County, Texas, they were able to purchase land for $1 per acre. They claimed the area as "Wendenland" and named their town Serbin the capital. Then, after associating themselves with the Missouri Synod of the Lutheran Church, many dispersed out across Texas.

Zoarites - the group formerly known as the Society of Separatists of Zoar. The Zoarites were German religious dissenters who emigrated in 1817. They settled in Tuscarawa County, Ohio and formed a communal-type agrarian society of socialists, pietists and mystics.

Native Americans

The Bureau of Indian Affairs began using the term "Native American" to denote American Indians and Alaskan Natives. In fact, the federal government has officially recognized over 550 tribes of Native Alaskans and American Indians. However, more recently, the term Native American has come to include Native Hawaiians and even Pacific Islanders living in US Protectorates.

American Indians

While the Bureau of the Census counts anyone who claims to be an Indian, each tribe has its own criteria for membership into the tribe. However, the Bureau of Indian Affairs and the professional anthropologist have their own criteria which do not always agree. According to the Bureau of Indian Affairs, a person must
* have a Certificate of Degree of Indian Blood indicating the person is a member of a federally-recognized tribe and
* have one-fourth to one-half or more Indian blood, depending upon tribal requirements.

Specific information cannot usually be found at the Bureau of Indian Affairs. Most of their records have been sent to the National Archives. Tribes maintain their own records. Membership in individual tribes usually requires lineal descent from a member of the tribes base roll or original members named in the tribal constitution and sometimes require
* a percentage of tribal blood
* tribal residency
* continued tribal contact

So before applying for tribal enrollment, specific tribal membership criteria needs to be found.

Seven Most Populous Indian Tribes in the United States (all with more than 50,000 in the tribe, according to 1990 census figures)

Cherokee	Chippewa	Choctaw	Pueblo
Navajo	Sioux	Apache	

Alaskan Natives

The Bureau of Indian Affairs divides Native Alaskans into three groups with their own distinct cultural traditions, languages and art.
* Aleuts were a maritime people who were native to the Aleutian Islands stretching over 1100 miles southwest of the Alaska mainland. Through the years, many moved to the Alaskan mainland. They were ethnically related to, but distinct culturally from, the Alaskan Eskimo.
* Eskimos belong to the Inuit/Inupiat and Yupik people of Alaska. Since the term "Eskimo" is thought of as pejorative in some places, they are called Inuit in Canada and Greenlander or Kalaallisut in Greenland. The Eskimo culture dates from at least 6000 B.C.
* Indians of Alaska include the Athabascan, Haida, Tlingit and Tsemshian tribes.

Localized populations of mixed Black, White and Indian origins have been established in remote areas of the United States. In 1953, Edward T. Price of Los Angeles State College estimated between 50,000 and 100,000 persons considered themselves members of one of these groups. However, racist practices frightened or shamed many into denying their heritage.

Groups include the Cane River Creoles of Louisiana, the Brown People of Kentucky, the Nanticokes and Moors of Delaware, the Wesorts of southeastern Maryland, the Brass Ankles and Turks of South Carolina, the Buckheads and the Carmel Indians of Ohio. Many belonged to one of the 245 "Indian" tribes which the US government still has not formally recognized. However, some have been recognized by individual states.

Several have Indian blood mixed with Whites, Blacks or both. But others, like the Issues of the eastern Blue Ridge of Virginia, were primarily Mulattos with only possible Indian blood.

It is quite probable that the more inland groups originated on or near a coast. But as the Caucasians moved further West, so did these groups - just ahead of settlers until they were finally uncovered.

Signals That a Family Has Hidden Their Racial or Ethnic Origin

- Changes in race designation in census records (i.e. Mulatto in 1870, Indian in 1880),
- Family tradition of having Indian, Black Dutch or Black Irish ancestry,
- Different racial designations within families (siblings, aunts, cousins) in the Federal Census,
- Rejected Indian land claims
- Change of surname for no clear reason,
- Vague family traditions that do not "check out",
- Lack of family history

Groups of Mixed Race

Terms, frequently used in a derogatory manner, have been developed for almost every possible racial combination. A few included

Mestizo	White and American Indian parents
Mulatto	White and Black parents
Cuarteron	White and Mulatto parents
Mameluco	Black and South American Indian parents
Cubra	Black and Mulatto parents
Chino-blanco	White and Chinese parents

However, some pockets of people are not so easy to define. They include -

"Cajans" of the Spanish frontier of Alabama (as opposed to Cajuns of Louisiana) - purportedly formed by the intermarriage of children of a Mulatto family named Reed / Reid, a free Black family named Bryd, and a Weaver family which settled in the Lower Tombigbee River Region of rural southern Alabama. Indians and white loggers, cattlemen and railroad men added to the mix.

Guineas of West Virginia - considered as Blacks or Mulattos on official records, but probably also contained some Indian blood. They were found in the western portion of Virginia before the 1800's. The surname Mayles/Mall/ Male was common among the Guineas.

Jackson's White / Ramapo of New York and New Jersey - a reclusive mountain group with Dutch sounding names such as DeFreese, Van Donck and de Groot. Their hermatic ways led to intermarriage and genetic abnormalities, such as additional or web fingers, mental retardation and albinism. Their 18th century style speech is often referred to as "Jersey Dutch".

Although more Caucasian in appearance, they attended segregated Black schools in New York as late as 1947. In reality, many Jackson Whites or Ramapos (Ramapough) had features of Mohawk Indians. Black, Dutch and, possibly Hessian soldiers or deserters could have been part of the mix. They considered themselves as descendants of the Delaware and Tuscarora tribes.

One story is that Jackson's Whites were descendants of runaway slaves and white female followers of Washington's forces. Upon Washington's retreat, these outcasts were forced to take refuge on Ramapough Mountain where they insulated and armed themselves against the rest of the world.

Lumbees or Croatans of North Carolina - discovered living along the Lumber River in the Robeson County area as early as the 1730's. In the 1990 census, more than 48,000 Indians identified themselves as Lumbees and they made up 90% of Pembroke in Robeson County, North Carolina.

Others were found in Hoke, Scotland and Sampson Counties, North Carolina and Bulloch and Evans Counties in Georgia. In Georgia, they worked in the terpentine industry, although General Sherman burned their terpentine forests during the Civil War.

Even though labeled as Indians by the North Carolina State (1888) and South Carolina (1896) Legislatures, the Croatans / Lumbees were not recognized by the Federal Government until 1956. Some researchers have suggested the Lumbees were descendants of the local Indians and survivors of the Lost Colony of Ft. Raleigh. Legend has it that when Gov. John White returned to England, he left orders that if the settlers found it necessary to leave the fort, they should carve their destination upon a tree. Supposedly, when White returned, he found the colonists gone and the words "Croatoan" and "Cro" carved on two trees. But the colonists were never found. The most common Croatan surnames - Locklear and Oxendene - were not connected to the Lost Colony.

Lumbees may have been related to the Cheraw Indians who left the Danville, Virginia, area circa 1703 to go to what would become Cheraw, South Carolina. In 1737, the Cheraws sold their land along the Great Pee Dee River of South Carolina, and moved to settle along the Drowning Creek of North Carolina. In fact, in1890, *The Statesboro Eagle* described Croatans as

> "the color of Indians, and the women and children who were not exposed to much of the sun are real bright in color. The men and women have straight hair and are intelligent people... Captain McKennon tells us that they are a distinct race in North Carolina."

The Locklear, Osendine, Chavis and Lowry names were common among the Lumbees. The Lumbees even had their own version of Robin Hood in Harry Berry Lowrie who fought oppression from 1862 to 1872.

Melungeons / Malungeons of Appalachia - a group found living in cabins in Hancock County Tennessee, who spoke an Elizabethan form of English and called themselves "Portyghees" as early as the 1790's.

The *American Heritage Dictionary* defined Melungeons as "a group of dark skinned people of uncertain origin." The *Dictionary of the English Language* reported the name may have originated with the French "melange" meaning "mixed", the Greek "melas" meaning "dark" or "black" or the Afro-Portuguese "mulango" meaning "shipmate." But Brent Kennedy on the Melungeon Internet homepage reported the name stemmed from the Turkish "melun can" meaning "one whose life has been cursed."

While Melungeons of Appalachia - primarily in Lee, Scott, and Wise County, Virginia; Hancock (Hawkins) County, Tennessee; Ashe County, North Carolina and Letcher County, Kentucky - can resemble Indians, their white ancestry is also quite evident. They do appear to have some Mediterranean features and suffer from several genetic diseases distinctive to the Mediterranean area. At various times, Melungeon ancestors were imagined to be

- Progeny of members of the lost colony of Roanoke and Native Americans;
- Portuguese or Moors brought to the New World by the Spanish, perhaps to the Santa Elena settlement off South Carolina, to build roads to forts and missions;
- Colonists who came with Welsh explorer Madoc;

- Offspring of African-American, Native American and Caucasian intermarriages;
- Shipwrecked Portuguese sailors;
- Turks, African and South American natives left on North American soil by Sir Francis Drake.

It is easier to say what they are not. They are not uniquely Native American, Caucasian or African-American.

Although they were given the designation of "Free Person of Color" (FPC), Melungeons were given none of the basic rights of White America. With cross marriages, "passing" as White became easier and many Melungeons opted to move to a new area and conceal their true ancestry. However, the surnames Collins, Goins, Mullins and Gibson are recorded as the most common among the Melungeons.

Redbones of southwestern Louisiana and Texas - a group who were probably of mixed White and African-American descent but may have had Asian, Native American, Basque, Spanish, Gypsy, Moor or Portuguese blood also.

Today most have cooper-colored skin, high cheekbones and dark hair and eyes. But light-skinned, blond-haired, blue-eyed Redbones are not unheard of. Similarly, Redbones with prominent Negroid features are also found.

Always Protestant, frequently Baptist, Redbones were first considered to be freed Blacks with English surnames, such as Ashworth, Willis, Boswell and Stanley. Depending upon the source, Redbones may have originated in South Carolina, Georgia or the Carolinas.

In 1806, the United States and Spain agreed to set-up a Neutral Zone in Southwestern Louisiana while talks were conducted setting a boundary between their two territories. Although populated chiefly by Indians and having no law in the area, outlaws, stray Mediterranean seamen, runaway slaves, Texans fleeing the Spanish and privateers sought refuge in the area. The Neutral Zone became the home of the Redbones. It was there that they farmed and became a socially isolated society.

Topic Sources and Additional Reading

Afrigeneas Homepage. <www.Afrigeneas.com> African Ancestored Genealogy. Updated 17 June 2000. Copyrighted 1999-2000.

Alaska natives. <www.uaa.alaska.edu/just/links/natives.html> Justice Center Web page, University of Alaska Anchorage. <ayjust@uaa.alaska.edu> Updated 10 May 2000. Copyrighted 1996-2000.

Baldwin, Patricia A. Hopkins. "The Mysterious Melungeons" <www.bright.net/ ~kat/mystery.htm> Printout dated 16 December 1999.

Berry, Ellen Thomas and David Allen Berry. *Our Quaker Ancestors: Finding Them in Quaker Records*. Baltimore: Genealogical Publishing Company, 1987.

Bowen, Gary. Words for Mixed Blood Peoples: A Work in Progress <www. netgsi.com/~fcowboy/mixedwords.html> Printout dated 20 April 2000.

Fields, Bill. So What Is a Melungeon Anyway? <www.melungeons. org/underonesky> Reprint from original. *Under One Sky*. Vol 1 No.1 1997.

History of Croatan Lodge #117 <www.croatan.org> Order of The Arrow Croatan Lodge #117. East Carolina Council <cdecker@Croatan.org> Last revised 21 June 2000.

Hornbeck, Shirley. Hornbeck's This and That Genealogy Tips on Black Dutch and Irish, Melungeons, Moravians, Pennsylvania Dutch. <homepages. rootsweb.com/~hornbeck/blkdutch.htm> Printout dated 16 May 2000.

Jones, Linda W. Genealogy: Acadian & French - Canadian Style. GEDCOM CD-ROM Project. <ourworld/compuserve.com/homepages/ lwjones> Printout dated 17 December 1999.

Larson, Frances. *The Genealogist's Dictionary*. N.p. 1986.

Lammert, Ron. Who are the Wends? Sponsored by My Herritage in cooperation with Texas Wendish Heritage Society, Inc. site created by Tim Harris. 1998 <home.sprynet.com/~harrisfarm/awend2.htm> Copyrighted 1998.

Knittle, Walter Allen. *Eighteenth Century Palatine Emigration*. Baltimore: Genealogical Publishing Company, 1965.

Mabry, Dr. Kemp. "Croatan Indians of Bulloch County". Reprint of Statesboro, Georgia: *Statesboro Herald*,: Online. <www.georgianetweb. com/bulloch> Printout dated 14 February 2000.

Marler, Don C. The Louisiana Redbones. <donwoodpress.myriad.net> Copyrighted 1997.

Martin, Kay. "On Black Dutch". *Under One Sky*. (April 1997).

Mika, Nick and Helma. United Empire Loyalist Pioneers of Upper Canada. Belleville, Ontario: Mika Publishing Company, 1976.

Price, Edward R. "A Geographic Analysis of White-Negro-Indian Racial Mixture in Eastern United States." Annals: Association of American Geographers. Vol 43. (June 1953) p. 138-55

Reaman, G. Elmore. *The Trail of the Black Walnut.* Baltimore: Genealogical Publishing Company, 1993.

Transportation Time Lines

Transportation regulations have been in effect in the United States for many years. For instance, Congress created the Interstate Commerce Commission in 1887 to oversee delivery of goods between states. Now, the government oversees nearly all modes of travel and delivery under the auspices of the United States Department of Transportation, which was created in 1966.

Air

1783	First parachute used in jump off a tower (France)
1783	A hydrogen balloon, without passengers, went to 3000 feet and traveled 15 miles
1783	First passenger hot air balloon carried a rooster and a duck
1797	First parachute jump was from a balloon at 2230 feet
1852	World's first airship flight took place (France)
1852	First practical dirigible balloon powered by steam constructed
1900	First dirigible built by county von Zeppelin (German)
1903	Wright brothers made world's first powered, controlled and sustained flight (US)
1909	First airplane crossed the English Channel
1910	First aerial warfare was fought in Italo-Turkish War
1911	First single-shell fuselage for airplane was introduced (France)
1911	Italians dropped aerial bombs
1915	First metal aircraft built (Germany)
1919	First nonstop transatlantic crossing of an airplane achieved
1926	World's first liquid fueled rocket launched (US)
1927	First solo transatlantic flight made
1938	Maiden flight of pressurized airliner in commercial service occurred
1939	First jet plane flown
1941	First jet powered aircraft flown (US)
1941	Rocket-powered vehicle was sent 240 miles into air (US)
1944	Rocket propelled airplane broke sound barrier
1957	First artificial satellite was launched (USSR)
1961	First manned spaceflight achieved (USSR)
1965	Mariner 4 space probe went past Mars (US)
1969	First moon landing accomplished (US)
1976	Supersonic transportation introduced

1620	Submarine invented (Holland)
1783	First paddle-driven steamboat built and sailed (France)
1789	US Lighthouse Service established as part of the Department of the Treasury (US)
1807	Robert Fulton began world's first continuously, commercially-successful passenger steamboat service (US)
1819	First steamship crossed the Atlantic
1825	Erie Canal completed
1836	Screw propeller patented (Sweden and US)
1838	Steamship made first transatlantic crossing
1845	First clipper ship launched (US)
1845	Screw-driven ship made first transatlantic crossing
1848	St. Lawrence Seaway opened
1852	American clipper ships broke transatlantic speed record (13 days)
1853	Steamboat Act established Steamboat Inspection Service (US)
1863	First mechanically-driven submarine used engine powered by compressed air (France)
1884	Bureau of Navigation established in Department of the Treasury (US)
1902	Congress authorized construction of Panama Canal (US)
1908	Gyroscope compass produced (Germany)
1912	Unsinkable Titanic sunk
1914	Panama Canal opened
1917-1919	Coast Guard transferred to the Navy Department from the Treasury Department (US)
1941-1946	Coast Guard transferred to the Navy Department from the Treasury Department (US)
1959	Hovercraft first demonstrated
1959	Full 2038 nautical mile St. Lawrence Seaway opened to deep navigation (US and Canada)
1967	Coast Guard transferred permanently to the Department of Transportation
1989	Oil tanker Exxon Valdez ran aground in Gulf of Alaska

Rail

1779	Earliest steam engine operated (England)
1789	First iron rail laid (England)
1789	Earliest public railway pulled by horses (England)
1803	First steam locomotive constructed (England)
1807	Railway passenger service began (Wales)
1815	First rail track laid (US)

1825	Stephenson's First steam railway opened (England)
1827	Baltimore & Ohio, first US Railway, chartered
1829	Stephenson's *Rocket* locomotive set a new speed record (35 mph)
1830	World's first railroad passenger service established (England)
1832	First mail carried by rail
1838	Congress affirmed railroads as Post Roads
1850	Congress passed land grant for development of railroads (US)
1853	New York-Chicago rail link completed (US)
1855	First train crossed Niagara Falls bridge
1857	First steel rails laid (England)
1863	First underground train opened (London)
1865	George Pullman's sleeping car introduced (US)
1865	World's first train robbery occurred
1869	George Westinghouse patented the air brake, making high-speed train travel possible (US)
1870	Boston, Massachusetts and Oakland, California railroad link completed
1879	First electric railroad demonstrated (Germany)
1883	First public electric railroad begins (England)
	Maiden trip of the Orient Express
1885	Canadian Pacific Railroad reaches across continent (Canada)
1892	Diesel engine patented (Germany)
1895	Baltimore & Ohio Railroad introduced electric service (US)
1898	Boston opened first US subway
1904	Trans-Siberian Railway, the world's longest, was completed (Russia)
1917	Railroads federalized during World War I (US)
1920	Railroads returned to owners under new regulations (US)
1920	Use of diesel locomotives began
1926	Congress passed US Railway Labor Act
1935	Diesel electric locomotives introduced for long distance use (US)
1971	Amtrack (National Rail Passenger Corporation) created (US)

Road

1839	Bicycle invented (Scotland)
1844	Charles Goodyear patented his vulcanization process, leading to rubber products, such as tires
1878	Karl Benz began working on motorized tricycle (Germany)
1887	Gottlieb Daimler and Karl Benz produced first successful automobile (Germany)

1888	Pneumatic bicycle tire invented
1893	Federal Highway Administration opened in the Department of Agriculture (US)
1895	First automobile race organized (France)
1898	First automobile fatality occurred (England)
1903	Detroit became center of auto industry (US)
1908	First Model-T sold (US)
1908	First assembly line for manufacturing automobiles opened (US)
1910	First self-starter installed in an automobile
1913	Ford created assembly line (US)
1915	Tractor introduced (US)
1916	First tanks used in warfare
1931	Post Office purchased 1000 Ford Model AA to be used to deliver mail (US)
1938	Volkswagen "Beetle" designed to Hitler's specifications (Germany)

Order In Which States Were Admitted to the Union

Delaware	December 7, 1787
Pennsylvania	December 12, 1787
New Jersey	December 18, 1787
Georgia	January 2, 1788
Connecticut	January 9, 1788
Massachusetts	February 6, 1788
Maryland	April 28, 1788
South Carolina	May 23, 1788
New Hampshire	June 21, 1788
Virginia	June 25, 1788
New York	July 26, 1788
North Carolina	November 21, 1789
Rhode Island	May 29, 1790
Vermont	March 4, 1791
Kentucky	June 1, 1792
Tennessee	June 1, 1796
Ohio	March 1, 1803
Louisiana	April 3, 1812
Indiana	December 11, 1816
Mississippi	December 10, 1817
Illinois	December 3, 1818
Alabama	December 14, 1819
Maine	March 15, 1820
Missouri	August 10, 1821

Arkansas	June 15, 1836
Michigan	January 26, 1837
Florida	March 3, 1845
Wisconsin	May 29, 1845
Texas	December 29, 1845
Iowa	December 28, 1846
California	September 9, 1850
Minnesota	May 11, 1858
Oregon	February 14, 1859
Kansas	January 29, 1861
West Virginia	June 20, 1863
Nevada	October 31, 1864
Nebraska	March 1, 1867
Colorado	August 1, 1870
North Dakota	November 2, 1889
South Dakota	November 2, 1889
Montana	November 8, 1889
Washington	November 11, 1889
Idaho	July 3, 1890
Wyoming	July, 1890
Utah	January 4, 1896
Oklahoma	January 16, 1907
New Mexico	January 6, 1912
Arizona	February 14, 1912
Alaska	January 3, 1959
Hawaii	August 21, 1959

United States History Time Line

1450-98	John Cabot explores North America for English
1492	Columbus lands in New World while searching for a western route to India
1494	Treaty divides the colonial world between Portugal and Spain
1494	Santo Domingo is settled by Europeans
1507	New World is named "America" for Amerigo Vespucci
1513	Ponce de Leon explores Florida and establishes St. Augustine
1513	Balboa crosses the Ismus of Panama
1541	Jacques Cartier attempts to colonize Quebec
1562-67	First black slaves are brought to Spanish West Indies by British John Hawkins
1565	St. Augustine, Florida is founded
1579	Sir Frances Drake claims California for Queen Elizabeth

1587	First English child is born in America and named Virginia Dare
1591	Roanoke Island colonists have disappeared
1598	New Mexico is explored by Spanish Juan de Onate
1603	Champlain explores St. Lawrence River
1607	Jamestown is established
1608	French establish Quebec
1609	Henry Hudson sails the Hudson River
1620	Mayflower lands
1624	Jamestown becomes a Royal Colony
1624	DeSoto discovers Mississippi River
1630	More than 1000 Puritans settle in Massachusetts
1636	Roger Williams establishes Providence, Rhode Island
1643	New England Confederacy is formed by Massachusetts, Plymouth, Connecticut, and New Haven
1660	Navigation Act restricts colonial trade
1669	Maine becomes part of Massachusetts Bay Colony
1673	Father Marquette and Louis Joliet sail Fox and Wisconsin Rivers and down the Mississippi nearly to the Gulf of Mexico
1682	William Penn arrives in Pennsylvania
1689	Establishment of the English Bill of Rights, precursor of the US Bill of Rights
1692-93	Salem Witch Trials
1699	Biloxi, Mississippi is settled
1701	Cadillac establishes Detroit
1718	Scotch-Irish immigrants begin to arrive in New World
1726	Spiritual awakening begins
1732	Georgia, originally a refuge for prisoners, is chartered
1733	British establishes the Molasses Act, taxing all rum and molasses
1735	Peter Zenger is acquitted in a libel suit
1740	South Carolina Slave Code is adopted
1741	Vitus Bering discovers Alaska
1752	Gregorian Calendar is adopted
1754	Benjamin Franklin proposes Plan of Union
1763	England receives Canada from France
1765	Sugar Act passes
1765	Stamp Act passes
1767	Townsend Revenue taxes imported glass, lead, paint, paper and tea
1769	First settlement of Tennessee
1770	Boston massacre
1773	Tea Act passes
1773	Boston Tea Party takes place
1774	"Intolerable Acts" passed
1774	Shakers begin first colony in America

1774	First Continental Congress meets
1775	Revolution opens at Lexington and Concord
1776	Thomas Pain publishes *Common Sense*
1776	Declaration of Independence is signed
1783	Treaty of Paris is signed ending Revolutionary War and making the United States a sovereign nation
1783	US begins trading with China
1783	US suffers depression having lost trade with West Indies after war
1784	Russians establish themselves in Alaska
1786	Alexander Henry and James Monroe ask Prince Henry of Prussia to become King of the United States
1787	Delegates draw up the Constitution and send to the States for ratification
1787	Alexander Hamilton writes the Federalist Papers
1787	James Madison and John Jay request a Bill of Rights
1788	US constitution goes into effect
1789	Second Continental Congress meets in New York
1791	Bill of Rights is established
1793	Washington, D.C. became the nation's capital
1793	Eli Whitney invents cotton gin
1795	Washington, D.C. is made the official capital city
1796	Washington delivers his Farewell Address
1800	Indiana and Ohio Territories are organized
1801	Jefferson becomes President in Washington, D.C.
1802	Georgia gives its western territory to US
1803	US acquires the Louisiana Purchase from France
	Lewis and Clark's Expedition begins
1805	Michigan Territory is organized
	Lewis and Clark reach the Pacific Ocean
1806	Lewis and Clark return from their expedition to the Pacific Ocean
1807	A law is passed forbidding the importation of slaves to the US
1809	Illinois Territory is organized
1812	Mississippi Territory is organized
	Missouri Territory is organized
	US declares war on Britain
	British and Indians capture Michigan Territory
1814	British burn Washington
	Treaty of Ghent ends the War of 1812
1815	Battle of New Orleans is fought
1816	"Year of Summer" is named when Connecticut has a blizzard in June and Georgia has a high of 46 degrees on July 4th
1817	Alabama Territory is organized
1819	US acquires East and West Florida

	Arkansas Territory is organized
1820	Missouri Compromise sets dividing point for slavery
1822	Stephen F. Austin establishes an American colony in Texas
1823	Monroe Doctrine
	Erie Canal is completed
1826	*Last of the Mohicans* is written by James Fennimore Cooper
1827	Democratic Party is formed
1830	Mormonism is founded by Joseph Smith in New York
1834	Indian Territory (Oklahoma) is organized
1836	Texas secedes from Mexico
	Colt patents the revolver
	Wisconsin Territory is organized
1837-1843	US depression
1838	Samuel Morse develops the Morse code making the telegraph possible
	Iowa Territory is organized
1840	Horace Greeley establishes *The New York Times*
1844	US annexes parts of Colorado, New Mexico, Kansas, Oklahoma and Texas
1845	Texas joins the United States
1846	US annexes parts of Arizona and New Mexico
1846-1847	Mass Irish emigration to US is due to potato famine
1847	First Mormons enter the Great Salt Lake Valley
1848	Mexican War ends with Treaty of Guadalupe Hidalgo which annexes parts of Colorado, New Mexico, Arizona, Wyoming; and all of California, Nevada, and Utah
	US annexes Oregon Territory
1848-1850	California Gold Rush
1849	Minnesota Territory is organized
1850	*Scarlet Letter* is written by Nathaniel Hawthorne
	Kansas and Nebraska Territories are organized
	Utah Territory is organized
1851	*Moby Dick* is written by Herman Melville
1853	Oregon and Washington Territories are organized
	US purchases parts of Arizona and New Mexico
1854	Republican Party is formed
	Walden is published by Henry David Thoreau
1855-1857	Dred Scott case brought by a slave causes Missouri Compromise to be declared unconstitutional
1857-1866	An underground telegraphic cable is laid across the Atlantic Ocean
1859	John Brown is executed following his raid at Harper's Ferry
1860	Abraham Lincoln is elected 16th President
	Southern states begin to secede from the Union
1861	Confederate States of America is organized
	South declares war on the Union

	Colorado and Nevada Territories are organized
	Dakota Territory is organized
	Transcontinental telegraph is completed
1862	Capt. Nathaniel Gordon becomes last American pirate to be hanged
1863	Battle of Gettysburg is fought
	Emancipation Proclamation frees slaves in Confederate states
1864	Sherman's troops burn Atlanta
	Indiana and Montana Territories are organized
1865	Slavery is abolished
	Confederate States surrender
	The Civil War ends
	Klu Klux Klan is founded
	Lincoln is assassinated
	Chicago's Union Stockyard opens
1866	France withdraws from Mexico
1867	Typewriter is developed by Christopher Sholes
	US purchases Alaska from Russia
1868	Wyoming Territory is organized
1871	US attempts to open Korea for trade fail
	Custer is killed at the Battle of Little Big Horn
1873	US depression begins
1874	Barbed wire is developed
1877	Phonograph is invented by Thomas Edison
1878	First labor union (Knights of Labor) is organized
1879	Light bulb is patented by Thomas Edison
1880	Gold is discovered in Alaska
1882	US Congress bans Chinese immigration for 10 years
1888	George Eastman introduces first inexpensive, simple camera
1890	US overtakes Britain in steel production
	Oklahoma Territory is organized
1893	Last Hawaiian queen is deposed by US Naval forces and American investors
1894	Eugene Debs leads violent Pullman Strike in Chicago
1895	Marconi invents wireless telegraph
1896	Supreme Court establishes the "Separate but equal doctrine"
	Alaskan Gold Rush begins
1897	John Phillips Sousa writes "The Stars and Stripes Forever"
1898	Hawaii is annexed
1899	Guam, the Philippines and Puerto Rico are annexed
	US fights war against Spain
1900	Hawaii Territory is organized
	Quantum Theory is proposed
1901	Radio signals span Atlantic
1905	Albert Einstein publishes "theory of relativity"

1907	700 people are killed in the San Francisco Earthquake
	Theodore Roosevelt bars immigration of Japanese laborers
1909	First US radio broadcasts
1912	Progressive Party is formed in an attempt to make social reforms
1914	Panama Canal is opened
	World War I begins in Europe
1915	Alexander Graham Bell patents first telephone
1919	Wilson's League of Nations begins without US participation
1920	19th Amendment to the US Constitution gives women the right to vote
1925	Scopes trial pits creation vs. evolution
1929	US stock market crashes
1933	President Roosevelt introduces "New Deal" of social and economic reform
1935	Congress passes Social Security
1941	Japanese attack Pearl Harbor, Hawaii, launching US entrance in World War II
1944	US and Britain invade Normandy, France
1945	War in Europe ends
	Atomic Bomb is tested in New Mexico and dropped on Japan
1948-49	Berlin airlift takes place
1954	Case of Brown vs the Board of Education of Topeka results in Supreme Court ruling against segregation
1957	Little Rock schools are desegregated
1960	Civil Rights Act increases voting right of blacks
1963	President Kennedy is assassinated
1965	Martin Luther King marches on Selma, Alabama
1971	US currency is devaluated
1972	Equal Rights Amendment is proposed
1974	President Nixon resigns in scandal
1980	Volcano Mt. St. Helens in Washington State erupts
1981	First surgery on unborn baby is performed
1982	Oil prices drop due to oil surplus
1992	US troops land in Somalia in humanitarian effort
1995	Federal building in Oklahoma City is bombed resulting in more than 180 deaths

Topic Sources and Additional Reading

DOT History: Chronology. Department of Transportation. <isweb.tasc. dot.gov/ historian/chronology.htm> Printout dated 2 March 2000.

Hone, E. Wade. *Land & Property Research in the United States.* Salt Lake City: Ancestry, 1997.

How to Make a Timeline. <dohistory.com/on-your-own/toolkit/timeline. html> Film Study Center. Harvard University. Created 04 February 2000. Copyrighted 2000.

Iannuzzo, C.T. The Wars of Religion. <www.lepg.org/wars.htm> Society for Creative Anachronism. Created 1998.

Railroad Maps 1828-1900. <memory.loc.gov/ammem/gmdhtml/rrhtml/ rrhome.html> American Memory Collection. Geography and Map Division, Library of Congress. Created 19 October 1998.

Random House Timetables of History. New York: Random House, 1996.

Archives

Definition

Archives can be defined as the documents or records of a group, or as the repository in which those records are kept. An archives can be large or small. A listing of the types of repositories having genealogical material pertaining to Americans might include

- The National Archives and Records Administration, which includes
  NARA I, in Washington, D.C.
  NARA II, in College Park, Maryland
  National Records Centers
  Regional Archives, which service 4-5 states
  Presidential Libraries
- State Archives
- Religious Denomination Archives
- University Archives
- Foreign Archives, such as the Archives of Ontario

State Archives

State Archives, usually situated in the state capital, genealogists might find

- Court records
- Land records
- Land grants
- Loyalty oaths*
- Periodicals
- State and local governmental papers
- State militia records
- State conducted censuses
- Tax lists
- Vital statistics, such as birth, marriage and death records

*After the Civil War, President Andrew Johnson declared amnesty for southerners who were Union sympathizers, Blacks and "the common man" All they had to do was sign an oath of loyalty to the United States.

National Archives and Records Administration

The National Archives (NARA) contains millions of historical records pertaining to the United States from the Revolutionary War to the present. The NARA considers only two to five percent of those records generated by the Federal government of enduring enough value to be archived. The materials are housed in repositories in Washington, D.C., in College Park, Maryland and in Regional Archives.

Although the National Archives system is massive, there are aids to help a genealogist find the material needed. *The Guide to Federal Archives* is an indexed three volume set of books which can be found in many larger libraries. The inexpensive *National Archives Microfilm Resources for Research: A Comprehensive Catalog* is 136 page soft cover book is available through the National Archives Trust fund. Among the many helpful publications, the Trust Fund has a 304 page *Guide to Genealogical Research in the National Archives* which can be purchased in soft or hard cover.

In addition, the NARA offers genealogical workshops at the main archives and the thirteen regional centers. Private consultations are also available. There is also a microfilm rental program used by many genealogists who are unable to travel to Washington, D.C. or one of the Regional Archives. Basically, the three major areas in which information can be found are

- The National Archives Building (Archives 1) in Washington, D.C. has the Declaration of Independence, Constitution and Bill of Rights on display. Archives 1 houses material related to

Genealogy & local history	Federal Courts
Congress	Native Americans
Pre-World War II military	District of Columbia
New Deal	Census
Maritime records	Land entry files

- National Archives (Archives 2) in College Park, Maryland which houses material related to

Aerial photography	Foreign relations
Commerce	Labor
Fiscal policy	Classified records
Cartography	Architecture
Nixon presidential tapes	Kennedy assassination
Berlin	Motion and still pictures
World War II military	Electronic records

- The 12 National Regional Archives, covering 9 regions, are found in the following cities

Northeast Region	Boston
	New York
Mid-Atlantic	Philadelphia
Southeastern	Atlanta
Great Lakes	Chicago
Central Plains	Kansas City
Southwest	Fort Worth
Rocky Mountain	Denver
Pacific	Laguna Niguel
	San Francisco

Pacific Alaska   Seattle
                       Anchorage
These Regional Archives have records of those Federal
Government programs on the local or regional level, such as
Field offices of Federal Agencies
District, territorial and circuit courts
Regional Bureau of Indian Affairs
Bureau of Customs
Records unique to the region, such as the Tennessee Valley
Authority (TVA) in the Southeastern Region

Black Studies

The National Archives has records from the Customs Bureau, Southern Claims Commission, Military Adjutant General, Freedman's Bureau, Comptroller of Currency and Confederate Government which aid the genealogist searching for information about Black ancestors. They may be part of records of The General Accounting Office, the House of Representatives, the US Court of Claims, the Department of the Treasury or the Office of the Adjutant General

Of particular interest, the Southern Claims Commission was established to review claims of Southern Loyalists who aided the US Army and Navy during the Civil War. Proof of loss of property and of loyalty to the Federal government was required. A number of former slaves and free blacks filed claims and others were among the 220,000 witnesses who testified. Genealogical information can include

- Names
- Ages
- Place of residence
- Former owners
- Plantation conditions

Records of the Commissioners of Claims (Southern Claims Commission, 1871-1880 are available on Microfilm at NARA. Even disallowed claims are available. Summaries of those have been bound in four volumes.

The Freedmen's Bureau (more formally known as The Bureau of Refugees, Freedmen and Abandoned Lands) supervised and managed affairs involving refugees, freedmen and abandoned or seized lands during the Civil War. Most of the bureau's work was accomplished from mid 1865 and late 1868. Among its duties, the bureau

- Operated hospitals and refugee camps
- Helped establish schools
- Attempted to reunite families torn apart by slavery
- Obtained back pay and pensions for Black soldiers
- Legalized marriages of freemen

Most of the records are indexed and they include records entitled - Blacks Who Were Awarded the Congressional Medal of Honor

Deaths, Col'd Trps 1861-65
Desc. Col'd Volunteers 1864
Destitute in SC 1866
Field District Registers
Freedmens Bureau Bank
Records 1865-74
Laborers, Gulf & LA 1864-67
Letter, Colo'd Recruits 1863-68
Marriage Certificates 1861-69

Misc. Claims Files 1866-69
Morning Rep. Engineer Hospitals
(Slaves, AL & MSD) 1864-65
Pension Claims 1866-72
Reg. Free Neg. Enrolled VA
Reg. Of Col'd Officers 1863-65
Slave Manifests 1789-1808

Census

Census records are probably the genealogist's greatest source of information. They have been conducted every ten years since 1790. Censuses are taken geographically by state, county, township, town, neighborhood and, finally, road.

Unfortunately, Congress has passed privacy laws prohibiting access to census records for seventy-two years after being recorded. Before that date the information is closed to the public. So, the 1930 census will not be released until 2002, the 1940 in 2012 and the 1950 in 2022. But censuses at least seventy-two years old are open to the public for research.

Questions asked by the government varied from census to census, which is good and bad for the genealogist. It is bad because early censuses supply very little information. But beginning in 1850, the variety of questions asked every ten years progressively added more and more information. Then, beginning in 1880, the information became even more detailed.

All of the censuses have been indexed whether in book form by state, soundex or miracode. However, indexes, especially the ones in book form can be incorrect and/or incomplete.

Information Given in Census Years

Census Year	Information on the Census
1790	Residence; name of head of household; numbers of white males 16 years of age and up and males under 6; of free white females; of slaves; of other persons
1800 & 1810	Residence; name of head of household; numbers of free white males and females in the under 10, 10-16, 16-26, 26-45, 45+ age brackets; of slaves; of other persons

Census Year	Information on the Census
1820	Residence; name of head of household; numbers of white males and females in same age brackets as 1810; of foreign citizens; of male and female slaves and of free African-Americans in the under 14, 14-26, 26-45, 45+ age brackets; of other persons; of persons engaged in agriculture, manufacturing and commerce.
1830	Residence; name of head of household; numbers of white males and females in age groups of 5 or 10 years, ending with 100+ years of age; of slaves in 6 age groups; of "deaf & dumb" in three age groups; of blind; of foreign citizens
1840	Residence; name of head of household; numbers of free males and females in 1830 age brackets; of slaves or freed blacks in 6 age brackets; of "deaf and dumb"; of blind; of person employed in 7 classes of occupations; of children attending school; of whites over 20 years of age who were illiterate; of those considered insane or "idiotic" in public or private care; Revolutionary War or military pensioners
1850	Residence; names of all members of the household with their ages, sex, color (white, black, mulatto), occupation, value in real estate, place of birth. Also included were notations if they had married or attended school within the last year; if they were illiterate, "deaf and dumb", blind, insane or "idiotic; if they were a pauper or convict. Other schedules were written for slaves which gave age, sex, and color (black or mulatto). It was also noted if they were fugitive slaves, freed, "deaf and dumb" or "idiotic".
1860	Same as 1850 with the addition of value of personal property and number of slave houses. There are also supplemental schedules for slaves and persons who died during the year (mortality schedule).
1870	Same as 1860 with the addition of whether parents were foreign born, month of birth or marriage if the event took place during the previous year, number of males over the age of 21 and those denied the right to vote for some reason other than the rebellion. There is a supplemental mortality schedule for those who died during that year.
1880	Same as 1870 with the addition of citizenship information, street address, relationship to head of the household, place of birth of parents, and any disability. There is a supplemental mortality schedule.

Census Year	Information on the Census
1890	Same as 1880 for those that have survived. Most general schedules have been destroyed. Additional schedules of Civil War union soldiers and their widows have survived.
1900	Residence including street address; names of all members of the household with the ages, sex, color or race (white, black, Chinese, Japanese, Indian), month, year and place of birth, marital status, years married, number of children, number of living children, place of parents' birth, citizenship; year of immigration, years in US; occupation; number of months unemployed; ability to speak English; education; home and property ownership. There were separate censuses done for Indian reservations, military bases and institutions.
1910	Same as 1900 with the addition of language spoken by person and parents, school attendance, employment and Union or Confederate service.
1920	Residence with street address; names of all members of the household with the relationship to the head of the household; sex; race; age on January 1, 1920; marital status; foreign birth; year of immigration; year of naturalization; school attendance; literacy; birthplace of person and their parents; mother tongue if foreign born; ability to speak English; occupation; mortgaged or free home ownership.
1930	Residence with street address; names of all members of the household with relationship to head of household; sex; race; marital status; age at first marriage; home ownership or rent value; school attendance; literacy; birthplace of person and parents; language spoken in home; ability to speak English; occupation and class of worker; last regular working day; veteran status; tribal affiliation for full or part Indians.

Using the Census to Get the Most Out of It

Once you have your ancestor's name it is very easy to find information about them in the censuses.
- Begin with the most recent census and work back decade by decade.
- Locate siblings, even if they have married. Where they live and who they married can help.
- Search for others with the same surnames in the county.

- Photocopy or copy all information about everyone in the household. That boarder or even servant may end up marrying someone in the family or be a relative of some sort.
- Write down names of neighbors. They can be blood relations, in-laws or friendly families.
- Record roll numbers, census date, actual date, state, county, page number, enumeration district and line for each family.
- Compare all names, birth places, and ages of family members from census year to census year. Sometimes that is the only way to make sure it is the same family when errors find their way into records.

Problems with Using the Census

Although it is probably the most useful tool for a genealogist, the US census still had it's problems too.
- Names changed. Given names and surnames can be misspelled by the enumerator. A nickname might be given instead of the given name.
- Ages changed. The source giving the age can be misunderstood, or just plain wrong. The most knowledgeable member of the family was not always the one at home when the enumerator came to record the information. The questions could have been answered by a step-parent, older child or even neighbor. In order to determine the correct year of birth, sometimes it is necessary to go through a number of censuses.
- Mothers changed. Unfortunately, life expectancy, especially among women of childbearing age, was not very good. The wife/mother of the family could easily change between censuses.
- Indexes were often incorrect or incomplete. The reason might have been difficulty in reading handwriting or just sloppy work on the part of the indexer.
- There were no Federal Censuses before 1790. So the information from colonial days is not as complete.
- Early censuses gave little detail. This made it much more difficult to determine which family was the right one, especially if the surname was a common one.
- If a family was not at home when the census taker called, they could have been completely left out of that census.
- Poor quality of ink and poor handwriting makes deciphering the census takers longhand notations more difficult.
- Because of the nature of the census, it is much harder to find someone living in a large city than a small town.
- Most of the 1890 census is missing. Although a special Schedule of Union Veterans and Widows fills in a few of the blanks, even portions of it have been damaged.

- Census takers were not necessarily familiar with foreign accents, names and languages encountered unfamiliarity can cause distortions.
- As with today, given names were not always indications of sex. Add to that the unfamiliarity with foreign names and a female Freiderieke could be listed as a male named Frederick, Johanna could become Johann.
- Census enumerators could not request proof of age, naturalization or other information. So they could only record what was told to them.
- Land shifted from one country to another, particularly during and after wars. For instance, at time Alsace Lorraine was part of both France and Germany. People born in Latvia might or might not have been born in the Soviet Union. So individuals could have been confused as what to list as their parents and their own birthplaces.
- Service men were often missed completely or listed as residents of their duty posts.

Soundex

Soundex is an index developed by the Works Progress Administration (WPA) in the late 1930's in an attempt to group similar sounding surnames and surnames with various spellings together. For the genealogist, misspelled or mislead names might be found with the correct spelling. The names Smythe, Smithe, Smith, and Smit would be found under Soundex code S530, although alphabetically they would be separated. Likewise, the names Little, and Lidel would be found together.

In addition, all persons within a state with the same surname would be found together. Brothers who settled in neighboring counties would still be indexed under the same grouping.

In the Soundex, each surname is represented by a letter followed by three numbers. Under the Soundex system the letters A, E, I, O, H, W, and Y are not coded, but are used if they are the first letters of the surname.

Number	Letters
1	BPFV
2	CSKGJQXZ
3	DT
4	L
5	MN
6	R

The rules for coding a name is as follows -
- The first letter of the surname becomes the first and only letter in the code.
    "Davis" would begin with "D"
    "Adams" would begin with "A".
- The three numbers of the code are assigned to the remaining consonants in the surname, with the exception of H, W, and Y.
    -If there are not three following consonants, zeros are used to fill out the three numbers.

    | Cole | = | C400 |
    | Hook | = | H200 |
    | Joy | = | J000 |

    -If a name has more than three following consonants, only the first three are used in the code.

    | Jacobson | = | J212 |

    -When two or more consonants of equal chart value appear together, only the first consonant is used for the code.

    | Scout | = | S300 |
    | Little | = | L340 |

- Surnames with prefixes may be found coded with or without the prefix.
    "Van Dyke" might be coded under V532 or D200

Civilians in War

• British and American Claims - Civil War	1871-85
• British and American Alabama Claims - Civil War	no date
• French and American Claims - Civil War	1880-83
• Southern Claims (approved) - Civil War	1871-80
• Southern Claims (disallowed) - Civil War	no dates

Diplomatic Records

- Collection of Seized Foreign Records, such as
    1. Collection of Italian Military Records 1935-1943
    2. Records of Private Individuals - Captured German Records
    3. Records of the German Navy, 1850-1927
    4. Name Index of Jews Whose German Nationality Was Annulled by the Nazi Regime
- Records of the Russian American Company 1802-1867
- List of US Consular Officers 1789-1939

District of Columbia

- Records of the City of Georgetown (District of Columbia) 1800-1879
- Distribution of Columbia Building Permits 1877-1949
- Guardianship Papers 1802-1878
- Naturalization Records
- Wills 1801-1888

Federal Court Records

- Naturalization Records of the US District Courts
- Index Cards to Criminal Case Files of US District Courts
- Private Land Grant Cases in the Circuit Court
- Index Cards to Bankruptcy, Civil and Criminal Cases Files of US District Court
- Criminal Case Files of the US Circuit Court
- Records of the US District Court for the District of Columbia Relating to Slaves, 1851-1863
- Revolutionary War Prize Cases: Records of the Court of Appeal Cases of Capture, 1776-1787

Federal Bureau of Investigation

- Index to Federal Bureau of Investigation Class 61 - Treason or Misprision of Treason, 1921-1931
- Investigative Case Files of the Bureau of Investigation, 1908-1922

Federal Land Records

Records from the US General Land Office and the Bureau of Land Management are found in the Textual Reference Branch of the National Archives. There was no Federal land in the original thirteen states, Maine, Vermont, West Virginia, Kentucky, Tennessee, Texas and Hawaii.

Homestead records from between 1800-1908 are arranged by state and land office. Military bounty lands are indexed by war and person. They contain a great deal of useful genealogical information.

Immigrant Affairs

Immigrants to the United States must register. The National Archives has the Alien Registrations from 1812-1814. The Federal Government did not even require the keeping of ship passenger lists until 1820. Immigration and Naturalization Service lists include foreign visitors,

immigrants and returning US citizens. Information on them usually includes whether the
- passengers had been in the US before,
- final US destination,
- names of relatives already in the US, and,
- after 1903, race.

In order to narrow search years, ask
- Did the ancestor come as a child or as an adult?
- Was the ancestor married?
- When and where were the ancestor's children born?
- Did the ancestor arrive with some or all of his children?

Census records can play an important part in this. If, for instance, the 1900 census indicates that four year old Marie was born in Germany, but her 2 year old brother Anton was born in Illinois, and if the 1910 and 1920 censuses agree, then the date of immigration was between 1896 and 1898.

After immigrating, those aliens who decide to become citizens of the United States leave behind a series of naturalization papers. Nineteenth century records only include the declaration of intention which may have the exact date of immigration listed. Those Naturalization Petitions in the National Archives from 1906 forward give more detail and include
- Declaration of intention
- Petition for naturalization
- Certificate of naturalization
- Oath of allegiance

Naturalization records generally include

| full name | date of birth | citizenship, if |
| age | nationality | granted |

Aliens who joined the US military were able to by-pass some immigrant requirements for becoming citizens. Some of their records can be found in
- Index to Naturalization of World War I Soldier, 1918

Northern border records begin with 1895 and the southern border ones with 1908. More recent naturalization records (C-files) are retained by the Immigration and Naturalization Service (INS) and can be viewed through Freedom of Information Act procedures.

Military Records

A Listing of Categories

No matter what rank, all servicemen have records. However, as with census records, by law there is a 72 year privacy gap for most of the records. Also, some early records were destroyed by fires. In an attempt to recompile records, the War Department abstracted information from other existing records. However, they were unable to reconstruct every record.

Some, but not all, of the military records in the National Archives which might help the genealogist are listed below. A complete listing is available through the NARA.

- American Naval Personnel Who Served During the Revolutionary War
- Amnesty Papers 1865-67
- Applications for Headstones 1879-1964
- Appointments to the District of Columbia Police 1861-1930
- Army Register, Officers 1800-1897
- Army Appointments 1829-1895
- Births, Children of Soldiers 1884-1912
- Cadet Applications 1800-1867
- Cadet Muster Rolls 1818-1849
- Cadet Rolls 1870-1915
- Case Files of Approved Pension Applications of Widows and Other Dependants of Civil War and Later Navy Veterans ("Navy Widows" Certificates, 1861-1910)
- Certificate of Disability 1812-1899
- Civil War Pension Files 1861-1934*
- Coast Guard Muster Rolls 1833-1932
- Confederate Hospital Records 1861-1865
- Confederate Soldiers Who Died in Federal Prisons, Hosp.
- Confederate Casualties 1861-1865
- Confederate Compiled Service Records
- Death Register of Marine Enlisted Men 1838-1942
- Death, Volunteers 1861-1865
- Deaths, Regular army 1860-1868
- Deserters 1861-1865
- Discharges, Regular Army 1861-1868
- E Books (Deaths) 1860-c.1900
- Enlistment Papers 1798-1912
- General Index to Pension Files
- Indian Wars 1892-1926
- Marine Muster Rolls 1789-1945
- Merchant Seaman Crew Lists 1803-
- Mexican War Pensions
- Navy Enlistment Register 1845-1885
- Old War Index to Pensions 1783-1861
- Patients, SD Barracks 1883-1886
- Records of the United States Military Academy
- Register of Commissioned Officers 1799-1915
- Register of Enlistments 1789-184???
- Register of Naval Officers 1815-1821

- Registration of Deceased Soldiers 1848-1861
- Retired Soldiers 1915-1920
- Retired Marine Enlisted Men 1798-1901
- Revolutionary War Pension & Bounty Land
- Revolutionary War Rolls, 1775-1783
- Roll of Honor (see Military Burials)
- Soldiers Dying Overseas 1917-1922
- Soldiers' Home Burials 1861-1918
- Soldiers' Home Hospital 1872-1943
- Statements of Birthplace, Naval Officers
- Union Compiled Service Records
- Veterans Who Served Between 1861 and 1900 (index)

*Pensions for those who fought for the Confederacy were given pensions by their states. So requirements of residency, proof of service and disability varied by state. So while the National Archives has Confederate service records, pension records can usually be found in state archives. The exceptions are union soldiers who came from or later settled in Confederate States.

Civil War

Researchers can become confused by designations of soldiers when examining through Civil War records.
- Volunteers initially enlisted for 6 months or less because they thought it would be a short war. A volunteer soldier or officer should have a compiled military service record which might contain a physical description, birthplace, reasons for a leave, battles fought, hospital and brig stays.
- Drafted soldiers were designated as volunteers.
- Regular Army papers are kept alphabetically. However, enlistment papers for Regular Army were not kept until 1863. Confederate or Union officers may have served in the Regular Army prior to the war.
- State Militias were also called up when the draft went into effect in 1863. However, all militias did not go.

World War I Draft Cards

World War I draft cards were microfilmed by LDS. These cards were filled out by every man aged 18-40. Each man was required to register for the draft prior to the US entry into the war. Information contained included -

Full name   Current address   Employer

Deformities	Physical description	Citizenship
Age	Next of kin	Race
Occupation	Birth date	

Military Burials

On September 11, 1861, a US War Department General Order made commanding officers responsible for the burial of the dead. After the Civil War, the twenty-seven volume Roll of Honor was published listing the burial place of many Union soldiers. The *Index to the Roll of Honor* was compiled by William and Martha Reamy.

Military Pension Applications

The National Archives is the repository of federal pensions given for the

Revolutionary War	Indian Wars
"Old Wars" (1783-1861)	Mexican War
War of 1812	Civil War (not Confederate)

These indexed pension papers can include

wife's name	physical description of veteran
place & date of marriage	description of military service
children's names & dates	affidavits from neighbors &
of birth	relatives

In the National Archives, pension applications are filed by war, state, and then alphabetically by pension applicant. In order to find an applicant's papers,

- Find the name in the alphabetical index for the correct period. There are also indexes compiled of application files for remarried widows, navy widows, other dependents and for disapproved pension files.
- Go to the roll or fiche of pension applications noted in the index.
- Check ledgers and payment cards. Even "invalid" pension payments are listed.
- Find the final payment voucher, which is a record of payments made to heirs after the pensioner's death.

Native American Affairs

At first (1789), the Bureau of Indian Affairs was assigned to the War Department. It became a separate agency in 1824. But tribal census and other records list only Indians who were enrolled members of officially recognized tribes with which the federal government had direct dealings. Sometimes the regular federal census of the entire US population remains the better source.

Early records pertaining to Native Americans housed at the National Archives include

- Agency Employee Records
- Annuity Payrolls 1848-1890
- B-M-D (Vital) Records
- Eastern Cherokee Applications Court of Claims 1906-1909
- Enrollment Cards and Allotment Applications
- Federal Censuses from 1885 through1940, also
    1   the 1860 Arkansas Roll 52 covered Indians in Indian Territory and
    2   the 1870-1900 censuses include reservations found in individual states and territories
- Final Rolls - Five Civilized Tribes
- Headquarters of Ft. Gibson, Indian Territory, 1830-1857
- Heirship Records
- Indian Agency School Reports
- Indian Census Records of Recognized Tribes 1885-1940
- Indian Census Rolls 1884-1940
- Indian Prisoners 1861-1865
- Marriage Register
- Records of Indian Trading Posts
- Records of The Five Civilized Tribes - Cherokee, Choctaw, Chickasaw, Creek, and Seminole, including
    1. Enrollment cards
    2. Guion Miller Roll
        - Cherokees living in Georgia, North Carolina and Tennessee circa 1900
        - Copies of enrollments from 1850, 1851, 1884
    3. Henderson Roll
        - Cherokee census of 1835
    4. Davis Commission
        - A census of members of the five tribes residing in Oklahoma circa 1895-1914 were censussed. In addition to name, age, and sex; census cards show members of the same family. The index is broken down by tribe and then into categories of relationship; such as related to tribe by blood, by marriage, as a minor or as a Freedman.
- Register of Enlistments of Indian Scouts and Soldiers in the US Army 1798-1914
- Removal of Cherokees of Oklahoma, such as Service Records of Soldiers Involved in Movement
- Records of Cherokee Indian Agency in Tennessee, 1801-1835
- School records

The National Archives also has maps of the Indian Reservations indicating land allotments and names of allottees.

Pardon Applications

Without a pardon, a Southerner was not allowed to own land, practice a profession, or hold public office after the Civil War. So between 1863 and 1870, fifteen thousand Southerners submitted applications and supporting documents seeking amnesty, even though they had been omitted from President Andrew Johnson's general amnesty. These applications are held by the National Archives and a great deal of genealogical information can be found in them.

Passenger Lists

Copies of passengers lists for basically all ships landing in the United States between 1819 and 1945 are preserved by the National Archives. After 1819, ship's captains were required to submit passenger lists to the Collector or Customs in any port in the US or one of its territories. Through the years, the US Customs Service has been part of the Departments of Treasury, Commerce and Labor, and Justice.

Many of the records of the US Customs Service are indexed under the alphabetical listing of ports. Dates of arrival and the vessel's name are given. Some are Soundexed. Some are in quarterly reports. Crews are listed. Many include ages, nationalities and occupations of the passengers. Ports of entry are listed below. However, there are infrequent gaps within the dates given, especially among the older records.

Baltimore, Maryland	1820-1957
Boston, Massachusetts	1820-1944
Detroit, Michigan	1906-1957
Galveston and its subports, Texas	1896-1951
Gloucester, Massachusetts	1918-1943
Gulfport and Pascagoula, Mississippi	1903-1935
Key West, Florida	1898-1945
New Bedford, Massachusetts	1902-1943
New Orleans, Louisiana	1820-1952
New York, New York	1789-1957
Philadelphia, Pennsylvania	1800-1945
Portland, Maine	1893-1954
Providence, Rhode Island	1911-1954
San Francisco, California	1882-1957
Savannah, Georgia	1906-1945
Seattle and neighboring ports, Washington	1882-1957
St. Albans, Vermont	1895-1954

In addition to port of arrival, examine several possible points of departure. Do not assume a point of departure. Dutch, Belgians and Germans may have left from Rotterdam, Antwerp, Hamburg, Bremen or even Le Havre. And many Russians and Scandinavians actually departed Europe from Britain.

Passport Applications

Since the Secretary of War was responsible for the Indians prior to 1824, the issuance of passports into their territory also fell within the War Department's jurisdiction. Those early passport applications were almost as full of potential genealogical information as the passports processed today. One early passport read

"Thomas Crittondon, Jeremiah Day & John Austin with their families consisting of twenty-two persons on Board a flat bottomed Boat, have permission to descend the River Tennessee & other waters lying in their way to Natchez..."

Among the passport papers and related documents in the National Archives are

- Passport Applications 1791-1925
- Emergency Passport Applications 1877-1905
- Notices to Citizens Abroad 1790-1940
- Register of US Citizens Abroad

Territorial Records

- General Correspondence of the Alaskan Territorial Governor 1909-1938
- State Department Territorial Papers
  Arizona 1864-72
  Colorado 1859-74
  Dakota 1861-73
  Florida 1777-1824
  Idaho 1863-72
  Kansas 1854-61
  Missouri 1812-20
  Montana 1864-72
  Nebraska 1854-67
  Nevada 1861-64
  New Mexico 1851-72
  Oregon 1848-58
  Orleans 1764-1813
  Northwest of the River Ohio 1787-1801
  Southwest of the River Ohio 1790-95
  Utah 1853-73

Washington 1854-72
Wyoming 1868-73
- Territorial Papers of the United States
  Iowa 1838-46
  Minnesota 1849-58
  Oregon 1848-59
  Wisconsin (Supplement) 1836-48
- Wisconsin Territorial Censuses of 1836, 1838, 1842, 1846, 1847

Topic Sources and Additional Reading

Allen, Desmond Walls "Confederate Pensions Held by the States" *Unlock Your Heritage... With Creative Problem Solving: Conference Syllabus.* The Federation of Genealogical Societies & The Dallas Genealogical Society 3-6 September 1997 p 427-430. Richardson, Texas: The Federation, 1997.

Collier, Leslie Smith "The US Census - Your New Best Friend" *Unlock Your Heritage... With Creative Problem Solving: Conference Syllabus.* The Federation of Genealogical Societies & The Dallas Genealogical Society 3-6 September 1997. p 105-108. Richardson, Texas: The Federation, 1997.

Digital Archive in Norway. <www.hist.uib.no/arkivverket/index_en.htm> Online. University of Bergen. Printout dated 09 December 1999.

Fitzhugh, Terrich V.H. *The Dictionary of Genealogy.* London: A&C Black, 1994.

Hey, David, ed. *The Oxford Companion to Local and Family History.* New York: Oxford University Press, 1996.

Ireland, Everett B. "Research in the Nation's Capital: Beyond the Beltway." *Unlock Your Heritage... With Creative Problem Solving: Conference Syllabus* The Federation of Genealogical Societies & The Dallas Genealogical Society 3-6 September 1997. p72-75. Richardson, Texas: The Federation, 1997.

Jacobson, Judy. *Genealogist's Refresher Course.* 2nd ed. Baltimore, Maryland: Clearfield Company, 1996.

Mills, Elizabeth Shown "Finding Birth, Marriage, and Death Records in the National Archives" *Unlock Your Heritage... With Creative Problem Solving: Conference Syllabus.* The Federation of Genealogical Societies & The

Dallas Genealogical Society 3-6 September 1997 p 331-334. Richardson, Texas: The Federation, 1997.

Mills, Elizabeth Shown. "How to Understand the Ethnic Terminology of Old Louisiana". *The Genealogical Helper.* Everton Publishing. (September-October, 1978). p.13-14.

National Archives and Records Administration Homepage. <www.nara.gov> National Archives and Records Administration. Printout dated 22 June 2000.

National Archives of Canada Homepage. <www.archives.ca> National Archives of Canada. Printout dated 22 June 2000.

Scott, Craig Roberts "Pension Records Research: You Stopped Too Soon" *Unlock Your Heritage... With Creative Problem Solving: Conference Syllabus.* The Federation of Genealogical Societies & The Dallas Genealogical Society 3-6 September 1997 p. 115-118. Richardson, Texas: The Federation, 1997.

United Kingdom's Public Record Office Home Page. <www.pro.gov.uk> Public Record Office. Printout dated 22 June 2000.

United States. National Archives and Records Administration. Microfilm Resources for Research: A Comprehensive Catalog. Washington, DC: National Archives Trust Fund Board, Revised 1996.

United States. National Archives and Records Administration. Immigrant and Passenger Arrivals. Washington, DC: National Archives Trust Fund Board, 1983. Rev. 1991.

Research in Washington, D. C.

The Basics of Getting Around

If you are going to Washington, D.C. to do genealogy research, there are several things you should know about the city before making the trip.

- Hotel and car rental rates are cheaper on the weekend.
- Hotels and motels are cheaper in the suburbs, but much less convenient.
- Many government buildings close on the Saturday, Sunday and Monday of three day government weekends. Washington, D.C. is crowded and more expensive during inaugurations and when the cherry trees are in bloom. The DAR closes completely for the week of their national convention. So plan trips around special events.
- Most federal government buildings have cafeterias or snack bars so lunch breaks can be brief, especially if taken before 11:45 a.m. or after 12:45 p.m.
- The Metro system of buses and the subway are inexpensive, clean and safe. The subway even makes stops at the airport and the train station. At each subway stop, debit cards (passes) can be purchased to save time.
- Taxi cabs have flat rate charges from the airports to each area of the city. Drivers can quote you the price of going to your hotel before you get into the cab at the airport.
- Taxi cabs raise their rates during rush hour. That's also the hardest time to find an empty cab and the busiest time for the Metro.
- Washington, D.C. was organized around a simple plan, making it easy to find your way around the city. It was divided into four quarters (NE, SE, NW, and SW). East-West streets are given letter names (such as, A, B, C Streets). North-South streets have numerical names (such as, 1st, 2nd, 3rd Streets). Large thoroughfares running diagonally across the city are named after states (such as, Florida, Pennsylvania and Connecticut Avenues).
- Maps showing most public buildings and Metro stops are usually available at area hotels.

Before Going to Washington, D. C.

- Make reservations ahead of time.
- Go to the internet web pages for facilities you intend to use.
  1. Search available card catalogues. The Library of Congress has put theirs on the internet.
  2. Find out days and hours facilities are open. Some are even open evenings and Sundays.
  3. Find out the address and directions to the facility.

- Plan your days in advance. But always leave at least ½ a day at the end of your trip to go back to one of the facilities. Sometimes you find you did not have quite enough time at one stop. Or perhaps you discover after visiting the Library of Congress that you should have searched for someone at the National Archives when you were there,
- Know what you want and where to find it.
- Look at the following books in your local library and copy names of books and call numbers that might be helpful. Possible sources include
    - *Genealogies in the Library of Congress*
    - *National Union Catalog*
    - *Periodical Source Index*
- Soundex all names you are going to be researching.
- Organize, organize, organize.

Once You Get There

- Get a Metro pass. It saves time and money.
- Arrive at the facility as early in the day as possible, or after 4 P.M. when the tourists have gone for the day.
- Get your researcher's cards (National Archives, Maryland State Archives and Library of Congress all require one).
- Pay your fees (DAR library).

Genealogical Sources in Washington, D. C.

In addition to the commonly thought of genealogical sources, Washington and its outlying areas have an abundance of often forgotten research sites. Sites in the district include -
- Afro-American Historical & Genealogical Society
- Catholic University of America Department of Archives, Manuscripts and Museum Collections
- Columbia Historical Society
- District of Columbia Genealogical Society
- District of Columbia Office of Public Records
- District of Columbia Public Library
- Episcopal Church Historian - Washington Cathedral
- Genealogical Speakers Guild
- Georgetown University Library Special Collections
- George Washington University Special Collections
- Immigration and Naturalization Office
- Library of Congress*
    - -American Folk Life Center
    - -Genealogy Reading Room
    - -Local History & Genealogy

- Moorland-Springarn Research Center at Howard University
- National Archives*
- National Register of Historic Places
- National Society, Children of the American Colonists
- National Society of the Daughters of the American Revolution Library*
- Naval Historical Center
- Smithsonian Institution Libraries, Special Collections
- United States Holocaust Memorial Museum Archives and Oral History Department and Archives

*Major resources

Genealogical Sources Near Washington, D.C. And Their Locations

Bureau of Land Management	Springfield, Virginia
College of William and Mary	Williamsburg, Virginia
Enoch Pratt Free Library	Baltimore, Maryland
George Peabody Library	Baltimore, Maryland
Maryland Historical Society	Baltimore, Maryland
Maryland State Archives	Annapolis, Maryland
National Archives II	College Park, Maryland
National Genealogical Society	Arlington, Virginia
Society of Mayflower Descendants	Reston, Virginia
Virginia Historical Society	Richmond, Virginia
Virginia State Library	Richmond, Virginia
Washington, D.C. Temple - Family History Center	Kensington, Maryland

Topic Sources and Additional Reading

Archives and Manuscript Repositories in the District of Columbia. <www.loc.gov/coll/nucmc/dcsites.html>. Library of Congress <lcweb@loc.gov> Updated 12 August 1998 .

Ireland, Everett B. "Research in the Nation's Capital: Beyond the Beltway". *Unlock Your Heritage... With Creative Problem Solving: Conference Syllabus* The Federation of Genealogical Societies & The Dallas Genealogical Society 3-6 September 1997. p72-75. Richardson, Texas: The Federation, 1997.

FHC Overview: Family History Center: Washington D.C. Temple: The Church of Jesus Christ of Latter-day Saints. site prepared by T. Giammo, Christine Enterprises. <www.access.digex.net/~giammot/FHC/> Last modified October 29, 1998.

Researching Genealogy on the Internet

Internet Address Ingredients

There are two types of internet addresses. One type is for e-mail. An e-mail address includes four components -
* the internet name of the person whose address it is,
* @, meaning "at,"
* the addressee's network provider, and
* the domain extension (URL).

So it might read with the following parts,

<user id @ network provider.url>

The other type of address is for a web page. A web page address has several of the same components as e-mail. It may begin with "www" signifying the World Wide Web is the host server. That will be followed by a two-part domain name, which identifies the internet server sites, and has been separated by a dot. The second part of the domain name will be one of the extensions (URL's) listed below.

.net	network service provider	.edu	educational
.gov	governmental	.com	commercial
.org	non-profit society/organization	.mil	military

So the primary web site address would be set out similar to

<host server. second level domain.url>

Sites can be divided into pages and an address can reflect the page of the site. For instance, "/~jacob" or "/~maillist" indicate personal web pages addressed with the page owner's name.

Another component is an identification of the site's country of origin. Even Antarctica has a two-letter domain for country (.aq). Domains for other countries can be found a <domainnotes.com>, a resource for domain names, notes and news. Some of the more commonly used include -

Australia	.au	Poland	.pl
Canada	.ca	Russian Federation	.ru
China	.cn	Spain	.es
Cuba	.cu	Switzerland	.ch
France	.fr	Turkey	.tr
Germany	.de	Uganda	.ug
Haiti	.ht	United Kingdom	.uk
Ireland	.ie	United States	.us
Japan	.jp	Vatican	.va
Mexico	.mx	Vietnam	.vn

Internet Sources

Since its beginnings, the internet has exploded. But with no concrete research standards and with the easy availability and access by both expert or charlatan, reliability should not be assumed. Since there is little citation and virtually no responsibility for accuracy on the internet, internet sources should be considered like published sources - to be used solely as a guide to the original or primary source.

On the bright side, sites like Fraudulent Lineages, the National Genealogical Societies Consumer Protection Committee and GenScams report on the most flagrant offenders. The Genealogy Hall of Shame at <blacksheep.rootsweb.com/shame> is known for its Red Flag alerts while the Federal Computer Investigations Committee investigates Internet crime. Yet with so many sites on the world wide web, policing every site is virtually impossible.

In addition, internet sites disappear - what was available today might be gone tomorrow. Although sites below were chosen for their long-lasting potential, that does not guarantee these sites will continue in the future. It also does not mean that they are the only good sites.

Types of Sites

Search Engines

Most search engines look for relevant sites by using either keywords or subjects. Some more frequently used which are not solely for members of specific internet providers, such as America On Line's <aolsearch.aol.com>, include -

Alta Vista	Magellan
Excite	MSN
Go Network	Northern Light
Google	Thunderstone
Hotbot	WebCrawler
Lycos	Yahoo

Multi-engine search sites simultaneously use many search engines, including those above, to give the largest number of matches in just a few moments. Although mega-searches sometimes look in lesser utilized databases, they are far more likely to use sites with many links. They are also more likely to use US and commercial sites.

Dogpile	www.dogpile.com
European Search Engine	www.euroseek.net
Ixquick	www.ixquick.com
MetaCrawler	www.metacrawler.com
Search Engines Worldwide	www.twics.com/~takakuwa/search/search.html
Search the Net	www.searchthe.net

279

Gateways to Genealogy

Gateways are lists of sites dedicated to a specific topic. Each listed site is automatically linked with that site. A double click of the mouse on the highlighted link should take the browser directly to the site. Unfortunately, internet sites simply disappear, so gateways or portals frequently list sites which no longer exist.

Despite its innocuous name, *Cyndi's List of Genealogy Sites* is probably the best genealogy gateway on the internet.

Ancestry Search	www.ancestry.com/main.htm
A Barrel of Genealogy Links	cpcug.org/user/jlacombe/mark.html
Cyndi's List of Genealogy Sites	www.cyndislist.com
Family History.Com	www.familyhistory.com
Family Tree Maker	www.familytreemaker.com
Genealogy Today	www.tic.com/gen.html
RootsWeb	Www.genealogy.com
Ultimate Family Tree	www.uftree.com
US Gen Web	www.usgenweb.org

Genealogical Publications on the Internet

Publications can include books, magazines or newsletters. And many of today's newsletters are being sent through e-mail.

Amazon.com Reference and Genealogy Books	www.amazon.com
Ancestry	www.ancestry.com
Canada's Family History News	www.eparrs.com/FHN
Clearfield Company	www.genealogical.com
Everton Publishing Co.	www.everton.com
Family Chronicle Magazine	www.familychronicle.com
Family Tree Maker	www.familytreemaker.com
Genealogy Today	www.genealogytoday.com
Heritage Quest	www.heritagequest.com
Higginson Book Company	www.higginsonbooks.com
Genealogical Publishing Co.	www.genealogical.com
International Internet Genealogical Society Newsletter	iigs.org/newsletter
Journal of Online Genealogy	www.onlinegenealogy.com
Mountain Press	www.mountainpress.com
Picton Press	www.pictonpress.com

Genealogical Societies

Most societies concern themselves with location or ethnic origins, such as The American Historical Society of Germans from Russia

<www.ahsgr.org> and The African-American Historical and Genealogical Society <www.rootsweb.com/~mdaahgs>. But there are also family associations. Fraternal groups, such as the Knights of Columbus <www.KofC.org> and lineage societies, such as the Associated Daughters of Early American Witches <www.adeaw.org> and the International Black Sheep Society of Genealogists homepages.rootsweb.com/~blksheep which can be good genealogy resources.

Federation of Family History Societies	www.ffhs.org.uk
Federation of Genealogical Societies	www.fgs.org
International Association of Jewish Genealogical Societies	www.jewishgen.org
National Genealogical Society	www.ngsgenealogy.org
National Society of The Daughters of the American Revolution	www.dar.org
New England Historic Genealogical Society	www.nehgs.org

Genealogical Supplies

Everton's Charts	www.everton.com/shopper/
Genealogy Software Springboard	www.gensoftsb.com
Genealogy Tools and Forms	www.genealogy.about.com/hobbies/ genealogy
Index of Forms	inman.surnameweb.org/form

Miscellaneous Genealogical Sites

AmeriSpeak	www.rootsweb.com/~genepool/ amerispeak.htm
Ancestry	Ancestry.com
Association of Professional Genealogists	www.apgen.org
Board of Certification for Genealogists	www.bcgcertification.org
Canadian GenWeb	www.rootsweb.com/~canwgw
Ellis Island Online	www.ellisislandrecords.org
GEDCOM Files	www.gedcoms.com
Immigrant Ships Transcribers Guild	istg.rootsweb.com
LDS Family History Centers	FamilySearch.org
Lineages Genealogy Query Page	www.lineages.com/queries/queries

Message Boards, Newsletter,Site Finder	www.genealogy.com
My Virtual Reference Desk - Genealogy	www.refdesk.com/factgene.html
Random Acts of Genealogical Kindness	www.raogk.com/before
ROOTS-L Genealogical Email Listings	www.rootsweb.com/~maillist
Rootsweb Homepage	www.rootsweb.com
Top Ten Genealogy Web Sites	www.familychronicle.com/webpicks .htm
Worldwide GenWeb	worldgenweb.org

Collections or Encyclopedic-Type Sources

American Life Histories, Federal	memory.loc.gov/ammem/wpaintro/ wpahome.html
Writer's Project 1936-1940	wpahome.html
"American Memory Collection"	memory.loc.gov
Infoplease Encyclopedia	www.infoplease.com
Kansas Collection	kuhttp.cc.ukans.edu/carrie/kancoll
Linkopedia	www.linkopedia.com
Making of America	moa.umdl.umich.edu
Repositories of Primary Sources	www.uidaho.edu/special- collections/Other.Repositories.html

Translation Sites

Alta Vista Translation Service	babelfish.altavista.com/translate. dyn?
Foreign Language Dictionaries	www.cis.hut.fi/~peura/dictionaries. html
Free Translation Tools	www.foreignworld.com
Immediate Translation	www.babelfish.com
Language Dictionaries and Translations	www.word2word.com/dictionary.html
Travlang's Translating Dictionary	dictionaries.travlang.com

Dictionaries

Dictionary	www.yourdictionary.com
Dictionaries, Etc.	www.cis.hut.fi/peura/dictionaries. html
Merriam-Webster Online	www.m-w.com
One Look Dictionary	www.onelook.com

General Information Sites

American Historical Society	www.theaha.org
Calculators On-Line Center	www-sci.lib.uci.edu/HSG/Ref Calculators2. html
Canada's National History Society	www.historysociety.ca
Copyright	lcweb.loc.gov/copyright
Electric Library	www.elibrary.com
FedWorld Information Network	www.fedworld.gov
History Place	historyplace.com
Info Services	info-s.com
Internet Public Library	www.ipl.org
Internet Public Library Reference Center	ipl.sils.umich.edu
LibDex	www.libdex.com
National Adoption Information Clearinghouse	www.calib.com/naic
Newspaper Association of America	www.naa.org/
Public Record	www.knowx.com
Research-It	www.iTools.com/research-it
US Geological Survey Geographic Resources with Geographic Names Information Services	mapping.usgs.gov
WhoWhere?	www.whowhere.com

All About the Internet

The Internet Society was formed in 1996 to help solve Internet issues and judge how to deal with its rapid growth. But sometimes all that is needed by the researcher is the availability of a few good sites.

Discussion and Information Lists	tile.net/lists/
Guide to Citing Electronic Sources	library.lib.binghamton.edu/search/citing. html
Library of Congress WWW Style Guide	www.loc.gov/loc/webstyle
Liszt for mailing lists	www.liszt.com
Search Engine Watch	www.searchenginewatch.com
Web Searching, Sleuthing...	www.thelearningsite.net/cyberlibrarian/ searching/ ismain.html
Yahoo: Beginner's Guide	dir.yahoo.com/Computers_and_Internet/Internet/

Harris, Robert. Evaluating Internet Research Sources. Vanguard University <www.sccu.edu/faculty/R_Harris/evalu8it.htm> Dated 1997.

Howells, Cyndi. Netting Your Ancestors: Genealogical Research on the Internet. Baltimore: Genealogical Publishing Company, 1997.

Howells, Mark. Standards for Technology in Genealogy. Version of article from March/April 1998 Ancestry Magazine. <www.oz.net/ ~markho/writing/ standard.htm> Printout dated 24 May 2000.

Kansas City Public Library. Introduction to Search Engines. <www. kcpl.lib. mo. us/ search/srchengines.htm> Printout dated 15 March 2000. Used 25 May 2000.

Kemp, Thomas Jay. Virtual Roots: A Guide to Genealogy and Local History on the World Wide Web. Wilmington, Delaware: Scholarly Resources, 1997.

Lamb, Terri Stephens. *Sams Teach Yourself E-Genealogy Today: Finding Your Family Roots Online.* Indianapolis: Sams Publishing, 1999.

Lawrence, Steve and Lee Files. "Accessibility and Distributor of Information on the Web" Reprint from *Nature.* Vol. 400 pp. 107-109. 1999. <www.wwwmetrics.com> Used 25 May 2000.

Renick, Barbara and Richard S. Wilson. *The Internet For Genealogists: A Beginner's Guide.* LaHabra, California: Compulogy, 1998.

Terms and Definitions: Basic Internet Terms for Newbies. <www.jworkman.com> Created by Julie Workman 25 May 2000.

Vander Hook, Sue. *Internet.* Mankato, Minnesota: Smart Apple Media, 2000.

Miscellaneous Sources and Additional Reading

Ancestors West, SSBCGS. South Bend, Indiana Area Genealogical Society, Vol. 20 No. 1; Feb 1993.

Christoph, Peter R. et al, editors. *New York Historical Manuscripts: Dutch: Translated by Dingman Versteeg.* Baltimore: Genealogical Publishing Company, 1976.

Flores, Norma P. and Patsy Ludwig. A Beginner's Guide to Hispanic Genealogy. San Mateo, California: Western Book / Journal Press, 1993.

Kirkham, E. Kay. *Research in American Genealogy: A Practical Approach to Genealogical Research.* Washington, D.C.: 5th Institute of Genealogical Research, 1954.

Reader's Digest Book of Facts. Pleasantville, New York: Reader's Digest Association, 1987.

Szuchs, Loretto Dennis, et. al, ed. The Source: A Guidebook of American Genealogy. Salt Lake City: Ancestry, 1996.

Wallenchinsky, David and Irving Wallace. *Peoples Almanac 3.* New York: Bantam Books, 1982.

Wallenchinsky, David, Irving Wallace and Amy Wallace. *The People's Almanac Presents The Book of Lists.* New York: William Morrow and Company, 1977.

Wallenchinsky, David and Irving Wallace. *Peoples Almanac 2.* New York: William Morrow and Company, 1978.

Index

A

ab napos, 21
ab nepos, 7
ab neptis, 7, 21
abatement, 154
abbreviations, 28-42, 50, 65
abepsia, 113
abettor, 154
abeyance, 145
abode, 66, 145
abridge, 29
abstract, 29, 87, 136, 137
Acadians, 233, 234
accelerated, 7
accents, 62, 263
accipitrary, 207
accomptant, 207
accoucheur, 207
accoucheuse, 207
account, 2, 17-19, 29, 86, 179, 204
Account books, 2, 204
accouter, 207
Accredited Genealogist, 30
achievements, 2, 83, 84
ackerman, 208
acre, 29, 66, 83, 145, 151, 152, 183-185, 188, 237
actuary, 208
Addison's Disease, 113
address, ix, 1, 2, 84, 86, 87, 91, 94, 251, 260, 261, 268, 275, 278
address books, 2
administrator, 30
adoption, 2, 29, 44, 55, 57, 61 154, 191, 283
adultery, 62
advertisements, 83, 84
advocate, 36, 155, 163, 208
adz, 25
aelaet, 7
aeronaut, 208

affeeror, 208
affidavit, 30, 155
Afghanistan, 133
Africa, 86, 125, 133, 177
African, 32, 130, 204, 233, 242, 260, 281
African-American, 204, 242, 281
Afrigeneas, 242
AG, 30
age, 7, 10, 16, 20, 29, 30, 65, 81, 82, 84, 87, 92, 102, 103, 139, 142, 143, 152, 169, 177, 178, 193-196, 259-263, 266, 269, 270
agencies, 86, 87, 258
agister, 208
aglutition, 113
agricultor, 208
agricultural schedule, 7
ague, 113, 120
ahnenlist, 7
ahnentafel, 7
Alabama, 69, 79, 113, 240, 248, 251, 254, 264
Alaska, 128, 187, 238, 242, 246, 249-251, 253, 258
Albania, 237
alblastere, 208
albumen, 92, 94
albums, 2, 3, 96, 204
alchemist, 208
Alexander the Great, 234
alias, 7, 10, 12, 30, 61, 155
aliquot parts, 145
almoner, 208
almshouse, 156
alnager, 208
Alsace Lorraine, 263
amanuensis, 208
ambrotype, 92, 94
American Antiquarian Society Proceedings, 29

American history, 72
American Legion, 30, 175
American Plague, 113
American Revolution, 15, 20, 21,
    31, 33, 74, 132, 197,
    235, 277, 281
American Society of
    Genealogists, 30
American War of Independence,
    19
Amish, 233, 234, 236
amnesty, 256, 267, 271
Anabaptists, 233
ananuensis, 208
anasarca, 113
ancestor, xiii, 1, 7, 12, 18, 21,
    22, 30
ancestor card, 75
ancestor chart, 7
ancestor file, 7
ancestry, 13, 45, 46, 54, 61, 78,
    139, 152, 234, 239,
    241, 242, 254, 280,
    281, 284, 285
anchorite, 208
ancient history, 70
andirons, 27
anemia, 116, 118
Anglican, 173
Anglo Saxon, 7, 191
anilepman, 208
animal qualities, 54
animals, 57, 148, 216, 219, 221,
    231
anniversary, 2, 83
Anno Regni, 30
announcements, 3-5, 17, 81, 87,
    156
annum, 18
anonymous, 30
anthropomorphic, 178
Antiquarian Society
    Proceedings, 29
antiquities, 30, 73
Apache, 130, 238
APG, 30

apiarian, 208
apoplexy, 114, 123
apothecary, 208
Appalachian Mountains, 185
appendix, 30
application, 4, 5, 63, 149, 269
appointment books, 2
appraisal, 145
apprentice, 2, 5, 30, 83, 84, 209,
    216
appurtenances, 25, 156
Arabic, 59-61
Archbishop, 29
archiator, 209
archives, viii, xi, 6, 8, 15, 16, 32,
    34, 38, 44, 75, 77,
    87, 139, 238, 256-
    274, 276, 277
archivists, 6, 8
aristocratic, 64
Aristotle, 91
Arkansas, 70, 79, 85, 168, 205,
    249, 252, 270
Armenian, 59
armiger, 8, 209
armoire, 25
armorer, 209
armory, 8
armourer, 209
arms, 8, 9, 11-13, 26, 31, 32, 64,
    108, 175, 180
army, 19, 33, 35, 130, 131, 210,
    212, 258, 267, 268,
    270
arpent, 183, 184, 187
arrest, 83, 136, 156, 165
arshin, 187
artificer, 209
artillery, 30, 34
artisan, 209
ascendant, 8
ASG, 30
assayer, 209
assessor, 30, 208
associated families, 7
association, 4, 30, 85, 87, 168,

273, 281
Black Death, 114
Black Dutch, 233, 239, 243
Black Fever, 114
Black Hawk War, 130
Black Irish, 239
Black Jaundice, 114, 125
black sheep, 138, 281
Blackwater Fever, 114
BLM, 31, 145, 152, 153
blood poisoning, 114, 122, 123
bloomers, 103, 109
Blue Laws, 157
blunderbuss, 25
BLW, 31
Board of Certified
    Genealogists, 31
boarder, 31, 262
bodeys, 211
Boer War, 133
Bohemia, 236
bona fide, 157
bonded, 19, 211
bondsman, 31, 157
books, iv, 2, 3, 14, 18, 31, 44,
    45, 72-80, 86, 89,
    90, 93, 111, 135,
    138, 153, 168, 172,
    182, 191, 204, 257,
    267, 276, 280, 285
born, vii, 12, 21, 24, 29, 31, 44,
    48, 54, 66, 82, 149,
    156, 160, 164, 165,
    169, 175-177, 193,
    194, 234, 250, 260,
    261, 263, 266
borough, 66, 157, 212
Boston Massacre, 130, 250
bound, 31, 137, 138, 157, 162,
    209, 258
boundaries, 6
boundary, 144, 154, 184, 242
boundary lines, 144
bounty, vi, 3, 31, 136, 141, 145,
    146, 148, 151, 265,
    268

bounty land, vi, 31, 141, 146,
    148, 151, 265, 268
Bounty Land Warrant, 31, 146
bounty warrants, 136
bowl, 28
box, 27
Boxer Rebellion, 133
brachygrapher, 212
braids, 100, 108
brass, 28, 202, 212, 239
Brass Ankles, 239
breakfront, 25
Brelorussian, 58
Brethren, 84, 234, 235
bride, 10, 39
Bright's disease, 115
Britain, 35, 131, 133, 191, 192,
    197, 198, 200, 233,
    251, 253, 254, 272
British, vii, 7, 18, 20, 31, 45, 65,
    78, 89, 130-133,
    170, 181, 184, 185,
    197, 200-203, 233,
    235, 236, 249-251,
    264
broadsides, 8, 218
broiler, 25
bronchitis, 115
Bronze John, 115
Brown Period, 96
Bruderhofs, 234, 235
Bubonic Plague, 114, 121, 127
Buckheads, 239
buckles, 97, 102, 104, 110
Bulgarian, 60
bulletins, 3
Bureau of Engraving and
    Printing, 199
Bureau of Indian Affairs, 31, 237,
    238, 258, 269
Bureau of Land Management,
    31, 145, 152, 153,
    265, 277
burial, 1, 10, 14, 19, 31, 43, 82,
    85, 173-175, 178-
    181, 227, 269

burial ground, 178
business, 3, 5, 11, 12, 18, 65,
83, 84, 137, 155,
157, 158, 207, 208,
217, 236
business license, 3, 5, 137
Buster Brown, 103

C

c., ix, 31, 32, 36, 37, 39, 40, 76,
92, 127, 175, 177,
190, 192, 200, 201,
238, 243, 251,
255-257, 267,
275-277, 285
ca., 31
caballero, 63
cabinet, 25, 92
cabinet card, 92
cadastral, 146
Cajuns, 234, 240
calamities, v, 113, 205
calendar, 10, 17, 31, 39, 160,
190-196, 250
calender, 213
California, 70, 90, 112, 128, 129,
176, 178, 186, 203-
206, 233, 247, 249,
252, 271, 284, 285
call slips, 76, 77
calotype, 92, 93
CALS, 31
camera, 91, 92, 111, 253
camera obscura, 91
Canada, 71, 78, 132, 133, 187,
201, 235, 236, 238,
243, 246, 247, 250,
274, 278
candle, 26, 28, 213, 227, 228
candlestick, 27, 28
canopy, 27, 228
carbine, 26
card, viii, 3, 8, 15, 75, 92, 94,
204, 213, 265, 268-
270, 275, 276
card backgrounds, 93

card borders, 93
card colors, 92
card corners, 93
card edges, 93
card size, 93
card stock, 92, 94, 95
carelessness, 63
Carmel Indians, 239
Carnival Period, 96
carriage, 26, 28, 217, 218, 223
carte de visite, 92, 94
cascading pedigree chart, 8
Cash Entry Act of 1820, 151
castle, 57, 66
casts, 83
catacomb, 179
catafalque, 179
catalog, 35, 37, 39, 72, 74, 84,
87, 257, 274, 276
cataloging systems, iv, 72
catarrh, 115, 118
Catholic, 40, 81, 131, 190, 191,
234, 276
Catholic League, 131
Caucasian, 15, 16, 240, 242
CD, 7, 31, 89, 243
cemetery, iv, vi, 5, 17, 32, 63,
68, 72, 79, 85, 141,
173-181, 182, 204
cemetery records, iv, 72, 79, 85,
173, 174, 181, 204
cenotaph, 179
census, viii, 4, 7-9, 11, 16, 18,
20, 28, 32, 33, 44,
62, 63, 73, 75, 76,
78, 85, 87, 88, 130,
137, 157, 160, 209,
238-240, 257, 259,
261-263, 266, 269,
270, 273
census enumerator, 9
census index, 7, 9
cent, 32, 95, 201, 202
century, 25, 26, 32, 70, 73, 96,
97, 99, 111, 112,
172, 179, 191, 196,

233-235, 240, 243, 266
cerecloth, 179
certificate, 5, 8, 18, 19, 31, 32, 36, 37, 43, 63, 145, 147, 148, 173, 238, 266, 267
Certificate of Degree, 238
certificates, 3
Certified American Lineage Specialist, 9, 31
Certified Genealogist, 32
CG, 32
chaffing dish, 26
chain, 146, 184, 185, 187, 188, 201
chain carrier, 146
chair, 25, 26, 211
chamber tomb, 179
chamberlain, 214
chambermaid, 214
chancery, 32, 137, 157, 216
chancery court, 157, 216
chandler, 214, 228
character, 56
characteristics, 54, 58, 94
chart, 4, 7, 8, 10, 18, 39, 133, 199, 214, 264
charter, 148, 157, 198
chattel, 157
Cheraw, 241
Cherokee, 54, 70, 234, 238, 270
chest, 26-28, 104, 105, 121, 152, 172, 178
Chicago, 79, 128, 129, 247, 253, 257
Chicano, 78
chiffonier, 26, 214
chifforobe, 26
chignons, 100, 101
chilblains, 115
childbirth, 122, 127, 173, 208, 214
children, 1, 2, 24, 32
Chile, 132
China, 78, 129, 133, 251, 278

Chinese, 9, 78, 132, 196, 204, 205, 239, 253, 261
Chinese Rebellion, 132
Chinese Opium War, 132
Chino, 9, 239
Chippewa, 238
chlorosis, 117
Choctaw, 87, 238, 270
cholera, 115, 116, 123, 125-128, 237
cholera infantum, 116
cholera morbus, 116, 123, 125
christened, 32, 43
christening, 43
Christian, vii, 9, 39, 43, 50, 55, 133, 175, 177, 190
chronology, 9, 190, 254
church, iv, 3, 8-14, 19, 20, 22, 32, 37, 43, 45, 63, 67, 68, 74, 79, 81, 85, 128, 157, 160, 161, 173, 177, 190, 193, 204, 210, 223, 234, 236, 237, 276, 277
church histories, iv, 79, 85
Church of England, 236
Church of Jesus Christ of Latter-day Saints, 9, 11, 14, 37, 45, 74, 79, 277
Church of the Brethren, 234
church records, 19, 32, 43, 63, 74, 173, 193, 204
cir, 32
circa, vii, 9, 31, 32, 55, 99, 106, 195, 241, 270
circuit, 137, 157, 258, 265
circuit court, 157, 265
citation, 6, 9, 20, 32, 46, 84, 279
citizen, 12, 16, 32, 147, 152, 159, 161
citizenship, 5, 8, 63, 64, 161, 164, 260, 261, 266, 269
city and county directories, iv, 80, 86

291

233

friends, 2, 3, 12, 14, 16, 81, 86, 94, 138, 141, 142, 176, 236
frock coat, 106
funeral, 3, 12, 82, 87, 173, 174, 179, 180, 182
funeral directors, 87, 182
funeral home, 173
furlongs, 183, 185, 188
furniture, 28, 91, 93, 207, 221

G

garnish, 27
gazetteer, 12, 36, 71, 88
Gem Period, 96
Genealogical Data Communication, 12
genealogical libraries, iv, 73, 74, 78, 85
Genealogical Periodical Annual Index, 35, 84, 89
genealogical publications, ix, 280
Genealogical Publishing Company, 35, 45, 46, 71, 90, 134, 182, 243, 244, 284, 285
genealogical records, 79
genealogical societies, ix, 12, 13, 34, 35, 38, 45, 46, 70, 71, 73, 75, 78, 79, 85, 112, 134, 139, 152, 168, 181, 189, 196, 232, 273, 274, 276, 277, 279-281, 285
Genealogical Society of Utah, 12, 35
genealogical supplies, ix, 281
genealogies, 3, 7, 19, 44, 73-75, 78, 204, 276
genealogists, v, xiii, 29-31, 34, 45, 56, 72, 76, 79, 84, 90, 112, 134-136, 152, 168, 172,

196, 256, 257, 281, 284
genealogy books, iv, 78, 79, 280
Genealogy Reading Room, 73, 76, 276
General Accounting Office, 258
General Land Office, 35, 152, 265
generation, 2, 12, 22, 35, 139, 143
gentleman, 11, 12, 35, 63-65
gentry, 65
geographic names, 6
geography, 57, 72, 73, 79, 255
geologic survey maps, 204
Georgia, 65, 81, 129, 151, 176, 236, 240, 242, 243, 248, 250, 251, 270, 271
Georgian, 17, 193, 194
Georgian Calendar, 193, 194
German, 7, 12, 22, 35, 38, 48, 54, 58-62, 71, 128, 132, 172, 220, 227, 233-237, 245, 264
German Measles, 128
German Peasant Wars, 132
Germanic, 7, 64, 202
Germany, 17, 19, 131, 191, 234-236, 245-248, 263, 266, 278
given name, 13, 17, 21, 48-54, 56, 60, 62, 262
glebe, 161
glossary, vii, 46, 152, 201, 232
godparent, 13, 24
Goodman, 56, 63, 64
Goodwife, 64
Goody, 64
governess, 35
government, iv, 5, 13, 18, 64, 84, 88, 89, 148, 149, 151, 158, 169, 198, 202, 237, 239, 240, 245, 256, 258, 259, 265, 269, 275

infantry, 36
inflation, 197, 199, 203
influenza, 113, 118, 126-128
information, iii-v, viii, ix, xi, 1, 2,
4, 6-9, 11, 14, 17-20,
30, 36, 38, 43-45,
72, 74-77, 79, 80,
85-87, 89, 91, 136,
138-141, 167, 168,
173-175, 178, 181,
204, 238, 257-263,
265-268, 271, 272,
283, 284
inhabit, 36
inherit, 19, 36, 136, 141, 149,
161, 165
inheritance, 143, 158, 161, 200
initials, 46, 86, 179
inmate, 14, 36, 162
inquest, 36
insanity, 113, 120
inscription, 38, 179, 199
institutions, 88, 136, 261
instrument, 27, 28, 162, 224,
229, 230
insurance, 3, 5, 43
intemperance, 114, 119
interlibrary loan, 14, 89
interment, 4, 180
international, v, 14, 36, 88, 127,
196, 280, 281
International Genealogical Index,
14, 36
internet, ix, xi, 3, 4, 7, 46, 72, 76,
89, 90, 140, 195,
241, 275, 278-284
interview, 1, 3
intestate, 138, 163, 165
Inuit, 238
Inupiat, 238
inventory, 14, 25, 36, 163
invitation, 4
Iowa, 36, 85, 88, 134, 249, 252,
273
Iran-Iraq War, 133
Iraq, 133

Ireland, 45, 129, 235-237, 273,
277, 278
Irish, 34, 45, 58-60, 132, 211,
235, 236, 239, 243,
250, 252
Irish Famine, 132
Irish Rebellion, 132
island, 37, 56, 68, 73, 78, 130,
131, 177, 178, 236,
248, 250, 271, 281
Israel-Arab Conflicts, 133
issue, xi, 14, 23, 33, 36, 39,
197-199
Italian, 58-60, 264
Italo-Ethiopian War, 133
Italo-Turkish War, 133, 245
Italy, 127

J

Jackson's Whites, 240
Jacobite Rebellion, 132
jail, 119, 229
Jamaica, 132
Jamestown, 65, 250
Japan, 129, 254, 278
jaundice, 114, 119, 125
Jefferson, 21, 55, 71, 76, 198,
251
jewelry, 3, 92, 95, 96, 110, 111,
165
Jewish, 30, 78, 88, 175, 192,
234, 281
Jewish Calendar, 192
joint tenancy, 148
Josephite, 14
Journal of Negro History, 36
journeyman, 221
judge, 32, 36, 39, 57, 63, 137,
156, 157, 163, 165,
283
judge advocate, 36, 163
judgements, 136, 147
judicial, 36
Julian, 10, 17, 39, 190-192, 194
Julian Calendar, 190, 191, 194
junior, 14, 23, 36, 44

311

Social Security, 3, 5, 20, 74, 76, 89, 254
Social Security Death Index, 5, 20, 74, 76
societies, ix, 1, 3, 13, 30, 33-35, 41, 43, 73, 85, 87, 88, 152, 189, 273, 274, 277, 279-281
Society of Friends, 12, 236
Society of Mayflower Descendants, 277
soldiers, 85, 146, 149, 204, 205, 240, 258, 261, 267-270
Sons of the American Revolution, 41, 42
soundex, viii, 20, 259, 263, 276
sources, 2, 3, 6, 54, 57
South Africa, 133
South Carolina, 126, 151, 176, 239-242, 248, 250
South Dakota, 71, 235, 249
Southern Claims Commission, 258
southwest, 186, 238, 257, 272
Soviet Union, 263
Spain, 132, 146, 149, 185, 186, 191, 197, 233, 234, 242, 249, 253, 278
Spanish, vi-8, 10, 11, 13, 14, 16, 17, 19-25, 29, 48, 59, 61-64, 69, 114, 118, 119, 123-125, 130-133, 146-150, 154-156, 161-163, 165-167, 179, 181, 186, 197, 198, 201, 202, 204, 208, 209, 213, 216, 219, 221, 223, 225, 228, 229, 233, 234, 236, 240-242, 249, 250
Spanish-American War, 130
Spanish Armada, 131
Spanish Civil War, 133
special collection, 76, 78, 203

spellings, 6, 29, 56, 61, 62, 84, 113, 154, 207, 263
spinster, 20
spoon, 26
spouse, 1, 22, 24, 25, 44, 138, 139, 141, 173
springs, 66
squire, 65, 209, 212
St. Anthony's Fire, 122
St. Vitus' Dance, 122, 125
stamp, 91, 94-96, 250
stamp box, 94, 95
Star of David, 175
state archives, 256
State Historical & Genealogical Societies, 73
state library/state library commissions, 70, 72, 89, 277
state militia, 256
stereograph card, 95
stool, 27
storage, 6, 8, 77
Strangers Fever, 123
students, 4, 83, 219
subpoena, 3
Sudden Death Syndrome, 136
suffixes, iii, iv, 41, 58, 66
summons, 3
Sunday School, 3
sunstroke, 116
superintendent of schools, 4, 137
surety, 157
surgeon, 41, 127
surname, iii, 6, 15, 17, 20, 41, 55-64, 74, 75, 84, 139, 142, 239, 240, 262-264
surrogate, 166
survey, v, vi, 143-146, 148-150, 184, 185, 204, 283
surveyor, 211, 215, 227, 230
survivor, 41, 158
swamp, 66, 69
Sweden, 191, 246

313

CPSIA information can be obtained at www.ICGtesting.com
Printed in the USA
BVOW03s0653060715

407394BV00009B/176/P